SENSING SACRED TEXTS

Comparative Research on Iconic and Performative Texts

Series Editor

James W. Watts, Syracuse University.

While humanistic scholarship has focused on the semantic meaning of written, printed, and electronic texts, it has neglected how people perform texts mentally, orally and theatrically and manipulate the material text through aesthetic engagement, ritual display, and physical decoration. This series encourages the twenty-first-century trend of studying the performative and iconic uses of material texts, especially as encouraged by the activities of the Society for Comparative Research on Iconic and Performative Texts (SCRIPT).

Published

Iconic Books and Texts

Edited by James W. Watts

Reframing Authority: The Role of Media and Materiality

Edited by Laura Feldt and Christian Høgel

Forthcoming

How and Why Books Matter: Essays on the Social Function of Iconic Texts

James W. Watts

SENSING SACRED TEXTS

EDITED BY
JAMES W. WATTS

SHEFFIELD UK   BRISTOL CT

Published by Equinox Publishing Ltd.

UK: Office 415, The Workstation, 15 Paternoster Row, Sheffield, S1 2BX
USA: ISD, 70 Enterprise Drive, Bristol, CT 06010

www.equinoxpub.com

First published in Volume 8.1–2 of the journal *Postscripts*.
© Equinox Publishing Ltd 2017.

© James W. Watts and individual contributors 2018.

ISBN 9781781797426 (ePDF) | ISBN 9781781795750 (hb) | ISBN 9781781795767 (pb)

British Library Cataloguing-in-Publication Data

A catalogue record for this book is available from the British Library.

Library of Congress Cataloging-in-Publication Data

Names: Watts, James W. (James Washington), 1960- editor.
Title: Sensing sacred texts / edited by James W. Watts.
Description: Bristol : Equinox Publishing Ltd., 2018. | Series: Comparative
  research on iconic and performative texts | Includes bibliographical
  references and index.
Identifiers: LCCN 2018007806 (print) | LCCN 2018032306 (ebook)
ISBN 9781781797426 (ePDF) | ISBN 9781781795750 (hb) |
ISBN 9781781795767 (pb)
Subjects: LCSH: Sacred books—Comparative studies.
Classification: LCC BL71 (ebook) | LCC BL71 .S46 2018 (print)
| DDC
  208/.2—dc23
LC record available at https://lccn.loc.gov/2018007806

Edited and Typeset by Queenston Publishing, Hamilton Canada.

Printed by Lightning Source Inc. (La Vergne, TN), Lightning Source UK Ltd.
  (Milton Keynes).

CONTENTS

Contents

List of Figures

List of Figures

Introduction

James W. Watts

The essays in this book were commissioned for a symposium on the theme, "Seeing, Touching, Holding and Tasting Sacred Texts," that took place in the Käte Hamburger Kolleg on Dynamics in the History of Religions at the Center for Religious Studies (CERES) at Ruhr University in Bochum on April 7–8, 2016. During the 2015–2016 academic year, the Kolleg focused its research on the theme "Religion and the Senses," to which this workshop contributed.

The workshop papers concentrated on how books engage the human senses of sight, touch and taste. We omitted the sense of hearing from the call for papers because orality and aurality has received more attention than any other sense in research on textuality and scriptures. Though still very underdeveloped compared to the traditional focus in humanistic disciplines on the semantic meaning of texts, oral performance and aural reception has been gaining increasing recognition for its formative role in how religious texts function. The studies of Wilfred Cantwell Smith and William Graham in the 1980s inspired a growing body of research that shows that sacred texts frequently gain and maintain that status through oral performance.

Books, however, also engage other human senses. The material nature of written texts necessarily engages the senses of sight and touch. Less obvious but nevertheless common is the religious and secular trope of tasting and consuming texts. These aspects of textual culture have received very little scholarly attention, especially in cross-cultural studies and comparative religions. So the workshop and volume invited contributors to give attention to sight, to touch and handling, and to taste and oral consumption.

James W. Watts is Professor of Religion at Syracuse University in Syracuse, New York, and was in 2015–2016 a Visiting Fellow in the Käte Hamburger Kolleg at the Center for Religious Studies at Ruhr University Bochum, Germany.

The essays that appear here do that, and much more.

Brent Plate describes and categorizes the sensorium evoked by book arts and its implications for understanding the impact of books in general and sacred texts in particular. He argues that the aesthetic dimension of iconic books needs separate analysis to understand their impact.

Dorina Miller Parmenter applies affect theory to the iconic dimension of bibles. Though not excluding the role of affect in performative and even semantic ritualization, she argues that affect theory provides an entrée into the distinctive role of the material book in the formation of people's religious identity.

Marianne Schleicher provides a detailed analysis of the ritualized processes of creating and installing a Torah scroll in a Jewish congregation. By grounding the artefactual uses of the scroll in each of the five senses, her essay demonstrates the pre-cognitive ways in which sensation shapes religious experiences of the text.

Christian Frevel shows that the books of the Pentateuch in the Hebrew Bible already emphasize the visual representation, materiality and sensual experience of script. This biblical model for writings' role in the construction and representation of ritual reality has resonated through religious cultures ever since.

David Ganz examines the artefactual as well as documentary evidence for the ritual handling of late medieval gospel books and other liturgical books. He demonstrates how construction of the volumes intended to engage haptic perception and how the art in and on the books models the importance and significance of touching them.

Katharina Wilkens deploys an analogy with linguistic code-switching to analyze the frequent clashes between semantic-purist and somatic-iconic ideologies over Quranic medicine in Muslim cultures, especially in East Africa. Her argument provides a model for understanding conflicts between scholars and practitioners over book rituals in a wide variety of religious traditions.

Cathy Cantwell surveys Tibetan ritual practices with books to show that ritualized interactions with sacred books express and reinforce Tibetan Buddhist identity and veneration of the Dharma. They also serve pragmatic medical ends. Her detailed discussion concludes by drawing comparisons and contrasts with the use of iconic books in other cultures, including the observation that Tibetan texts become more sacred through their ritual use.

Yohan Yoo examines the instructions of two influential Neo-Confucian sages on the discipline of reading Confucian texts. They recommended imaginatively tasting the text while visualizing its author and hearing the author's voice reciting the contents rather than the reader's own. Yoo emphasizes that this discipline went beyond metaphor to employ the senses imaginatively in ritual reading.

James Watts concludes the collection by drawing on C. S. Pierce's theory of signs and Roy Rappaport's theory of ritual to argue that touching sacred texts and the sight of people touching them indexes their religious identity. Through ritual touching, these books become material manifestations of deity and transcendence which, in many traditions, become the most important religious artefacts.

This collection adds to previous collections about iconic books (Myrold 2010; Watts 2013) by expanding the analysis to a broader range of cultures and traditions, including Tibetan Buddhism (Cantwell), Islam in sub-Saharan Africa (Wilkens), and medieval Confucian traditions in Korea (Yoo). It advances theoretical discussion of the phenomenon of iconic books by applying the insights derived from affect theory (Parmenter) and linguistic code switching (Wilkens). The essays on Jewish sacred texts show how the artefactual use of texts establishes transitivity between a scripture and people's beliefs and identities (Schleicher, Frevel, Watts). Papers on decorated medieval codices and modern book art document the contribution of the aesthetic dimension to the definition of sacred texts (Plate) and the importance of the sense of touch to their aesthetic appreciation and religious significance (Ganz).

We are grateful to Prof. Volkhard Krech and the staff and faculty of the Kolleg at CERES for their generous intellectual, moral, administrative and financial support for the workshop and this project, including contributing some of the papers published here. The workshop and this volume contribute to the growing body of collaborative research associated with SCRIPT, the Society for Comparative Research on Iconic and Performative Texts, founded in 2010 (www. script-site.net). All the essays in this volume were originally published in 2017 in a special issue of the journal *Postscripts* 8.1–2.

References

Graham, William A. 1987. *Beyond the Written Word: Oral Aspects of Scripture in the History of Religion.* Cambridge: Cambridge University Press.

Myrvold, Kristina, ed. 2010. *The Death of Sacred Texts: Ritual Disposal and Renovation of Texts in World Religions.* London: Ashgate.

Smith, Wilfred Cantwell. 1989. "Scripture as Form and Concept: Their Emergence for the Western World." In *Rethinking Scripture: Essays from a Comparative Perspective,* edited by M. Levering, 29–57. Albany: State University of New York Press.

Watts, James W., ed. 2013. *Iconic Books and Texts.* London: Equinox.

What the Book Arts Can Teach Us About Sacred Texts: The Aesthetic Dimension of Scripture

S. Brent Plate

Religion and art became separated in the modern age, or so the secularized story goes. But looking at a history of books, including their artistic creation, we find interesting ongoing parallels occurring between religious and artistic texts. Illustrations and scripts, bindings and papers, printmaking and performance, all serve artistic and religious ends. The artistic and the religious are tied together, ultimately, by appealing to the senses, bringing texts and reading into the realm of the aesthetic (Gk. aesthetikos: pertaining to sense perception). Books are powerful and enjoyable as well as dangerous and condemned, because they are felt, seen, tasted, heard, and touched. By looking at contemporary "book arts" and noting their sensual affects, we can understand "sacred texts" in better ways. Ultimately we find modern secular arts are not so far from religious experiences. Examples come from modern book artists such as John Latham, Brian Dettmer, Luigi Serafini, Meg Hitchcock, and Guy Laramée.

My hope lies in the materiality of language, in the fact that words are things too, are a kind of nature. ... Everything physical takes precedence: rhythm, weight, mass, shape, and then the paper on which one writes, the trail of ink, the book. Maurice Blanchot (1995, 327)

What is it about the *Encyclopedia Britannica* that draws such reverence and revolt? Such respect and ridicule? Weight. Mass. Spine. Space. Symbol of knowledge and social advancement. But also emblem of an older age of knowledge. In 2012, after 244-years of printing the oldest, continuously published encyclopedia in the world, the Encyclopedia Britannica, Inc., announced it would no longer publish printed editions.

S. **Brent Plate** Associate Professor by special appointment in Religious Studies and Cinema & Media Studies, at Hamilton College in Clinton, New York, and is the managing editor of the journal, *Material Religion*.

Figure 2.1   Julian Baggini, *Bibliocide*. 2013. Video Still.

In response, British philosopher Julian Baggini staged what he called a "bibliocide" with a set of encyclopedias that belonged to his family. The volumes had been sitting in plastic tubs for years, filled with mold. He takes them out and performs a non-nostalgic ceremony, stacking them, dosing with lighter fluid, and watching them burn (Figure 2.1). In a short video, Baggini's words accompany the burning. He calls it a "funeral pyre," as he reads the "liturgy of the spine," turning not just "ashes to ashes," but "Arctic to Biosphere, Birds to Chess, Chicago to Death, Decorative to Edison," and so on. As the mass of volumes burns, the philosopher indicates their symbolic value and that in their burning we are also saying goodbye to older forms of authority, ways of gathering information, and "books as precious objects to be looked after," "books as status symbols." It's a great liturgical performance made by a self-professed atheist.[1]

In the same year, Quebecoise artist Guy Laramée created his own homage to/destruction of the *Encyclopedia Britannica* in a work called *Adieu* (Figure 2.2). He glued together a set of encyclopedia volumes and, as he does with books, uses them as a sculptural medium to create landscapes whittled out of the pages. The volumes are cut into, carved, and formed into something new, at the same time as their bookish use is destroyed. Besides being beautiful sculptures, part of the concept is to show the ways knowledge and lan-

---

1. The video of Baggini's "Bibliocide" can be see at: https://youtu.be/cuakjcMGneI, accessed 10 October, 2016. A short essay was also published (Baggini 2013).

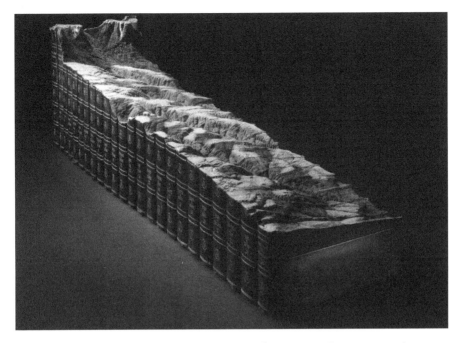

Figure 2.2   Guy Laramée, Adieu. 2013. Photo and permission by Guy Laramée. www.
         guylaramee.com

guage are ideally meant to open out into space, into a larger environment. The use of old books is key to his work since in days past "people made books that would last, because knowledge was still sacred."

This encyclo-mourning/sculpting/burning was in play well before the Britannica, Inc. announced its cessation of print. Already in the 1960s, British artist John Latham was toying with the encyclopedia's gravitas, its generative work of knowledge, even as he portrayed it against its own best interests. Between 1964–1968 he staged a series of what can only be called rituals, in which he stacked a 3-meter high pile of reference books, often including a set of encyclopedias, and lit them on fire. He conducted these rituals in public spaces: outside the British Museum and outside the Senate House in London, for example. This was a time when Nazi book burning was still fresh in the cultural memory.

A few years later, Latham turned again to the encyclopedia, but this time in a different medium. His 1971 work, *Encyclopedia Britannica*, is a 16mm film in which every frame of the film corresponds to one page of the massive reference work. The camera ran at a speed of seventeen frames per second (and thus seventeen images flash before the viewers' eyes every second) and so any text becomes unreadable. Latham takes a universal reference work that supplies access to great knowledge, but renders unusable for its intended sense. Instead, the book becomes object, and conjures a different mode of visual perception.

I begin with these approaches to the *Encyclopedia Britannica* for a few reasons that set out the interests of this article. First, the artworks can roughly be linked together through the term "book arts," that is, art that uses books as its primary medium, whether using pre-made books for sculptures and performances or making new books artistically. I'll discuss this further in the next section, alongside an initial definition of sacred texts. Second, book arts question how books can be used in sacred ways, turning us away from semantic meanings of texts toward aesthetic engagement with the materiality, and hence sensuality, of books. With the book arts as a guide, and a survey of a number of recent artists working in the field, the following section develops an "aesthetic dimension of sacred texts," noting the connection to the senses and the ongoing need for rituals. Creating artworks through the use of books makes broader social, cultural, and religious comments about knowledge production and forms of power, and ultimately extends our definition of sacred texts.

Books arts and sacred texts in the modern world

"Book arts" is an ambiguous term, and takes its place alongside a number of other ambiguous phrases such as artists' books and *livre d'artiste* (Drucker 2004), fine bookmaking and book objects (Phillpot 2013), and the recent neologism "blooks," objects that are made to *look* like books but have other uses (Dubansky 2016). Surveying much of the artwork and critical responses to it, Garrett Stewart uses the term "bookwork" since these objects *do* something, they perform (Stewart 2011). Cutting across some of these other categories, what I am grouping together here under the name "book arts" has two interrelated characteristics. First, the artworks use books as a primary medium, either as the end product (what is usually, strictly speaking, called an "artists' book," a created work usually of paper and binding that takes its final form as a book), or using ready-made books as the means to a sculptural, performative, and/or conceptual end (as in the examples of Baggini, Laramée, and Latham). The former might be thought of as the "craft" of bookmaking, while the latter is part of artistic "expression," though I'd hesitate to draw too strong a distinction between them. I'm interested in artworks that could be found in museums as easily as in the special collections of a library. What I do not include are examples of "fine printing" or "editorial editions" of books, or what might generally come from the tradition of the *livre d'artiste*.

Second, and closely related, the book arts I am looking at, to use the words of Johanna Drucker, interrogate "the conceptual or material form of the book as part of its intention, thematic interests, or production activities" (Drucker 2004, 3). In one form or other, I'm interested in those arts that call the very understanding of the book and related issues of *reading* into question, asking not only what it *is*, but also what it *does*. I mean this in both conceptual and material aspects. These questions arise out of a particular late or post-modernist environment in which the status of the book's authority has been called into question—the cessation of printing the *Encyclopedia Britannica* being emblematic of this epochal shift. In and through these modern interrogations we can begin to rethink a definition of sacred texts. To do so, I turn to the second key term in my title.

Sacred texts are found in many religious traditions around the world, with substantial variations (see especially Myrvold 2010, 2–5; cf. Bowker 2014; Levering 1989). In some traditions (e.g., Protestant Christianity and Sunni Islam) the texts are considered foundational to the tradition itself, given through direct communication from a single God. In other traditions (e.g., Mahayana Buddhism, Jainism) the texts are "sacred" not because they come directly from on high, but because they are useful for teaching and may point toward enlightenment. Some texts are understood to be primarily "oral" (e.g., the Quran, the Vedas), while others are at their essence in scripted, bound form (e.g., The Golden Plates of the Book of Mormon, Guru Granth Sahib). At the risk of reductionism, and strange as it may be to make such a definition in a "journal of sacred texts," I here offer a heuristic definition of sacred texts that may be useful in thinking about the place of texts, and books, in religious life. At the very least, it is the definition I am thinking about in relation to the arguments in this article. By sacred texts, I initially mean:

- a collection of words and symbols,
- that are written, etched, printed, spoken, or chanted,
- hold authority and provide meaning,
- prescribe behaviors for relating to human and/or superhuman beings,
- are embedded in a particular tradition,
- are valued by a community of adherents,
- who perform rituals with and through the text,
- and the material texts are tied to a conceptual, social imaginary.

This definition includes the Bible and Talmud, but it is broad enough to include encyclopedias and national constitutions. Note too that the material form of a "text" is broader than "books," and can include recitations, scrolls, and loose leafs, but the bound shape of the book has become one of the most prominent forms of sacred text in the modern world, so even, for example, the oral nature of the Quran is often encountered by Muslims in book form. And modernity is the setting for my argument.

In the modern age, with high literacy rates, cheap print, and mass transportation leading to changes in the *material* mode of book production, sacred texts have undergone massive *conceptual* changes. In modernity, books, and human relations to them, have been drastically altered. The relationship has become disembodied, at least as believed on a conceptual level, as if texts were only static words on a page that needed to be read and comprehended by a mind. As the medieval art historian Michael Camille suggests, "Perhaps only today, with the fast-approaching 'death of the book' and after centuries of idealist incorporeal aesthetics that denied the body in favor of a myth of pure mind, are we able to begin to appreciate and partially recover the cultural history of this submerged corporeality that links textuality to the five senses" (Camille 1998, 42). Camille, among other medievalists, has sought to recover the different relations to texts in the past, highlighting the sensual apprehension of books by literate and illiterate persons alike.

One of the key elements in the contemporary, late/post-modern recovery of the relation between the senses and texts has to do with the role of books within rituals. Scholar of Sikh traditions and material texts, Kristina Myrvold, states: "At the junction of ritual and texts we also find a vital tension between tradition and modernity. Ritual practices do not fade away or disappear in the face of modernization, but rather transform and even become revitalized. ... People may reclaim tradition by inventing rituals that respond to their needs in a rapidly changing world" (Myrvold 2010, 8). Sacred texts are partly defined based on their *content*, but they are also part of living traditions, and people *use* the texts within performative environments.

This revitalization is part of what Baggini, Latham, and Laramée are up to with their book arts, as their secular performances begin edging toward the religious and the ritualistic. At least, as I'm arguing here, their artworks give us the opportunity to reconceptualize the nature and function of books, and thus reconceptualize the place of sacred texts, not as words simply to be semantically meaningful, but as sensuous, emotional, sometimes even beautiful, engagements. Writing about his performance piece, Baggini states, "no matter how much I try to frame my act of bibliocide positively, I still can't shake the feeling that I did something wrong. If any secular object deserves the status of the sacred, surely it is the book, which aside from all those practical innovations that feed, clothe, warm and heal us, is the most important human creation of all time" (Baggini). Precisely in and through his taboo ritual, the sacrality of books, as material objects, comes to the forefront, revealing their long time lofty status in the social imaginary. I suggest that it is an artistic impulse that allows rituals to be reinvented and traditions revitalized. The book arts provide a way to reimagine the place of sacred texts, particularly as they touch on the aesthetic dimension.

The aesthetic dimension of sacred texts

As the limits of modernity have been glimpsed, if not altogether surpassed, there have been several new modes of research that have resituated the role of the book in the past and present. One of these has been a growing interest in the materiality of sacred texts, thinking through the ways texts look and feel, and how they find their way into rituals, not as instruction manuals but as objects to be used in performances. Much of this research was nicely summed up in the 2006 article, "The Three Dimensions of Scriptures" by James Watts. In his helpful taxonomy there are what he calls the *semantic, performative,* and *iconic* dimensions. As Watts puts it: "The *semantic dimension* of scriptures has to do with the meaning of what is written, and thus includes all aspects of interpretation and commentary as well as appeals to the text's contents in preaching and other forms of persuasive rhetoric" (141). This dimension is generally how religious studies—and related scholarly fields from biblical studies to history—has approached texts in the past, something along the lines of what Camille called an "idealist incorporeal aesthetics." But new approaches to sacred texts have begun to uncover the material elements of textuality, something that religious practitioners have long understood. So, Watts relates two further dimensions: "The *performative dimension* of scriptures has to do with the performance of what is written. ... The *iconic dimension* of scriptures finds expression in the physical form, ritual manipulation, and artistic representation of scriptures" (141–142).

Here I am adding a fourth, interconnected dimension I'll call the "aesthetic dimension," taken from the Greek etymology of *aesthetikos* that relates it to "sense perception." The aesthetic dimension signals the sensual connection between human bodies and texts, intersecting with each of the three other dimensions, but emphasizing all the senses and not only the visual. By using the term "aesthetic," I also mean to trigger what we moderns commonly think of when we use that term, that is, the connotation of aesthetics as related to the arts. It is this two-part aspect of the aesthetic (sense perception *and* art) that I mean to evoke.

The aesthetic dimension, like the other three dimensions, sometimes intersects with, sometimes overlays, sometimes lie dormant, and other times stands at the fore of the others. For example, there is no *semantic* dimension without ears and eyes. Even if one is struggling for the seemingly "invisible" meaning of translations and contexts, texts are perceived primarily through the eyes in modern scholarly thought, and secondarily the ears. Even so, most semantic approaches, like most biblical studies, operate in an aesthetic vacuum, presuming scholars' brains are directly downloading deep meaning—no senses needed. Or so it is believed.

The *iconic* dimension on first glance points merely to the eyes. However, icons in the traditional sense of Christianity's Eastern Orthodoxy—which is to say nothing of enacting *darshan* in South Asia or *baraka* in North African Sufi contexts—is very much about the other senses as well. As Bissera Pentchava's work on the *Sensual Icon* in Byzantium details, one connects to icons through the lips as well as the eyes, through the nostrils that sniff the incense and ears that hear the prayers occurring in the presence of the icon (Pentchava 2010). Icons, and thus also iconic texts, are always already multi-sensual. And much of the aesthetic dimension can be seen in the *performative* dimension of scripture. But I think it useful to bracket out and highlight the sensorium, that in-between, liminal locus that, as I've argued elsewhere, is the crux of religious experience itself. The senses form what I've called the "skin of religion," a semi-permeable membrane that mediates input and output, the flows of religious behavior and belief, and the creation of sacred environments (Plate 2011). We use the senses at home altars and great pilgrimage sites, in private devotions and in megachurches. And we can only engage with books, pages, and texts, when we use our senses.

Artists and their books

The examples of the *Encyclopedia Britannica* already move us in several aesthetic directions as books are embedded in new forms of myth, ritual, and symbol, engaged by people's bodies. Here I explore several further examples of book arts which provoke questions about the nature and function of sacred texts. For heuristic purposes, I have outlined three categories of book arts, providing brief descriptions of the categories and giving three examples of artists in each category. The aim is not to provide an exhaustive overview of book arts, but to stimulate further thinking about the ways artists have used and created books, and how that might impact an understanding of sacred texts.

The book as medium and means

John Latham used books as sculptural elements beginning in the 1950s. In works such as *Bible* and *Belief System*, both from 1959, Latham disfigures, partially destroys, and then mounts old books in sculptural fixity to generate questions about stale knowledge and about information as static. Library and gallery alike can create an immobile culture. So he started working beyond sculpture to create performance pieces like the "skoob" project. As part of his critique of books and social knowledge production, during this time he also critiqued an art world and art theory that emphasized formalism (Abstract Expressionism and then minimalism were the reigning champions of artistic styles), especially as articulated by one of the most prominent art critics at the time: Clement Greenberg.

In August 1966, Latham gathered with some students at his home. They took a library copy of Greenberg's book, *Art and Culture*, tore it into tiny bits, chewed the paper and spit it out. They collected the discarded material, added yeast, and let it ferment. Latham had checked the book out from the library at St Martin's School of Art, where he was teaching at the time, and eventually the book came to be overdue. Latham went to the library and gave them a small phial of the masticated material, returning what he called the "essence" of the book. For this performance he was subsequently dismissed from his teaching post at St Martin's. Nonetheless, he created an artistic document of the performance, included letters from the library and the phial, and collected it all in a work titled *Still and Chew: Art and Culture 1966–1967*. It is now in the collection of the Museum of Modern Art in New York.[2]

Beginning in 1990, Latham turned to the sacred books of Western religions and began to create sculptures, incorporating Qurans, Bibles, Torahs, and Talmuds into the work. In the process of creating his artworks he challenged commonly held notions of the sacredness of these texts. This was his "God is Great" series, with most versions containing one or more sacred texts, cut in half, with each piece glued to both sides of a glass plate so that the books have the appearance of being sliced through with the glass. These were conceptual works that depended on book destruction as their trigger. In 2005, "God is Great (#2)"—consisting of a Quran, Bible, and Talmud volume sliced through with a glass plate—was about to be put on display at Tate Modern, but museum officials took it down before anyone saw it because they were afraid of "offending" anyone in an age of Islamist terrorism. More recently, at the Portikus Gallery in Frankfurt in 2014, three men (sometimes identified as "Islamist" though that wasn't entirely clear) entered the

---

2. From Tate Gallery. http://www.tate.org.uk/context-comment/articles/and-word-was-made-art Accessed 14 March 2016. Latham critiqued what he called the "Mental Furniture Industry." He saw books as the repositories of a kind of static knowledge that is uncritical and lacking intuition.

gallery, agitated the workers, and stole the Quran from the installation, "God is Great (#4)," one of the last works Latham made before he died in 2006. In these instances, an inert, three-dimensional sculpture stirs emotions, prompting bodily action by others.

Throughout his career, Latham challenged the status of books by disfiguring them and thus attempting to "free" a culture that had grown complacent with its acceptance of books, sacred and otherwise, as a key form of knowledge. As one commentator of John Latham sums up the artist's work with books:

> The printed book and its ongoing twentieth-century identity crisis was Latham's muse, and the trail of dismembered, mutilated volumes he left behind him was not evidence of destruction, but *of a sustained effort to rethink and reinvent*. He probed, pushed, and stretched its boundaries, ferociously experimenting with new forms it might assume. Battered and charred, his books were no longer quite themselves, but a variety of strange, unreadable, hybrid and inter-medial objects. (Partington 2014, 72; emphasis added)

Between sacred and profane, but also between library and museum, destruction and regeneration, Latham's experiments with books draw attention to what books have come to mean in broad cultural parlance.

Guy Laramée picks up on many of the same themes as Latham, though he executes his work in strikingly different ways, moving us further toward an aesthetic and ritualized approach to books and knowledge. Laramée says, "In a way, what I do belongs to sacrifice, in the anthropological lore. In the sacrifice, the victim becomes sacred precisely because she is sacrificed. So these books that nobody cared about anymore become sacred objects in a way, because I transform them into art."[3] Destruction is tied to sacrifice. Death becomes ritualized and through this, transformations might occur.

In other works and writings, Laramée has created a mythology of a people he calls the "Biblios." "Once upon a time there was a tribe that collected words," Laramée starts his story. "The Biblios had all sorts of words and when some were lacking they made up more." Laramée goes on to tell how they were at first an oral people, but the Biblios eventually discovered writing, which led to books, which led to collecting, which led to them creating imposing library structures in which they all lived. To connect with each other they had to excavate through the books, creating massive tunnels. This allowed them to be with each other, but as a result, many words were lost in the tunnel digging. In the end, Laramée says, "It's generally agreed that the Biblios perished under the weight of their knowledge."[4]

3. http://www.itsnicethat.com/articles/guy-laramee
4. http://www.guylaramee.com/index.php/biblios/biblios/ accessed 14 March 2016.

Figure 2.3 Guy Laramée, *The Holy Bible (The Arid Road to Freedom)*. 2015. Photo and permission by Guy Laramée, www.guylaramee.com .

Neither Laramée nor Latham are against knowledge per se. They are critiquing a stale and overly-amassed knowledge, and they see these problems most glaringly in the form of the modern printed book. For Laramée, the books become landscapes, with the negative spaces cut away to suggest erosion, just as his "destruction" allows an opening of the book into a larger space beyond (Figure 2.3).

Similar to Laramée, Brian Dettmer has found old books to be useful objects through which to reinterpret the past, while pointing toward the future. He too participated in memorializing the end of the encyclopedia in his 2012 piece *Tower #1*, a work that creates a tower of encyclopedias in ways similar to Latham's skoob towers, though Dettmer's books were "destroyed" not through fire but by knife. Dettmer finds old books and goes page by page, cutting through a book with an x-acto knife, revealing images, words, and ultimately relations across and between the pages. Though he does not necessarily read the books before he begins his work, Dettmer offers an "interpretation" of the books as he cuts into them. He works through encyclopedias, bibles (e.g., *The Picture Bible*, 2005; Figure 2.4), classic literary works like *Tristan Shandy*, as well as old medical textbooks, highlighting words and images that stand out, excavating themes that are found by enacting the texts. He discusses his method as "a more tactile way of learning by actually having an experience with the material" (quoted in Brown 2008).

Figure 2.4   Brian Dettmer, *Picture Bible*. 2005. Photo and permission by Brian Dettmer.

In a TED talk he gave in 2014 to a group of youth, Dettmer comments on why people seem to be disturbed by the destruction of books, even in an artistic fashion such as his. It is because, he suggests, "we think of books as living things [….] They are created to relate to our body […]. they also have the potential to continue to grow, to become new things."[5] Dettmer's books then, are aesthetic objects, bodies that correspond to human bodies, and the connection is an aesthetic one.

Each of these artists, and many others as well, work through processes of, as one commentator put it, "excavation, surgery, erasure, and mutila-

5. https://www.ted.com/talks/brian_dettmer_old_books_reborn_as_intricate_art

tion" (Martin n.d., 4). Through these sometimes taboo activities, new variations of the sacred emerge. The book is sacrificed, giving new takes on life by the artists as well as the audiences who come to interact with the works.

Artists' books

I switch here from artists who take "found" books and carve into them to form something new, to artists who are creating their own books from the ground up. This is what is more properly termed "artists' books," works that begin from raw materials to create a book, generally with pages that are bound together in a codex form. Here "books" (this term is used especially loosely in this instance) are not the means to a final product but are the final product themselves. And here, instead of a certain element of "destruction," we find creation. Like the previous grouping, the artists noted here connect books with larger forces of space, culture, and identity.

Islam Aly has created a number of books that reflect and comment on Arabic and Muslim modes of knowledge and ritual. Books such as *Marginalia 1* (2013) and *28 Letters* (2013) use Arabic calligraphy styles and laser cutting techniques to create negative spaces in pages made from flax paper. The Arabic characters are the empty spaces in the page, cut away from the book itself. The relation of letters to page is inverted, as Aly takes older forms of artistic forms and styles and reframes them. He states, "I wish to explore new ways to use the rich structures of historical books in contemporary artists' book practice and incorporate contemporary content into strictly historical structures."[6] In each of these, the cut out characters are legible, though not entirely readable, turning semantic meanings into aesthetic engagements.

In 2014, Aly made *Orientation Cube*, a book with Johannot paper pages, laser-engraved edges, bound in plexi-glass, with Coptic stitching, and placed in a folding box (Figures 2.5a-d). Aly discusses how his book is made in light of the Kaaba, the ancient shrine that stands at the center of the Great Mosque in Mecca. In the artwork, he says, "A tiny black cube is positioned at the center of the inner back board, around which are concentric circles cut in the thirty sections of the book to reflect the process of circumambulation." As with Laramée's works, book space and geographical space coincide; the book becomes a landscape, an embodied world that connects with the bodies of the audience. And like good ritual, it is a condensation of space and time, a way of focusing energies. "Reading" a book in this instance involves opening the box, unfolding the pages, even playing with the designs to create a space that is mindful of prayerful orientation.

6. http://www.islamaly.com/about.html

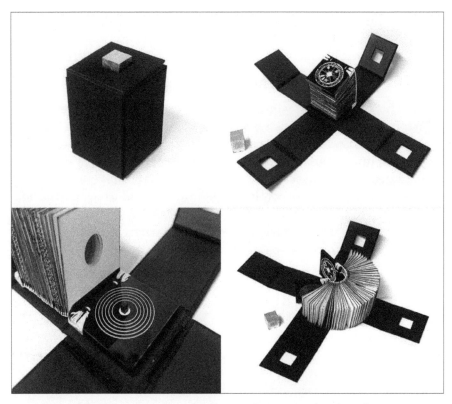

Figure 2.5 a-d. Islam Aly, *Orientation Cube*. Photo and permission by Islam Aly.

Not unlike Aly, Robert Kirschbaum's *The 42-Letter Name* is an artist's book that mixes and merges book pages with architectural space. In Kirschbaum's case, he begins with the *idea* of words, more specifically the idea of one particular word, a mystical 42-letter name of God found in Jewish prayer traditions. On first glance, the pages are simple line drawings, geometric cube shapes that seem in want of adding up to something, a "fragment of creation" as the artist considers. And indeed, the three-dimensional spaces that they cubically conjure in their final form of a nine-square grid is reminiscent of Ezekiel's geometrical, symmetrical vision of the third Temple in Jerusalem (Ezekiel 40-47). "Following the grid pattern," Kirschbaum says, "I then begin to carve out, weigh, transform, permute, and depict forms initially intended to function as plans for discrete objects that are fragments of a more perfect whole" (Kirschbaum 2009, n.p.; Figure 2.6).

Kirschbaum's "book" bends toward architecture, and in a fascinating mode of comparative, interreligious analysis we find him working from a Jewish perspective but also coming to the geometry of the "cube" as an

Figure 2.6 Robert Kirschbaum, *The 42-Letter Name*. Permission by Robert Kirschbaum.

ideal form, similar to the Kaaba of Mecca (*kaaba* literally means "cube"). He's drawing on Ezekiel's description of the Temple, but here Kirschbaum subtracts parts of the complete cube in each rendering, showing the incomplete nature of the world today. There are fragments that can mystically be "read" together, adding up to a harmonious whole, though perhaps only in an ideal form.

While there is little to semantically read in the examples given so far, other artists bring us closer to the literate and semantic dimensions by channeling our energies toward the words on pages, even though this is a long way from literate reading. Jan Owen's *Prayer Palimpsest* (2013), as one example, is a handmade book of twenty-six pages, sewn together with a Hollytex cover. Inspired by calligraphy styles from Asia and medieval European manuscripts, she handwrites a collection of prayers and poems with Sumi ink. The resulting work has a good deal of legibility—the individual letters and words are decipherable—though it would be difficult to sit and read for long. Apart from literal reading, the book becomes an object to be looked at, while the polyester pages provide a slightly jarring effect, most unlike the paper typically used in manuscripts, and foreign to the fingers of most readers.

With these examples of artists' books, we begin to suspect that in the modern age, the act of reading itself might be in question as much as the object of the book. Reading goes beyond pure vision, as the precisely developed visual typefaces of modern books give way to pages that are translucent, shot through with multiple layers, or made to be part of a construction set, fingered and touched.

The book's imaginary

The last group of artists I'll note brings us further into the imaginary, from the physicality of the artists' book as we have just seen, to the ideality of characters, books, and readability. These artworks rely on the imaginary of legible characters, as well as the imaginary of the book; the book itself being a concept that is based on an object. Ultimately, to approach many of these works, we the audiences/participants must *believe* and *imagine* that books have a bounded nature, and that the characters inscribed within them lead to words, which lead to sentences that mean something on a semantic level.

Seguing from Jan Owen's work, Sher offers a telling contrast. Like Owen, Sher creates a compact "book" that is lovely to behold, shows the signs of handmade creation, and creates the sense of a personal, devotional work. And yet Sher puts much of that into question with her 2013 piece, *Blog* (Figure 2.7). Several years ago, Elizabeth Sher was in an arts residence in Barcelona and began to write in an automatic language on a daily basis. She made up the characters, which look a lot like Chinese characters for those of us who don't know anything about Chinese, and each day this practice solidified for her. Intriguingly, in an age of New Media she thought of herself not as writing/journaling but as "blogging." And then she turned her automatic writing back into an old medium by writing with a bamboo pen, using sepia ink, and writing on rice paper. In a further transformation, she turned the written pages into a scroll, rolled it and placed it in a plain pinewood box, conjuring Jewish burial, and in Hebrew lettering wrote the word "blog" on the top. In each permutation, ideas are *suggested*, not symbolized, relying on the imaginary of the audience to make connections.

Taking automatic writing to a severe degree, we note the *Codex Seraphanianus*, produced from 1976 to 1978 in Rome by designer and artist Luigi Serafini. The book is 360-pages of undecipherable writings and bizarre images. It looks like an encyclopedia, with naturalist drawings, and the hint of technical details. But these are fantastical images, and unreadable text. Serafini, under the influence of psychedelic drugs and long travels, saw himself as a medium to the characters, surrealistically not in control of what he was producing at the time. Ultimately, unlike the other works I have noted, which are handmade in small artist's sets, Serafini's work was mass-produced by a number of publishing houses around the world. Prominent

Figure 2.7   Elizabeth Sher. *Blog*. 2013. Permission by Elizabeth Sher.

literary figures such as Roland Barthes and Italo Calvino, among others, have written about it (see Taylor 2007).

In this case, it is not the imaginary of the book that is in question, but the imaginary of semantic meaning. For decades, scholars and tech-geeks have tried to de-code the *Codex*, certain that among the scribblings is a legitimate alphabet with coherent commentary. Serafini himself has said there is no hidden meaning in the text (it is, he says, "asemic") though this hasn't stopped many from seeking its Rosetta Stone, the key that will allow the unlocking of the meaning. After all, we must have semantic meaning! The *Codex Seraphanianus* seems to hold out a secret for a careful hermeneut to decode. The text appeals to the mystery-solving attitude of the literary scholar.

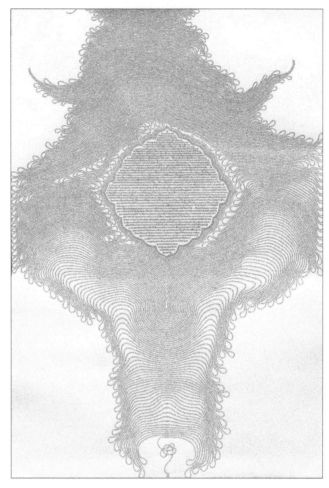

Figure 2.8   Meg Hitchcock, *Throne: The Book of Revelation*. 2012. Permission by Meg Hitchcock.

Finally, I turn to Meg Hitchcock, who brings us back to legibility and semantic meaning, while relying on an imaginary idea of a book that is necessary to bring her transformations to light. Hitchcock comes from a fundamentalist Christian upbringing, and so knows what it is to have a high regard for the Bible. As she moved away from her background, she still retained a respect for sacred texts, and uses them throughout her artworks as she takes one sacred text, cuts out letters from it, then takes the letters and glues them into another configuration that spells out passages from another sacred text. For example, the 2012 work, *Throne: The Book of Revelation*, (Figure 2.8) reads literally as the book of Revelation from the Christian Bible: starting at top left is chapter one, verse one, and extending to the end of chapter 22 at the bottom of the picture. All of the letters (Roman characters, in English) were initially cut from pages of an English translation of the Quran. Then, at the center is a mandala-type form that contains "The Throne Verse" from the Quran (*ayat al-kursi*; 2:225), and all of these characters were cut from a Christian Bible. The result is an image that can be looked at, but also read. Its conceptual hook is based on the idea that there was an intact Quran and Bible that were cut up and its constituent parts reordered into another whole.

Between destruction and creation, Hitchcock's work, like many others I have discussed here, challenges the ideal concept of books and literal meanings by bringing us to aesthetically encounter a grouping of symbols that are visible and tangible. The physicality of letters, pages, and bindings affects an experience that is not always congruent with the ideality we keep in our mind as we confront these pieces. To get at the discrepancies between body and mind, and between aesthetics and semantics, ritual is again invoked, even when this ritual is the artist working in their studio. The painstaking work of cutting out thousands of individual letters and repasting them in another place is a long process, which Hitchcock makes clear is also a meditative process.

Conclusions: Redefining sacred texts

In the arts, as in religious rituals (see the other contributions in this volume for examples) if not in libraries, books are chewed up and spit out, set aflame, fondled, dug into, cut up, and gazed upon, as bodies engage their artistic forms and intellectual aspirations. There has been a widespread and increasing artistic interest in books in the past half century that reflects an anxiety and excitement over the "death of the book," which also spells a certain end of reading. Books are now sculptural matter and fodder for performance, but also a final hoped-for form that requires pages, bindings, symbolic markings, and a lot of decisions about how to put all that together. Meanwhile, the artists are clearly engaging in larger cultural comment and critique about the status of knowledge and the role of media, and through their creative destructions they point toward new inventions of texts in the material world and social imaginary alike.

Many of the artists noted here have been challenged and critiqued for their destruction of books. Even the YouTube site for Julian Baggini's *Bibliocide* is filled with vindictive comments about how awful it is that Baggini burned those encyclopedias. There is a secular imaginary of the book as sacred in the contemporary world, and this attitude is not merely directed toward "sacred" texts. The destruction is a sacrifice, as so many of the artists note, which is always destruction, demise, and death. But what is going on is something less like *desecration* and more like the sacred act of *deconsecration*. The "con" is crucial here, as it is for religious traditions. To take something apart, and do it ritualistically, is to "deconsecrate." It is a sacred activity. Something comes from the sacrifice.

And while these artists are creating, destroying, and provoking in new ways, for new sets of media consumers, aesthetic engagement with books has been around since there have been sacred texts. Michelle Brown speaks to the imagery of the fourteenth-century, "Holkham Bible Picture Book," in ways that resonate across many sacred texts, and into the modern age:

> To view [the Holkham Bible] merely as a religious picture book, designed to help instruct an illiterate audience in the basics of Bible stories, is to miss the point of the work that marks a radical shift in modes of communication. It is to mistake an early Flash Gordon comic strip for George Lucas's *Star Wars* epic. For during the early fourteenth century, when the book was made, artists and spiritual directors were taking art into spheres as innovative as film would prove to be seven centuries later ... Art, like music, can provide an immediacy and profundity of access to the senses and to emotional response. (Brown 2007, 1)

Similarly, describing the engagement with medieval books by the literate and illiterate alike, Michael Camille notes how, "Reading a text was a charged somatic experience in which every turn of the page was sensational, from the feel of the flesh and hair side of the parchment on one's fingertips to the lubricious labial mouthing of the written words with one's tongue" (Camille 1998, 38). "Reading" has long been a multi-sensual affair.

This article is connected with the others in this volume which outline the myriads ways that texts are sensually engaged. We don't need the book arts to tell us this, we just need to go back to review the place of text in religious traditions. Yet, my suggestion is that if we begin from the insights of book arts and then turn to look at sacred texts, we will ask different questions. We might pay better attention to the bindings, the literal and legible alongside the non-sensical and translucent.

So, what makes a text sacred? Recall my initial comments at the beginning of this article. In the end, I want to amend the definition to include the aesthetic dimension. Thus, a sacred text is:

> a collection of words and symbols, that are written, etched, printed, spoken, or chanted, hold authority and provide meaning, prescribe behaviors for relating to human and/or superhuman beings, are embedded in a particular tradition, are valued by a community of adherents, who perform rituals with and through the material texts that are tied to a conceptual, social imaginary, *and appeals to the senses of human bodies.*

The sacred is in part created within the material texts' sensual appeal to the bodies of people: whether by bonfire, ingesting, hearing, looking, or even reading the books. The aesthetic dimension is not merely the "artistic" element. However, through the arts we begin to see the "sensational" element of aesthetics, the ways the material books in all their myriad forms appeal to the sights and sounds and smells and tastes and touch of the human body.

References

Baggini, Julian. 2013. "Bibliocide," *Aeon.* 6 March, https://aeon.co/essays/burning-books-is-a-wickedly-complicated-task, accessed on 10 October 2016.

Blanchot, Maurice. 1995. *The Work of Fire.* Translated by Charlotte Mandell. Stanford, CA: Stanford University Press.

Bowker, John. 2014. *The Message and the Book: Sacred Texts of the World's Religions.* New Haven, CT: Yale University Press.

Brown, Ellen Firsching. 2008. "The Cut-up Artist." *Fine Books & Collections,* 33 (May/June): 48.

Brown, Michelle. 2007. "Introduction to *The Holkham Bible Picture Book. A Facsimile.*" London: British Library.

Camille, Michael. 1998. "Sensations of the page: Imaging technologies and Medieval illuminated manuscripts." In *The Iconic Page in Manuscript, Print, and Digital Culture,* edited by George Bornstein and Theresa Tinkle, 33–53. Ann Arbor: University of Michigan Press.

Drucker, Johanna. 2004. *The Century of Artists' Books.* New York: Granary.

Dubansky, Mindell. 2016. *Blooks: The Art of Books that Aren't.* New York: Mindell Dubansky.

Howes, David. 2003. "Coming to our senses: The sensual turn in anthropological understanding." In *Sensual Relations: Engaging the Senses in Culture and Social Theory,* edited by David Howes, 29–59. Ann Arbor: University of Michigan Press. https://doi.org/10.3998/mpub.11852

Jansen, Thomas. 2012. "Sacred Text." In *The Wiley-Blackwell Companion to Chinese Religions,* edited by Randall L. Nadeau. Oxford: Blackwell. https://doi.org/10.1002/9781444361995.ch13

Kirschbaum, Robert. 2009. "The 42-Letter Name." Artist's limited edition.

Levering, Miriam. 1989. *Rethinking Scripture.* Albany: State University of New York Press.

Martin, Nicholas. n.d. "From front to back: Art and design under the influence of books." In *Charisma of the Book,* Exhibition catalog. Abu Dhabi: New York University Art Gallery.

Myrvold, Kristina. 2010. "Introduction." In *The Death of Sacred Texts: Ritual Disposal and Renovation of Texts in World Religions,* edited by Kristina Myrvold, 1–10. Abingdon: Routledge.

Partington, Gill. 2014. "From books to skoob; Or, media theory with a circular saw." In *Book Destruction from the Medieval to the Contemporary,* edited by

Gill Partington and Adam Smyth, 57–73. New York: Palgrave. https://doi.org/10.1057/9781137367662_4

Pentchava, Bissera. 2010. *The Sensual Icon: Space, Ritual, and the Senses in Byzantium*. University Park: Penn State University Press.

Phillpot, Clive. 2013. *Booktrek: Selected Essays on Artists' Books since 1972*. Zurich: J.R.P. Ringier.

Plate, S. Brent. 2011. "The skin of religion: Aesthetic mediations of the sacred." *CrossCurrents*. 62(2): 162–180. https://doi.org/10.1111/j.1939-3881.2012.00228.x

Stewart, Garrett. 2011. *Bookwork: Medium to Object to Concept to Art*. Chicago, IL: University of Chicago Press. https://doi.org/10.7208/chicago/9780226773933.001.0001

Taylor, Justin. 2007. "The Codex Seraphinianus." *The Believer*. (May): http://www.believermag.com/issues/200705/?read=article_taylor

Watts, James. 2006. "The Three Dimensions of Scripture." *Postscripts* 2(2–3): 135–159.

3

How the Bible Feels:
The Christian Bible as Effective and Affective Object

DORINA MILLER PARMENTER

Despite Christian leaders' insistence that what is important about the Bible are the messages of the text, throughout Christian history the Bible as a material object, engaged by the senses, frequently has been perceived to be an effective object able to protect its users from bodily harm. This paper explores several examples where Christians view their Bibles as protective shields, and will situate those interpretations within the history of the material uses of the Bible. It will also explore how recent studies in affect theory might add to the understanding of what is communicated through sensory engagement with the Bible.

In a plenary address given to the Society of Biblical Literature in 2008, Jonathan Z. Smith reflected upon recent changes in the academic study of the Bible and called for a conscious redescription of biblical studies as part of the study of religion. Rather than continuing to favor biblical studies as an exceptional subject within the study of religion, Smith (2009) said that there ought to be a "concern for sacred texts as embodied material objects commensurate with interests in those texts as documents of faith and history" (26). Since Smith's pronouncement, concern for the Bible as an embodied material object—as object engaged by the senses in the complex realm of social bodies—has been a bourgeoning area of research as part of the "materialist turn" within religious studies that is aligned with cultural studies (see Schaefer 2015; Vasquez 2011). There are many twists and disparate routes in this material turn, but what unites them is a conscious movement away from the privileging of reading and interpreting texts that has been dominant in Western history (Morgan 2010a; Parmenter 2015; Schaefer

Dorina Miller Parmenter is Associate Professor of Religious Studies at Spalding University in Louisville, Kentucky.

2015; Vasquez 2011). Focusing on materiality and the senses is a shift away from the epistemology of the rational subject who orders the world through acts of signification and textual interpretation, toward a more "embodied epistemology" where "[s]ensation is an integrated process, interweaving the different senses and incorporating memory ... and emotion into the relationships human beings have with the physical world" (Morgan 2010a, 8). Since the texts of and textual practices with the Christian Bible have shaped the dominant hermeneutic that material culture studies attempts to dethrone, the Bible is an acute object for analysis from a material perspective. In this paper I will be following this material turn to examine several examples where Christians view their Bible-books as effective objects for protection, and will situate those interpretations within the history of the material uses of the Bible. I will also begin to explore how one aspect of cultural studies called "affect theory" might contribute to understandings of people's uses of the Bible.

Thinking through the Bible as an effective object

In the courses that I teach where the primary text is the Bible, I usually start the classes by asking students to write reflection papers on their experiences with this book. Knowing the assignment can easily result in lists of the Christian students' beliefs that they assume are biblical, I specifically tell them not to do this, but instead to reflect on their prior engagement with or exposure to the material *book* of the Bible—do they own a Bible, where do they usually see a Bible or a representation of a Bible, what does it look like, what do they or what have they seen others do with it, and so on. Students usually struggle with this task, because generally they have not thought about the book of the Bible before—it has been taken for granted, whether in the foreground of a student's personal religious life, or in the background of a life lived in American culture. But occasionally I get priceless reflections that I imagine are typical of many Americans' experiences with the Bible, even though they may not always articulate them. Here is an excerpt from one of those insightful papers:

> From my grandmother I received a very nice leather bound Bible with my name in beautiful gold letters on the front. That book has been to more places with me than any other piece of literature that has been in my hands; however, I have never actually opened it . . . to read it. It traveled with me nearly across the world as I was part of Operation Iraqi Freedom in 2004 for no other purpose than I thought it would in some way protect me. I never was overly religious but through that experience I learned that I was definitely spiritual, and I called on that book as a safe place, or perhaps a security. (Ortiz 2011)

In his 1980 address to the Society of Biblical Literature called "America's Iconic Book," noted scholar of American religions Martin Marty (1982) described this attitude about the Bible in American culture as a "carapace," or "a protective covering, the sort of cocoon that individuals, subcultures, and in their own way societies need for the structuring of experience.... The Bible, in American history and in much of present-day culture, ... and its presumed contents, that for which one would consult if one did consult it, remove the 'just happening' dimension from human existence" (6–7). James Watts (2006) takes this view of the iconic dimension of the Bible a step further to emphasize how ritualizing scriptures' vessels via sight and touch are social practices that legitimate their users, producing feelings of power, purpose, comfort, and confidence.

The book-as-object in Christianity refers to Bibles or Gospels in a codex form, a technology that developed along with Christianity and became firmly attached to its scriptures by the fourth century. Despite early Christian leaders' insistence that the Gospel message was not bound to written texts, Christians developed a reliance on the written word to combat heresy and stabilize orthodox teachings. In a society where few could read, those with literacy skills held religious and social power, and those who possessed the Book had a potent tool (Gamble 1995; Parmenter 2006).

After Constantine, Church councils as well as legal proceedings enthroned a Bible in their ritual spaces to call upon Christ's presence to legitimate their decisions, without recourse to the text itself. In private Bible uses for protection and healing, the tension between scripture as a saving object, which harnesses an effective external presence, and scripture as a saving text, which affects the user from within the heart, is evident in Church Fathers' advice. For example, John Chrysostom complains that many Christians have Gospel-books for protective charms but scarcely read them, so he tries to redirect attention back to the text and its incorporation: "For if the devil will not dare to approach a house where a Gospel is lying, much less will any evil spirit, or any sinful nature, ever touch or enter a soul which bears about with it such sentiments as it contains" (*Homily on John* 32:3, in *NPNF* ser. 1, vol. 14, 114). The textual and material evidence shows that many Christians did make amulets out of scriptures,[1] despite criticism from church leaders like Chrysostom:

> Do you not see how women and little children suspend Gospels from their necks as a powerful amulet, and carry them about in all places wherever

---

1. Some scriptural charms have survived the centuries, such as the amulet of the Letter of Agbar to Jesus (*Oxyrhynchus Papyri* vol. 65 no.4469, trans. Maltomini 1998, 122–129) and miniature codices created to serve as amulets (Haines-Eitzen 2005).

they go[?] Thus do thou write the commands of the Gospel and its laws upon your mind. Here there is no need of gold or property, or of buying a book; but of the will only, and the affections of the soul awakened, and the Gospel will be your surer guardian, carrying it as you will then do, not outside, but treasured up within; yea, in the soul's secret chambers.

(John Chrysostom, *Homily on Statues* 19.14, in Schaff, *NPNF*, ser. 1, vol. 9, 470)

In addition to the inspiration and assurance provided by the text, the immediacy of the Bible as an effective object gives people what they need in their material lives: stories abound of Gospels driving away the devil, putting out fires, being untouched by fire or water, and providing the antidote to snakebite or cures of other illnesses (see Parmenter 2006).

Similar examples of protective book rituals can be found in the fusion of Roman Christian traditions with Celtic and Anglo-Saxon culture in the British Isles between the sixth and ninth centuries. Following the precedent set by the ancient Israelites, who carried the Ark of the Covenant to war (1 Sam 4:1–11) just as their enemies carried statues of their gods (2 Sam 5:21; Toorn 1997; Parmenter 2015), here biblical books and their cases acted as battle standards and shields in times of war. Most notorious is the Irish Cathach (battle) reliquary believed to contain a controversial copy of the Psalms penned by St. Columba around 560, and now found in the National Museum of Ireland in Dublin. Tradition holds that Columba copied this psalter without the owner's permission, which led to a war. Columba was victorious, and therefore in the following centuries the manuscript was carried into other battles in the Cathach shrine on the breast of one of the O'Donnell family, so the book-shrine was also a breastplate. One *Life* of St. Columba claims, "if carried three times to the right around the army ... going into battle, it was certain that they would return victorious" (Raferty 1941, 51).

Stories of soldiers being saved by a bullet in a Bible begin in the nineteenth century, when they become a favorite topic within Protestant evangelicalism, especially in the new Bible Societies forming in the United States and Britain. One anecdote from 1805 refers to the pocket "Bibles" carried by Oliver Cromwell's Protestant troops during the English Civil War of the seventeenth century: one of Cromwell's soldiers, a "wild, wicked young fellow," at the end of the day noticed a bullet hole in his Bible, which had stopped at Ecclesiastes 11:9, "walk in the ways of thy heart, and in the sight of thine eyes, but know ... that for all these things God will bring thee into judgment." The tale climaxes in the conversion of the formerly wicked soldier, so that "the Bible was the mean of saving his soul and body too" (Buck 1805, 59–60). Apparently, the storyteller was not aware that Cromwell's soldiers' Bibles were quite thin—only sixteen pages, consisting of selected verses applicable to soldiers—and did not contain Ecclesiastes (Daniell 2003, 471).

Cromwell's Soldiers' Bible seems to have set a model for providing Bibles to soldiers, for the seventeenth century editions were reprinted during the American Civil War in both the North and South. During this time Bible publishing was booming in the U.S., with a multitude of Bibles available through private purchase or distributed by various Bible societies (see Gutjahr 1999).[2] The monthly reports of these groups promoting the Bible, designed to affirm their own work and gain further support, create a repository for bullet-in-a-Bible stories. Here is just one example, from a speech to the Bible Society of Massachusetts and included in their January 1863 Annual Report:

> Here is [a Bible], which a wife sewed in the pocket of her husband's uniform, who was reluctant to take a Bible with him. He bore it away to the battlefield, and the bullet that would have struck his heart entered the Word of God, and stopped at the words [from Acts 20:24]— "But none of these things move me, neither count I my life dear unto myself, so that I might finish my course with joy;" and then, after that Bible had saved the man's mortal life, better still, it was the precious means of saving his immortal life. That Bible had a history. It was given to his wife when she was a girl in the Sabbath school, by her teacher, who had gone to glory; and so it went on from one to another, doing its immortal work. (*Annual Report of the BSM* 1863, 26–27)

The popular phrase of the American Bible Society, "the Bible doing its work," could affirm either the Bible as a "supernatural object" or the idea that "God is 'embodied' in the very words of scripture" to provide guidance and spiritual protection (Fea 2016, 62–63). This again demonstrates the tension between scripture as a saving object, engaged by the senses, or scripture as a saving text, engaged by the mind and heart. In a history of the American Bible Society, regarding its efforts among soldiers in the Civil War, John Fea writes: "Many soldiers viewed the Bible as a holy book with spiritual power apart from the words contained therein. Even if the Bible was not being read, it still had the mystical power to provide spiritual solace in the most frightening of times as long as it was somehow connected to one's body during the thick of the battle" (2016, 82).

The tradition of bullet in a Bible stories continued through World War I, along with reports of where the bullet stopped in the text. This combination shows the desire for edification through the semantic dimension where the material tends to dominate, and harkens back to Christian practices

---

2. The books distributed by Bible societies were generally New Testaments only, designed to fit into a vest pocket, but soldiers did carry larger Bibles as well (Daniell 2003, 722–726; Fea 2016, 81).

of biblical divination since at least since the fourth century. For example, an Australian soldier in World War I had a near-death experience when a shrapnel bullet pierced the New Testament and Psalms in his shirt pocket, going through the back of the book through Acts where "the Gospel pages stopped the bullet" (Harris 2015, 31). Similarly, another Australian soldier was saved when shrapnel stopped not far from Ephesians 6:16–17: "Above all taking the shield of faith wherewith ye shall be able to quench all the fiery darts of the wicked. And take the helmet of salvation and the sword of the Spirit, which is the word of God" (Harris 2015, 91).

It wasn't enough to have faith that the Bible could stop a bullet; you could ensure that your loved one had the proper piece of equipment by buying him an armored Bible. The Heart Shield Bible with a gold-plated steel front cover, engraved with "may this keep you safe from harm" was produced by Protecto Bible Company for soldiers during World War II. Advertisements claimed the covers were constructed of "bullet proof" metal that "protects his heart, saves lives!" (Dault 2013). Several publishers sell metal-covered Bibles today, but do not claim that they are bullet-proof.[3]

Stories of being saved by a bullet in a Bible continue to get a lot of media coverage and spark the interest of people today (see Quigley 2010). Certainly, Christians are intrigued by the stories and continue to circulate them in sermons and on the internet. One blogger's response to reading about a soldier's Bible stopping a bullet helps us to segue into an examination of the affective power of the Bible: "I do know reading the account reaffirmed my own love for the Bible. Not just the Word it contains, but the physical book and the comfort it may bring" (Buxton 2008).

Feeling through the Bible as an affective object

It is clear that many people desire physical contact with and security from their Bibles, even when those practices do not necessarily align with the sanctioned or authorized uses of Bibles as texts to be read, contemplated, and lived out. Tracing the perception that a material engagement with the Christian Bible is effective against bodily harm is an interesting task, but it does not explain the users' motivations for wanting the physical comfort and protection of the Book. My student soldier or the bearers of the Cathach shrine did not value their scriptures as saving objects because they knew the stories that I have recounted, yet neither are these Bible uses random occurrences; the ritualization of Bibles as saving objects are shared social practices. Something is communicated in these practices, but whatever sec-

---

3. Several popular videos have debunked the idea that a Bible or other book can stop a bullet (see Mythbusters 2004; Deuce and Guns 2016).

ond-order historical sketch I have generated is not the content of that communication. There is a desire for and communication of feeling—for how the Bible feels. The feeling is not magically attached to the Bible itself, the feeling is not owned by the individual Bible user, and the feeling is not a response to a prior intellectualization about history or theology.

Recent studies in what is called "affect theory" help to give us some tools for thinking about this priority of feeling. The editors of the *Affect Theory Reader* define affect as "the name we give to those forces—visceral forces beneath, alongside, or generally other than conscious knowing, vital forces beyond emotion—that can serve to drive us toward movement" (Gregg and Seigworth 2010, 1). Bringing affect theory into religious studies is thus a part of the "materialist turn" away from a prioritization of religious texts, hermeneutics, and linguistic propositions that we call "belief" toward an emphasis on embodiment and material practices. In a recent book called *Religious Affects: Animality, Evolution, and Power*, Donovan Schaefer asks:

> What if religion is not only about language, books, or belief? In what way is religion about the way things feel, the things we want, the way our bodies are guided through thickly textured, magnetized worlds? ... How is religion made up of clustered material forms, aspects of our embodied life, such as other bodies, food, community, labor, movement, music, sex, natural land-scapes, architecture, and objects? ... How is religion something that carries us on its back rather than something that we think, choose, or command?
>
> (2015, 3)

Or, as Schaefer asks throughout his book: What if we consider that religion, as a thing of the senses, "feels before it thinks, believes, or speaks" (2015, 8, 212)?

Theoreticians of affect make a point of distinguishing affect from emotion, aligning emotion with identifiable signifiers, like sadness, joy and anger, which fall into the realm of a thinking subject who creates the world through language. Instead, affect is "not so much experienced by the individual as constitutive of the individual" (Supp-Montgomerie 2015, 337) through the social circulation of energy between bodies. Because this view decenters the thinking subject, "bodies" are not just human bodies, but also include material objects; thus we rely on our sensory interactions with multifarious aspects of the material world to build our lives, to complete our incomplete selves (Morgan 2012, 52; Plate 2014, 1–22), to make us feel that our existence matters.

All the bodies in question here are social bodies, constituted through relationships that exceed the individual substantiations of particular actions (Supp-Montgomerie 2015, 338). So what is transmitted without being taught in words in Bible rituals is affect, or the power of what it feels like to be a body within a group that exists through its material interactions with other bodies. As David Morgan (2010b) puts it, "[o]bjects and spaces are not static, with abstract meanings encoded within them. Indeed their 'meanings' are often not singular or intellectual meanings at all, but rather the stories of their travels through time" (68; see also Morgan 2012, 66).[4] These stories are not always narratives in language, but worlds constructed through feelings. Sometimes the stories are stories communicated in language, as linguistic by-products of the affective force attached to objects, which then maintain and continue the generation of the power felt in relation to the thing. For example, the stock stories of a Bible stopping a bullet—including the disposition of the intended victim before and after the encounter with the bullet, the place in the text where the bullet stopped, the faith of the giver of the Bible to the recipient, the afterlife of the Bible as it is circulated among others after the war—are a way of articulating as well as producing affects related to other kinds of Bible uses.

Theorist Sara Ahmed's essay "Happy Objects" (2010) is relevant to a study about the affects generated by the Bible, which then lead to the perception of the Bible as effective, or a powerful, saving agent. She writes that "good" objects are those whose affects have been socially habituated—where people have oriented themselves toward those objects that the group has deemed "necessary for a good life" (34). It is not difficult to see how the Bible fits into this description of good objects. Christians' experiences with the Bible—whether political, social, or psychological, and undoubtedly tied to the semantic and performative dimensions of the text—consolidate into the lesson that the Bible is "good." For Protestants, the Bible is an indispensable object, for only through the Bible is the promise of salvation available. This affective quality, the feeling that the Bible is an agent of salvation, is cultivated through the iconic dimension of scripture; or, to put it another way, material and visual interactions with the Bible reflect and produce an orientation toward that object as that which promises a good life, that which saves.

In his analysis called *How the Bible Works*, ethnographer Brian Malley describes a weekly Sunday School activity called *Pat the Bible* for two-year-olds in an evangelical church. During the lesson each child is handed a

---

4. Stories of particular Bibles' travels through time is another favorite genre of nineteenth century evangelism in the U.S. and England. We saw this above in with the Civil War Bible sewn into the soldier's uniform (Taylor 1863, 27); see also *The Story of a Pocket Bible* (Sargent n.d.), *The Story of a Red Velvet Bible* (M. H. 1885a), and its sequel, *Richard Blake and his Little Green Bible* (M. H. 1885b).

pocket-sized Gideon New Testament, and a variety of songs are sung while the children are taught to lovingly pat their "Bibles" (2004, 46). Having this activity with pre-readers sets the stage for future interactions with the Bible as text that will be grounded in the prior affective response and orientation to touching the Bible as good. While this affective habituation (Ahmed 2010, 35) is readily apparent in children's ritual practices, I would like to assert that this production of affect is one of the primary functions of the iconic dimension of scripture. Because the affect of seeing, touching, and engaging with material scripture is cultivated in community, this sensation is tied up with access to power—with a social good, with that which maximizes life. This iconic affect thus influences what the Bible does for people, offering salvation in a multitude of ways.

In the example of my student taking her unread Bible to war, it is likely that her action was affect-based or a response to an impulse triggered by past social experiences, rather than cognitively-based (Hill and Hood 1999). The physical form of the Bible protects and comforts, so that she feels safe. To dismiss her practice as magic or superstitious or her Bible as a talisman, charm, or fetish (see Schneiders 1991, 43)—all terms that indicate affect, not "proper" thinking—is to dismiss the affective nature of the material practices in which we are constantly embroiled.

References

Ahmed, Sara. 2010. "Happy objects." In *The Affect Theory Reader*, edited by Gregg and Seigworth, 29–51. Durham, NC: Duke University Press. https://doi.org/10.1215/9780822392781-002

Annual Report of the Bible Society of Massachusetts. 1863. Boston: T. R. Marvin and Son.

Buck, Charles, ed. 1805. *Anecdotes, Religious, Moral, and Entertaining; Alphabetically Arranged, and Interspersed with a Variety of Useful Observations*, vol. 1. Third edition. London: Knight and Compton.

Buxton, Shirley. 2008. "A Bible Instead of Bullets." *God Things.* 13 March. https://shirleybuxton.wordpress.com/2008/03/13/a-bible-instead-of-bullets/. Accessed 11 March 2013.

Daniell, David. 2003. *The Bible in English*. New Haven, CT: Yale University Press.

Dault, David. 2013. "'Battlezone' Bibles and bulletproof covers: The material rhetoric of armor plating in contemporary Bible production." Conference paper presented at the Southeastern Commission for the Study of Religion Annual Meeting, Greenville, South Carolina, March.

Deuce and Guns. 2016. "WWII Bible bullet proof?" *YouTube.* 25 February. https://youtu.be/Z-xKLHz5Yxw. Accessed 17 October 2016.

Fea, John. 2016. *The Bible Cause: A History of the American Bible Society*. Oxford: Oxford University Press. https://doi.org/10.1093/acprof:oso/9780190253066.001.0001

Gamble, Harry Y. 1995. *Books and Readers in the Early Church.* New Haven, CT: Yale University Press.

Gregg, Melissa and Gregory J. Seigworth. 2010. "An inventory of shimmers." In *The Affect Theory Reader*, edited by Gregg and Seigworth, 1–28. Durham, NC: Duke University Press.

Gutjahr, Paul. 1999. *An American Bible: A History of the Good Book in the United States, 1777–1880.* Stanford, CT: Stanford University Press.

Haines-Eitzen, Kim. 2005. "Miniature books and rituals of private reading in late antiquity." Conference paper presented at the American Academy of Religion Annual Meeting, Philadelphia, Pennsylvania, November.

Harris, John, ed. 2015. *Their Sacrifice: The Brave and their Bibles.* Minto: Bible Society Australia.

Hill, Peter C. and Ralph W. Hood. 1999. "Affect, religion, and unconscious processes." *Journal of Personality* 67: 1015–1046. https://doi.org/10.1111/1467-6494.00081

Horsbrugh, Marjory. 1885a. *The Story of a Red Velvet Bible.* London: Hodder and Stoughton.

———. 1885b. *Richard Blake and his Little Green Bible: A Sequel.* London: Hodder and Stoughton.

John Chrysostom. 1886–1889. *Homily on John.* In *Nicene and Post-Nicene Fathers*, First Series, edited by Philip Schaff, volume 14, 1–334. Edinburgh: T & T Clark. [Reprint ed.: Grand Rapids, MI: Eerdmans, 1989].

———. 1886–1889. *Homily on the Statues.* In *Nicene and Post-Nicene Fathers*, First Series, ed. Philip Schaff, volume 9. Edinburgh: T & T Clark. [Reprint ed.: Grand Rapids, MI: Eerdmans, 1989].

Malley, Brian. 2004. *How the Bible Works: An Anthropological Study of Evangelical Biblicism.* New York: Altamira Press.

Maltomini, F., ed. and trans. 1998. "Letter of Abgar to Jesus." In *The Oxyrhynchs Papyri*, edited by M. W. Haslam, A. Jones, F. Maltomini and M. L. West, vol. LXV, no. 4469, 122–129. London: The British Academy.

Marty, Martin. 1982. "America's iconic book." In *Humanizing America's Iconic Book: Society of Biblical Literature Centennial Addresses 1980*, edited by Gene M. Tucker and Douglas A. Knight, 1–23. Chico, CA: Scholars Press.

Morgan, David. 2010a. "Introduction: The matter of belief." In *Religion and Material Culture: The Matter of Belief*, edited by David Morgan, 1–17. New York: Routledge.

———. 2010b. "Materiality, social analysis, and the study of religion." In *Religion and Material Culture: The Matter of Belief*, edited by David Morgan, 55–74. New York: Routledge, 2010.

———. 2012. *The Embodied Eye: Religious Visual Culture and the Social Life of Feeling.* Berkley: University of California Press. https://doi.org/10.1525/california/9780520272224.001.0001

MythBusters. 2004. "What is bulletproof?" *Discovery Channel.* 29 September. http://www.discovery.com/tv-shows/mythbusters/mythbusters-database/is-anything-really-bulletproof/. Accessed 17 October 2016.

Ortiz, Angel. 2011. Student paper for The Synoptic Gospels. Spalding University, Louisville, Kentucky. December.

Parmenter, Dorina Miller. 2006. "The iconic book: The image of the Bible in early Christian rituals." *Postscripts* 2: 160–189. [Reprinted in *Iconic Books and Texts*, edited by James W. Watts, 63–92. Sheffield: Equinox, 2013].

———. 2015. "Material scripture." In *The Oxford Encyclopedia of the Bible and the Arts*, vol. 2, edited by Timothy Beal, 24–35. Oxford: Oxford University Press.

Plate, Brent S. 2014. *A History of Religion in 5 ½ Objects*. Boston, MA: Beacon Press.

Quigley, Chris. 2010. "Bibles stopping bullets." *Quigley's Cabinet*. 29 March. http://quigleyscabinet.blogspot.com/2010/03/bibles-stopping-bullets.html. Accessed 17 October 2016.

Raftery, Joseph. 1941. *Christian Art in Ancient Ireland,* vol. 2. Dublin: Stationary Office of Ireland.

Sargent. George E. n.d. *The Story of a Pocket Bible.* London: The Religious Tract Society.

Schaefer, Donovan O. 2015. *Religious Affects: Animality, Evolution, and Power*. Durham, NC: Duke University Press. https://doi.org/10.1215/9780822374909

Schneiders, Sandra M. 1991. *The Revelatory Text: Interpreting the New Testament as Sacred Scripture.* San Francisco, CA: HarperSanFrancisco.

Smith, Jonathan Z. 2009. "Religion and Bible." *Journal of Biblical Literature* 128: 5–27. https://doi.org/10.2307/25610162

Supp-Montgomerie, Jenna. 2015. "Affect and the study of religion." *Religion Compass* 9/10: 335–345. https://doi.org/10.1111/rec3.12166

Toorn, Karel van der. 1997. "The iconic book: Analogies between the Babylonian cult of images and the veneration of the Torah." In *The Image and the Book: Iconic Cults, Aniconism, and the Rise of Book Religion in Israel and the Ancient Near East*, edited by Karel van der Toorn, 229–248. Louven: Peeters.

Vasquez, Manuel A. 2011. *More than Belief: A Materialist Theory of Religion*. Oxford: Oxford University Press.

Watts, James W. 2006. "The three dimensions of scriptures." *Postscripts* 2: 135–159. [Reprinted in *Iconic Books and Texts*, edited by James W. Watts, 9–32. Sheffield: Equinox, 2013].

4

Engaging All the Senses: On Multi-sensory Stimulation in the Process of Making and Inaugurating a Torah Scroll

Marianne Schleicher

Based on an analysis of the process of making and inaugurating a Torah scroll, this article describes what is likely to trigger sensory responses in the participants in each phase of the process and the function of activating the five senses of touch, hearing, vision, smell, and taste. By distinguishing between hermeneutical and artefactual uses of sacred texts and drawing on sensory integration theory, it argues that multi-sensory stimulation in handling the Torah scroll brings people close and enables nonconscious internal negotiation between individual memories, cultural representations, and the immediate environment. In this way, sense-stimulation facilitates the transitivity crucial for individual subject formation as part of a greater collective.

Introduction

This article argues that the multi-sensory process of making and inaugurating a torah scroll enables nonconscious internal negotiation between individual memories, cultural representations, and the immediate environment in a way that facilitates the transitivity crucial for individual subject formation as part of a greater collective. The argument is based on a detailed analysis of the ritualized process of making and inaugurating a new torah scroll in contemporary Jewish religious practice which engages all five senses. Information on the entire process has not previously been collected and systematized into a standardized description, nor have scholars directed their attention to the coherence of the entire process or, for that matter, to the role of the senses in this process or similar rituals involving sacred

Marianne Schleicher is Associate Professor for the Study of Religion at Aarhus University, Denmark.

texts.[1] The empirical data derives from different, often documentary sources and offers only my reconstruction of an intelligible whole. The reconstruction also draws on background information from ancient Israelite-Jewish texts and traditions that have become normative for this process.

The purpose of the analysis is to identify what is likely to trigger sensory responses in the participants in the different phases of the process of making and inaugurating a torah scroll and then to explain the function of activating the five senses of touch, hearing, vision, smell, and taste. I am aware that I only have limited, at best partial, information about individual negotiations of the activated senses, just as I cannot possibly determine if authorities or norms interfere with how individuals interpret the tactile feelings, sounds, sights, smells, and tastes. I can and shall, however, detect sensory cues in the process and present some qualified suggestions as to what associations are evoked by the multi-sensory uses of the most sacred of Jewish texts based on the history of Jewish religion.

Theoretical framework

The first theoretical point of departure that informs the analysis is a distinction between hermeneutical and artefactual uses of scripture that I developed a decade ago[2] to counter a tendency within the study of religion to consider sacred texts only as important source material about religious rituals and doctrines. Sacred texts certainly constitute such source material for the study of religion, but the discipline hardly ever treats them as a religious phenomenon in their own right whose sacred status alters the premises and consequences of their use in contrast to other religious and non-religious texts.[3] In other words, a knowledge gap exists with regard to

---

1. I am deeply grateful to James Watts for inviting me to the Bochum Symposium in April 2016 on "Seeing, Touching, Holding, and Tasting Sacred Texts" and for the implied encouragement to pursue questions on the senses with regard to scriptural use. It has come as a surprise to me how useful this perspective can be for explaining the effects that follow from what I have called artefactual use (see next footnote) and from what Watts has called the iconic dimension (see Watts 2013). I will not go into the minor details of what separates our understanding and terminology because I believe that we share a more important wish to promote material perspectives on sacred texts and their use. Sharing this wish and the subsequent pursuit of answers with Watts have been the most stimulating event in my academic life for years.

2. The distinction was presented in English for the first time in Schleicher 2009a and 2009b. It has later been adapted to new contexts as in Schleicher 2010 and 2011.

3. The anthology edited by Miriam Levering: *Rethinking Scripture: Essays from a Comparative Perspective* from 1989 constitutes the main exception to this tendency. While every single contribution has much valuable insight to offer, the book, however, refrains from presenting the "static, universal characteristics" of scripture as a phenomenon. Levering feared that it would cloud the "dynamics of the relations that people have had with

the ritualized ways of handling sacred texts and what implications sacred texts as a phenomenon have for the religiosity of individuals and collectives. To a certain extent, this knowledge gap could be mended by drawing upon insights from the so-called "canon debate," where scholars have discussed the function of canonical texts as a storage place for and a symbol of society's religious norms (McDonald and Sanders 2002; Finkelberg and Stroumsa 2003). These scholars argued that society uses canons to recall such normativity and thereby to claim a culture and history. As such, canonical texts become a means for including or excluding present or potential members of a particular society based on an evaluation of whether or not their practices and beliefs remained within its boundaries (Ricoeur 1979, 271–276). The canon debate thus offered insights into how religious specialists have applied scripture to maintain and transmit religious normativity. Still, it reflects an elitist bias because of its focus on usage among specialists and because it offers practically no information about lay uses, which are the preponderance of individual and collective uses of sacred texts.

The discipline of anthropology was swift to appropriate the material turn with its interest in defining how matter comes to matter. In *How the Bible Works* from 2004, anthropologist Brian Malley decided to counter the approach to sacred texts in hermeneutic and literary theory by investigating "the social, psychological, and material processes by which a text holds a place in the discursive ground of a community" (Malley 2004, 9). Malley coined the term "transitivity" to address what he considered the main function of scripture. He pointed to scripture's relational nature and how its material aspects serve to establish links between dual contexts defined on the one hand as private and culturally transmitted beliefs and on the other hand the text, not so much as words, but as an artefact (Malley 2004, 73–74). I was convinced that Malley's concept of scripture as artefact and its function in generating transitivity was pivotal for addressing the interacting processes between scripture, its material embedding, and the associations of both elite and lay users that scriptural use provokes. However, I disagreed with Malley's refusal to address the function of what I call hermeneutical uses of sacred texts. Accordingly, I coined a distinction between hermeneutical and artefactual uses of them and reflected on their complementary functions.

texts, their ways of receiving texts in the context of their religious projects" (11). If a definition aims to describe the static essence of things, I agree that one risks either saying nothing or projecting knowledge from one's own background onto all scriptures. However, the study of religion has pursued functional definitions at least since Emile Durkheim, and such functional definitions would focus on the relations and receptions of texts among users in all strata of society.

The hermeneutical and artefactual uses of sacred texts are not mutually exclusive, but activated in turn or simultaneously depending on the needs of the user. I follow Paul Ricoeur in defining hermeneutical use of sacred texts as a two-step process of analyzing the text and considering its proposed religious worldview. The first step consists of a circular process of reconstructing a text's verbal architecture in order to decipher an implied semantic whole out of the textual parts. As a second step, the reader is encouraged to consider whether he or she should appropriate, transform, or refuse the text's proposed worldview (Ricoeur 1976, 77; 2003, 377–378). Only a few lay individuals engage in such a detailed as well as critical reading enterprise. Otherwise only members of the elite, i.e. religious or academic specialists who have received training in hermeneutics, engage in such conscious negotiation of norms crucial for individual and collective adaptation in times of crisis or altered environments.

Artefactual use of scripture designates the very handling of a sacred text as a physical object in collective or individual rituals and repetitive acts. Handling transforms it into a manipulable symbol. Triggered by the sensory aspects of the sacred text, such as form, texture, embellishment, smell, and enacted sounds, artefactual use allows individuals, be they lay or elite, to negotiate the sensory intakes of the environment in a more or less nonconscious way, which parallels the conscious negotiations available through hermeneutical use. The outcome of these negotiations influence how users project their needs, experiences, and hopes onto a particular sacred text in a way that often interferes with, even overrules, its textual content. Accordingly, sacred texts serve as a hub that establishes connections in all directions. Transitivity is thus the overall effect of artefactual use, attracting the projections of its users, tying them together with collective and cultural representations due to cues in the immediate surroundings. Sensory intakes from these cues even affect the users before they becomes conscious thereof, to which I shall turn soon. However, it should first be emphasized that because no reading or interpretative skills are required and because the artefactual use of sacred texts represents the use known best to most religious people in literate traditions, it is my estimate that the preponderance of all uses of sacred texts is artefactual, which is why the study of religion must direct attention to sacred texts as a phenomenon with important functions for individuals and collectives.

The second theoretical point of departure that informs my analysis goes into detail about the sensory integration involved in artefactual use and its function for meaning-making on a more or less nonconscious level. The senses are capable of receiving information about different forms of energy and chemicals in the environment and of passing such information about the physical state of the external world on to the central nervous system. In this way, the senses are seminal to facilitating our behavioral reactions and decisions in our environment and establishing our connection to the world (Keeley 2002).

The act of establishing transitivity seems to be the central function of the senses. Sensory integration is unique in each individual, and scholars tend to see sensory integration as a matter of establishing in individuals connections between previous experiences of similar sensory inputs and the planning of future transactions with the surrounding world, negotiated with normative interpretations of it (Waskul *et al.* 2009, 5–22). This negotiation is a kind of feedback-feedforward evaluative process that considers the give-and-takes with past, present, and future environmental elements. This evaluation is crucial to individual subject formation and the maintenance of self-continuity over time. It even conveys a feeling of control over the environment and stimulates the innate drive of the individual to explore his or her own capacities (Bundy *et al.* 2002, 5; 12–17).

The autonomic nervous system that governs the feedback-feedforward evaluative process is part of the peripheral nervous system that works in tandem with the central nervous system. As the name indicates, the autonomic nervous system responds to information about physical sensation in an autonomic, nonconscious way. Whenever we recall previous experiences, they surface to our consciousness, but what experiences, memories, individual or collective representations we recall is beyond our conscious control. That depends on what has previously been stored in each individual.

The modalities of the five senses serve different functions. The sense of touch receives information about pressure sensed by nerve endings in the skin. Depending on the degree of pressure, it stimulates calming as well as sexual arousal, it activates various defense mechanisms, and it enables the precise handling of physical objects, including people. It thus facilitates a physical connection to the outside world premised on nearness, even intimacy (Bundy *et al.* 2002, 51, 85).

The sense of hearing located in the ear processes information about sound waves and enables discriminations for location and direction, which affects the orientation of the head, eyes, and body required for individual and collective movement and action. Thanks to feedback loops, the ear differentiates between familiar and novel auditory input, thus allowing for selective auditory attention. The sense of hearing is not only responsible for transmitting information that is processed by the brain as verbal language, it also transmits non-verbal aspects of sounds such as vibration, frequency, intonation, harmony, and rhythm that can affect the brain waves of individuals and so their mental and emotional states (Bundy *et al.* 2002, 59–60).

The sense of vision depends on the eyes to mediate waves of light processed as contrast, color, form, and movement of different speeds and directions. The visual system enables nonconscious guidance of motor actions and depth perception, localization, direction, and identification of proximate objects, including humans. It furthermore enables conscious, higher order visual-spatial recognition to be used for wayfinding and memory of connections between features in the environment (Bundy *et al.* 2002, 61–67, 128–136).

The sense of smell has the nose as its organ, where chemical receptors distinguish between the seven basic odors: ethereal, floral, musky, pepperminty, camphoraceous, spicy and putrid. Odors can be sensed at both close and long distance because they are airborne. Smell differentiates between familiar and novel olfactory input, with great significance for basic in- and outgroup detection (Porteous 1985, 357–358). Furthermore, the sense of smell is the most important sentimental pathway to memories, probably because of the close connection between the olfactory bulb and the limbic system governing emotional life, its access to the amygdala responsible for processing emotions, and to the hippocampus that is generative of associative thinking between memories of previous scents, of people, places, and events in the past, and of new inputs (Waskul *et al.* 2009, 9).

Finally, the sense of taste has the mouth as its organ where taste receptors mainly on the tongue distinguish between sweetness, sourness, saltiness, bitterness, and umami to enable an identification of food as either appetitive, nourishing, putrid or even poisonous. While the primary function of taste is to stimulate an adequate intake of food that secures individual survival, the appetitive reaction to food does not only rely on perception of chemicals in what we eat or drink. Environmental influences from cultural traditions and close relationships affect our individual food preferences, binding us in a nonconscious way to collectives, just as we may acquire a liking for new tastes if we adapt to new environments. The plasticity of taste is important for both individual and collective survival (Hayes and Keast 2011).

On the basis of these two theoretical points of departure, I will distinguish between hermeneutical and artefactual uses of sacred texts, though I expect artefactual uses to dominate because the process of making and inaugurating a Torah scroll is a very material process. I will trace configurations of transitivity by asking how the sacred texts serve as hubs and what they channel and link. I will also look for particular cues for stimulating the senses and reflect on how sensory inputs matter for individual and/or collective negotiations of experience.

Analysis: The process of making and inaugurating a Torah scroll

The making of a Torah scroll

The act of making a Torah scroll fulfills God's last commandment to Moses in the Torah where God says: "Now write down this song and teach it to the Israelites and have them sing it" (Deut 31:19). Based on this quotation, the Babylonian Talmud (c. 7th century CE) prescribes that every Jewish man must write a Torah scroll for himself (*b Sanhedrin* 21b). Should he be unable to write one, he can pay a scribe to do so (*b Megillah* 27a). Contrary to hermeneutical use where words and sentences are interpreted in light of the immediate context, the Talmud ignores the fact that God only commands Moses to write down a song. Ignoring the immediate context renders the implicit quotation of the Torah an instance of artefactual use that seems to serve the function of addressing late antique concerns; i.e., how to bring male Jews to write Torah scrolls. Originally, the Talmudic prescription ensured the material distribution of Torah scrolls, enabling male members in Jewish families to engage in Torah studies. Today, Torah manufacturing has turned into a symbolic act: the commissioning of a Torah scroll is often dedicated to the memory of a deceased member of a family, a congregation, or even a nation.[4] As a result, the commissioning act establishes transitivity between the commissioning party, the memorialized person, and the context of its future use.

To begin making a scroll, a layperson, a tanner, or the scribe must find skins from kosher animals such as goats, cattle, or deer. To allow for the sacred status of the finished product, the agent must conduct the tanning process with the conscious intent of turning the skins into parchment for a Torah scroll (*b Megillah* 19a). The skins must first soak in water for a number of days. After this, they continue soaking for eighteen days in a new liquid mixture consisting of water, salt, sometimes calcium, and dates or dog or bird dung ("Parashat Bo," *Yalkut Shimoni*) to start the process that will enable the removal of hair and fat. Today, limewater is preferred over dog or bird dung. Then barley flour is added to open the pores to enable the later intake of high levels of resin and tannic acid, stemming from gallnuts, that help the skins contract and harden (*b Gittin* 19a). The hair and fat are then removed by scraping the skins with non-metal tools. After this, the processed skins are dried on a stretching rack. The parchment must

---

4. Cf. http://www.breakingisraelnews.com/40805/75-Torah-scrolls-dedicated-in-memory-of-war-victims-idf/#ZiayzocvVfktCMyR.97 (17 October 2016).

be prepared on both sides (bShabbat 79b) and cut into square sheets. It is beyond doubt that these chemicals and excrements from the process of tanning skins for the Torah scrolls generate strong smells. It is also likely that the scrolls retained these smells for some considerable time. I have not been able to find any comments in religious texts on such smells from scrolls. However, the Babylonian Talmud states that a woman is entitled to demand divorce from her husband or refuse levirate marriage if the husband or brother-in-law is a tanner (m Ketubot 9:10; b Ketubot 77a). Similarly, neighbors are entitled to object to their neighbor's wish to become a tanner or a tanner's wish to become a resident in their neighborhood (b Baba Bathra 21a–b). Today, when limewater has replaced dog or bird dung in the tanning process, the smell of lime still sticks to the sheets. At a Jewish Enrichment Center in Chicago just after the festival of Simchat Torah when the giving of the Torah is celebrated, a group of children were introduced to seeing, touching, hearing and smelling the scrolls of the Torah for the first time. When asked what the Torah smelled like, they responded that it smells like lemon make-up and yummy spices.[5] In other words, now that the smell is associated with something positive, institutional websites do not hesitate to report the smell of a Torah scroll, whereas premodern religious texts are suspiciously silent about its acrid smell of resin, acid, dog or bird dung, old dates and flour. Their silence about the smell of the scroll stands in remarkable contrast to the negative connotations of a tanner's odor. While habituation may explain how people could ignore the smell, it also seems that the interpretation of smell is negotiated between individually triggered responses and societal norms about the meaning of a particular smell. Maybe individual and collective veneration of the Torah simply stunted the sense of smell in this case, overruling the acridity of chemicals and excrements.[6] This could be an act of in-group courtesy to Jews who commit themselves to preparing skins for kosher parchment. How would a Jewish tanner otherwise avoid exclusion from marital and residential relations and endure the solitary process of soaking, scraping, stretching, and cutting the skins for the benefit of the entire community while affected by the same fumes that this community tries to avoid?

After tanning the skins, the scribe takes over the process. The scribe

---

5. http://jewishenrichment.org/2014/10/15/first-day-of-yedidim-nitzanim-explore-the-Torah-scroll-with-many-senses

6. In the medieval Kabbalistic book *Sefer haZohar* III: 115b, God is described as being able to ignore the acrid smell of tanners when God has to go to the streets of the tanners in search of his beloved, the *Shekhinah*, who resides there during the exile of the Jews.

needs his[7] sense of vision to make precise lines with a ruler in columns on each square sheet, leaving space for margins to surround and protect God's words to Moses (*b Menachot* 30a). Information about the visual characteristics of the letters derives from basic hermeneutic readings of the Mishnah (c. 200 C.E.) that specified that the sacred status of the Torah depended on its textual passages being written in the Assyrian script on parchment and in ink (*m Yadayim* 4:5). No vowels or accents are allowed in a scroll fit for ritual use. These meticulous rules generate a visual norm that establishes a recognizable, common denominator between scriptural scrolls that is supported by recollections of previous views of sacred scrolls. The visual characteristics seem crucial for the ability of users to recognize a scroll's status as sacred. Finally, the meticulousness of the rules and norms activate associations with cultic purity rules in the priestly tradition of Israelite religion where such meticulousness was a precondition for being close to God (e.g. Lev 8; 21). Auditory cues from the scratching of a reed or a quill from a kosher bird against the parchment blend into the writing process and emphasize the unique production methods now reserved for writing sacred texts. The commissioning party also depends on the mental preparation of the scribe before each session of writing the Torah text. Especially before writing the name of God, the scribe has to say aloud: "I now have the intent to write the holy name." Surely, the sense of hearing will soon become accustomed to the familiar phrase that nevertheless becomes an auditory element in the writing process. The writing of God's name is not to be interrupted. If an error occurs in the holy name or it transgresses into the margins, the sheet is unqualified for ritual use and has to be stored away or buried (*Shulkhan Arukh*, Yoreh Deah, 22).[8] Once the entire Torah text has been written—except for the last section in Deuteronomy—the very tactile process of making the scroll comes to an end in sewing the sheets together with threads of dried tendons from kosher animals and attaching a cylinder at each end (*b Baba Bathra* 14a).

---

7. I refer to a scribe as he, because this profession has almost exclusively consisted of men. According to the Babylonian Talmud, a Torah should be written by someone who dons tefillin, which explains why women cannot be scribes. Leili Avrin mentions that a few Medieval Jewish women wrote torot, including Paula bat Abraham from the thirteenth century, and that fifteen women scribes are known from the Renaissance, but she does not document this claim (Avrin 1991, 128). In modern times, it is not until 2007 that we hear of Jen Taylor Friedman from a Reconstructionist congregation finishing what seems to be the first scroll written by a woman (Friedman, n.d.). Orthodox Judaism does not consider scrolls kosher if they are written by a woman, according to a Babylonian ruling (*b Gittin* 45b).
8. For more, see Schleicher 2010.

The writing of the last letters (ketivat ha-otiyot)

The almost finished scroll is now moved to the home of the donor, who either finishes the last letters in the last section of Deuteronomy or sells this honor to one or more people as a way of funding the commissioning (*b Menachot* 30a on Deut 31:19. Selling this honor to community members makes sense given the costly affair of commissioning a Torah, usually 20,000 USD or more (Avrin 1991, 117). Yet, such financial transactions establish transitivity, allowing more people to connect through and to the scroll about to be inaugurated. To make the writing of the last letters more sellable, a parallel between correcting a letter in a scroll and finishing the writing process is often invoked. The parallel builds on an artefactual reference to the Talmud that ignores the semantic message of the sentence "Even if he corrected but one letter he is regarded as if he had written it" (*b Menachot* 30a), by interpreting the act of correcting a scribal error as identical to the writing of the last letters. Subsequently, transitivity is extended from the donor and his or her lifting of the Talmudic commandment to both the donor's house and to people who help finance the scroll's manufacture by buying the right to finish the scroll.

Dressing the Torah (gelilat ha-Torah)

The scroll must now be prepared for its journey to its context of use, typically a synagogue or a religious institution, and Jews do so by dressing it in ways analogous to the dress of the high priest in the Tabernacle, according to Exodus 28. Dressing the Torah scroll or simply wrapping the Torah scroll in linen has been known from the 2nd century onward.[9] The dressing involves a lot of touching, emphasizing the nearness, even intimacy, of the participants with the scroll. First, they take the scroll and wind a Torah binder around it. Second, they dress the scroll. In the Ashkenazi, i.e., German language influenced, region, they dress it in a mantle. Sephardic Jews, i.e., Jews with Spanish roots, erect it in a wooden or silver box. Local Ashkenazi women skilled in handicraft may embroider the name of the donor and the target institution on the mantle along with either decorative or floral motifs or images evoking narratives and scenes from the Torah,[10] while Jewish men, skilled in woodcarving, or silversmiths are responsible for similar ornamentation and inscription on the Sephardic Torah boxes.

---

9. Some of the Dead Sea Scrolls were found wrapped in linen while many others found at Qumran were enclosed in ceramic jars. A depiction in the Duro Europos Synagogue also indicates the praxis of wrapping/enclosing the scroll in that Ezra is depicted as standing next to a covered scroll (Avrin 1991, 64; 120; 129).

10. http://ijamuseum.org/museum/the-collection/textiles (18 October 2016).

Third, they place Torah crowns or pomegranates in precious metals on top of the two cylinders including small metal bells. Inverting the function of the bells in Exodus 28 where they sound to prepare God for Aarons coming, the bells now attached to the scroll sound to prepare the congregation for the coming of the sacred object. By convention, the sound of bells alert participants and bystanders to change their own behavior to ready for the procession. Finally, they hang a Torah shield made of precious metal on the cylinders. The Torah shield often visually depicts the two tablets with the Ten Commandments and the two pillars standing at the entrance of the Jerusalem temple. Its immediate function in Rabbinic Judaism was to indicate the weekly Torah portion and its accompanying portion from the Prophets to be read during synagogue service. Today, the engraving of the names of the donors on the shield has taken precedence over the liturgical function to ensure a visual marker of transitivity between donor and shield.

The Torah procession

Similar to the tactile experience of dressing the Torah scroll, holding a sacred artefact in a procession indicates a privileged nearness to the sacred that used to be granted to only leaders and religious specialists in archaic religions. In the oldest layers of Israelite religion, Moses, divinely sanctioned kings, and priests had such privileged access to sacred things and buildings.[11] As the Torah scroll from Late Antiquity onward acquired the status of a metonymy of God due to its content of divine speech (Stern 1987, 619), but was distributed widely to ensure every family's access to the normative foundation of Judaism, access to the sacred was potentially at hand at all times. However, in the Middle Ages a kind of re-archaization occurred that once again left the primary handling of the Torah as a sacred object to scribes and rabbis. It is therefore not surprising that it is in this period that processions with Torah scrolls appear in that processions enabled lay Jews occasional nearness to the sacred artifact of their tradition. Once dressed, the involved parties escort the scroll with the tiny bells sounding from the Torah crowns and pomegranates in an outdoor procession to its place of inauguration. On its way, it functions as a hub, connecting itself to the participants and the traversed spaces along the route to its future host institution. The donor and his or her family and friends carry the scroll under a canopy, while other participants congratulate the donor on fulfilling the commandment to write a Torah scroll. This is the moment where the proces-

---

11. Moses carried the tablets down from Mount Sinai (Exod 31:18). For more on the monopoly of religious specialists on their privileged access also to myths and their early written versions, see Assmann 2006, 106; 126–127.

sion enables all participants to approach and kiss the dressed Torah scroll, where the intimate experience of kissing expresses the hope that touching the scroll with one's lips may enable the scroll to transfer health and longevity onto the kissing people. The canopy usually marks weddings: under it, a bride and groom form a covenant. The canopy's association with weddings then symbolizes the bond between the scroll, the kissing participants, and its place of inauguration as a bond of intimacy, love, and commitment.

If the scroll is destined for a synagogue, children from the congregation lead the procession—in daytime with flags and at night with candles or torches. First, the exalted and happy sounds of people parading, congratulating, and kissing establish a joyous mood, the memory of which can be triggered again at similar sounds. Second, the young vanguard of the procession with their torches and lights creates transitivity to God in Exod 13:21–22 who led the Israelites for forty years in the desert as a pillar of smoke at day and as a pillar of fire at night. In Rabbinic Judaism, this cultural experience developed into the representation of the *Shekhinah*, God's female presence, who chose to be with her children in exile (Scholem 1952). Third, the procession also creates transitivity with the representation of the first torah procession as it is described in 2 Sam 6:14–15. Here, King David danced in front of the ark as it was led to Jerusalem. The ark contained the two tablets, but according to Deut 31:26, Moses commanded the Levites to place his handwritten Torah scroll next to the two tablets.[12] A Torah procession thus establishes additional transitivities to the scriptural and messianic figure of King David as well as to Jerusalem as an earthly and heavenly representation of divine promises to the Israelites. The current generation is inserted into this relational web of Mosaic and Davidic connotations. The donor must give sweets to the children, so that the tasty intake of candy helps store their ritual participation as a positive memory.

Once the procession reaches the entrance to the place of inauguration, typically a synagogue, other members of the congregation carry its old scrolls out to the entrance for the old scrolls to welcome the new scroll. Then the main actors carry the new and the old scrolls into the synagogue to become members of the same Torah cupboard, thus establishing transitivity even among scrolls.[13]

---

12. See Watts 2015, § 11–13 for his convincing analysis of the relation between the esoteric tablets and the exoteric scroll.

13. For more on processions, see Grimes 2005, who is among the few scholars of religion who has reflected on the function of procession as a religious phenomenon.

Circumambulation (hakafot)

In contemporary Judaism, sounds of prayers accompany the dancing men and boys of orthodox congregations and dancing members of all genders in more liberal denominations who move in circuits seven times around the reader's table where members of the procession still hold the new and the old scrolls close in their arms. During the circuits, the liturgy for Simchat Torah is recited. On the sixth circuit, Hasidic Jews recall the deaths of six million Jews during the Second World War. Once the seven circuits have been accomplished, those who carry the old scrolls return them to the Torah cupboard, also referred to as the ark (Elbogen 1993, 359). The Torah cupboard is placed on the wall pointing toward Jerusalem where the temple used to stand in which God's presence resided over the ark. The geographical direction thus connotes the temple's Holy of Holies, which explains the inscription above the cupboard in e.g. the Copenhagen Synagogue that says, "Know in front of whom you are standing." This indicates the presence not of an object, but of God. Similarly, the Torah curtain, often embroidered by the local women or the mother of the donor who are skilled in handicraft, is called the *parochet* just like the curtain in front of the Holy of Holies in the Tabernacle (Exod 40:21) and in the Jerusalem temple. Even though a synagogue is not a sacred place *per se*, the words of God in the Torah scrolls are taken as metonymies of God that alter the status of the room whenever the scrolls are taken out and undressed.

Once undressed in the inauguration ritual, the new scroll is placed on the reader's table. The donor says the blessing used to express gratitude for new events (*b Berachot* 54a; *b Pesachim* 7b; *b Sukkah* 46a.)—in this case, the new scroll and the new piece of clothing that the donor must be wearing. One participant reads Deuteronomy 34, the last portion of the Torah, thus standing in a line of readers who have obeyed the commandment to read the Torah aloud to men, women, and children to help them remember the covenant (Deut 31:10–12; Josh 8:34; Neh 8:8; 2 Kgs 23:2–3). This is the moment when the almost sanctified Torah is most exposed. Touching the text on the pages of the scroll is forbidden, so readers hold a Torah pointer in their hands to avoid touching the most sacred part of the sacred text, i.e., the letters. It is interesting that the numinosity of the very letters is considered so powerful that their proximity requires certain defense mechanisms from readers. By preventing them from touching it, from coming too near, the artefactual way of handling the Torah reflects the conception in Israelite-Jewish religion of an ontological difference between God and humans. This ontological difference explains the claims that no human being can see

God's face and live (Exod 33:20) and that the high priest will die if he does not sanctify himself according to strict procedures prior to entering the Holy of Holies (Lev 16:2).

Thus in the ritual phase of circumambulation, this artefactual use of the torah creates transitivity between the joyous day of Simchat Torah, the deaths of millions during the Shoah, Jerusalem, God's very presence, the sacred letters, the ontological difference between God and humans, and the oscillating sounds of familiar words in collective prayer and individual recitation and reading.

The raising of the Torah (hagba'ah)

After the reading, a layperson raises the scroll with three columns visible for everyone to see while the congregation bows down respectfully and states that this is the Torah. Some also believe that the vision of the very words of the Torah draws down divine lights upon the one who sees them (*Shulchan Arukh*, Orach Chaim, 134:2–3). It is very characteristic of a procession that it culminates in the display of the sacred object, in this case the lifting of the undressed Torah scroll. By lifting it, everyone is able to see the uniting artefact, a common visual experience that again establishes the participants as belonging to the same group.

A second dressing of the Torah (Gelilah)

Any participant may perform the second dressing of the new scroll, which was and still is considered an honorable act, entailing the same kind of nearness, even intimacy, with the rolled up scroll as during the first dressing. It once more emphasizes how lay people in this ritual have access to sensing, even touching the sacred artefact.

Inauguration (hachnasat ha-Torah)

The lay participant then passes the dressed scroll to the cantor who carries it to the Torah cupboard while the congregation accompanies this phase with dance and singing. Odors of sweating, familiar bodies and the sounds of local voices fill the synagogue, while the cantor hands over the new scroll to yet another lay participant who places it inside the Torah cupboard. The cantor then recites Psalm 24 about God's entry into Jerusalem with a tune familiar from a song sung on the festivals of Rosh Hashanah and Yom Kippur. Then he recites the prayer known as Aleinu and the Mourner's Kaddish. In this way, the liturgical recitals and readings by lay participants and professionals, intonated in ways associated with several of the high holidays and according to geographically specific musical traditions, are matters of artefactual use that point forward to the composite liturgical use of the Torah on both joyous and sad festivals in the in-group environment. Recitals and readings link the scroll with the distinct voices of the local congregation, just as they once again establish the Torah scroll as a metonymy of God through the literary imagery of Ps 24.

Festive meal (seudat mitzvah)

The entire process finishes with a festive meal where men, women, and children celebrate the fulfilment of the commandment to write a Torah scroll and the local accomplishment of transforming it into a fully sanctified object. It begins with everyone washing his or her hands. The donor then performs a blessing over the bread familiar to the participants from the beginning of the Sabbath meal. He or she then cuts a small piece for him- or herself and dips it three times in salt, before cutting out shares for all others who share in the meal, who then say the same blessing. The participants also dip the bread in salt three times before eating it. The dishes that follow are not regulated, but it is customary to bake a Torah scroll inauguration cake, known as a *hachnasat sefer Torah*-cake. Eating it evokes God's message to Ezekiel: "'Son of man, eat this scroll I am giving you and fill your stomach with it.' So I ate it, and it tasted as sweet as honey in my mouth" (Ezek 3:3). While food is crucial for survival in this world, the scroll that God gives Ezekiel to eat contains divine words, metonymies of God that taste sweet. Eating this sacred object transforms Ezekiel to enable him to contain and speak the words of God. Typical of artefactual uses of sacred texts, the participants at the festive meal ignore the immediate context of Ezekiel where Ezekiel is to speak to the Israelites who stubbornly refuse to listen to God's address. Instead, the participants consider themselves recipients of God's scroll because tasting the cake serves as an analogy for internalizing God's words just as Ezekiel did. Many other tasty and nice-smelling dishes are placed on the table at the festive meal that concludes the process. These tastes and smells are likely to trigger positive memories of the inauguration of the Torah scroll the next time similar tastes and smells are encountered. After eating, "grace after meal" is said, after which the rabbi and other Torah scholars initiate discussions on the importance of the Torah. Accordingly, the meal connects donor and participants with each other and with tasteful intakes of in-group types of food and food rituals, connoting transformation of in-group members through divine words and reflections on their meaning.

Conclusion

I have described the process of making and inaugurating a Torah scroll and in what phases different sensory responses become triggered. Touching the Torah scroll, either in the process of making it or of inaugurating it, evokes nearness, even intimacy, in a way that links it together with the people who handle or kiss it. Participants thus come into direct contact with the Torah, thus gaining access to the blessings that follow as long as one respects the ontological difference between God and humans and sanctifies oneself accordingly. Smelling the Torah scroll seems influenced by societal norms when it comes to evaluating a particular smell. A striking silence with regard to the acrid smell of chemicals and excrements on older scrolls stands in sharp contrast to the joy of addressing the lemon-like smell of modern scrolls. Past silence on smell could be a matter of in-group habituation and identification similar to past and present silence about the musky odors of sweating, familiar bodies in the crowded room of a synagogue. Seeing the Torah scroll is associated with aesthetic characteristics that enable users to identify a scroll's status as sacred. The relatively modern tradition of engraving the names of the donors on scroll-related items such as the Torah shield depicts visually how the donors are linked to the scroll. The shared experience of seeing the Torah scroll raised high also transforms it into a uniting artefact, which again establishes the participants as belonging to the same group. Hearing the words of the Torah scroll and the oscillating sounds associated with its making and inauguration is filtered through the selective auditory modality distinguishing between familiar sounds, signaling in-group activity, and unique sounds that call upon one's attention. Tasty food associated with the Torah such as sweets during the procession or the festive meal at its end are likely to help store ritual participation as a positive memory, just as it links together donors, those who receive, and in-group types of food and food rituals.

Hermeneutical use of scripture only occurred in a single instance during the process of making the Torah scroll, in specifying the visual characteristics of parchment, letters, margins, and ruled lines. Multiple artefactual uses, however, show how these sensory processes can generate transitivity between the scroll, participants, the synagogue, sad and joyous calendrical days, sad and joyous moments in history, and God's very presence. All these aspects seem highly relevant for individual meaning-making. The focus on the senses has furthermore revealed how bringing close seems to be a primary aspect of artefactual use, which again highlights a major difference from archaic religion, such as the oldest layers of Israelite religion prior to the Babylonian exile, where only specialists had access to the ark that contained the tablets of the covenant. While the process of making and inaugurating a Torah scroll only constitutes one example of how the senses become activated and the potential consequences of doing so, it nevertheless calls for future research on ritual stimulation of the senses. These processes of ritualizing Torah scrolls abound in information about religious meaning-making in settings where lay and elite participants handle sacred texts together. The shared handling seems to suspend cognitive negotiations of norms and instead offers artefactual, sense-stimulating uses of sacred texts where every participant gains access to nonconscious negotiations of sensory inputs that are crucial to individual meaning-making.

References

Assmann, Jan. 2006. *Religion and Cultural Memory*. Stanford, CA: Stanford University Press,

Avrin, Leila. 1991. *Scribes, Script and Books: The Book Arts from Antiquity to the Renaissance*. Chicago/London: American Library Association/The British Library.

Bundy, Anita B., Shelly J. Lane and Elizabeth A. Murray. 2002. *Sensory Integration: Theory and Practice*, 2nd edition. Philadelphia, PA: F.A. Davies Company.

Elbogen, Ismar. 1993. *Jewish Liturgy: A Comprehensive History*. Philadelphia, PA: The Jewish Publication Society.

Finkelberg, Margalit and Guy Stroumsa, eds. 2003. *Homer, the Bible and Beyond: Literary and Religious Canons in the Ancient World*. Leiden. Brill.

Friedman, Jen Taylor. nd. "Milestones." www.hasoferet.com. Accessed 17 October 2016.

Grimes, Ronald L. 2005. "Procession." *Encyclopedia of Religion*, 2nd edition, edited by Lindsay Jones, 7416–7418. Detroit, MI: Macmillan Reference.

Hayes, John E. and Russell S. J. Keast. 2011. "Two decades of supertasting: Where do we stand?" *Physiology & Behavior* 104(5): 1072–1074. https://doi.org/10.1016/j.physbeh.2011.08.003

Keeley, Brian L. 2002. "Making sense of the senses: Individuating modalities in humans and other animals." *Journal of Philosophy* 99(1): 5–28. https://doi.org/10.5840/jphil20029915

Malley, Brian. 2004. *How the Bible Works: An Anthropological Study of Evangelical Biblicism* Oxford: AltaMira Press.

McDonald, Lee Martin and James Sanders, eds. 2002. *The Canon Debate*. Peabody: Hendrickson.

Porteous, J. Douglas. 1985. "Smellscape." *Progress in Human Geography* 9(3): 356–378. https://doi.org/10.1177/030913258500900303

Ricoeur, Paul. 1979. "The 'Sacred' Text and the Community." In *The Critical Study of Sacred Texts*, edited by Wendy Doniger O'Flaherty. Berkeley: Graduate Theological Union.

———. 2003. *The Rule of Metaphor: The Creation of Meaning in Language.* London: Routledge.

———. 1976. *Interpretation Theory: Discourse and the Surplus of Meaning.* Fort Worth: The Texas Christian University Press.

Schleicher, Marianne. 2009a. "Artifactual and hermeneutical use of scripture in Jewish tradition." In *Jewish and Christian Scripture as Artifact and Canon*, edited by Craig A. Evans and H. Daniel Zacharias, 48–65. New York: Bloomsbury Academic.

———. 2009b. "The many faces of the Torah: Reception and transformation of the Torah in Jewish communities." In *Religion and Normativity: Receptions and Transformations of the Bible*, edited by Kirsten Nielsen, Vol. 2: 141–158. Aarhus: Aarhus University Press.

———. 2010. "Accounts of a dying scroll: On Jewish handling of sacred texts in need of restoration or disposal." In *The Death of Sacred Texts: Ritual Disposal and Renovation of Texts in World Religions*, edited by Kristina Myrvold, 11–29. London: Ashgate.

———. 2011. "Constructions of sex and gender: Attending to androgynes and *tumtumim* through Jewish scriptural use." *Literature and Theology* 25(4): 422–435. https://doi.org/10.1093/litthe/frr051

Scholem, Gershom. 1952. "Zur Entwicklungsgeschichte der kabbalistischen Konception der Schechina." *Eranos Jahrbuch* 21: 45–107.

Stern, David. 1987. "Midrash." In *Contemporary Jewish Religious Thought*, edited by Arthur A. Cohen and Paul Mendes-Flohr, 613–620. New York: Charles Scribner's Sons.

Waskul, Dennis D., Phillip Vannini and Janelle Wilson. 2009. "The aroma of recollection: Olfaction, nostalgia, and shaping of the sensuous self." *Senses and Society* 4(1): 5–22. https://doi.org/10.2752/174589309X388546

Watts, James W. 2013. "The three dimensions of scriptures." In *Iconic Books and Texts*, edited by James W. Watts, 9–32. London: Equinox

Watts, James W. 2015. "Iconic scriptures from decalogue to Bible." *Mémoires du livre / Studies in Book Culture* 6(2): 1–23. https://doi.org/10.7202/1032712ar

5

On Instant Scripture and Proximal Texts:
Some Insights into the Sensual Materiality of Texts and their Ritual Roles in the Hebrew Bible and Beyond

CHRISTIAN FREVEL

The paper discusses the importance of writing in the Hebrew Bible beyond the information storage aspect of script. Writing in the Torah is by no means limited to the textualization of tradition. The visual representation of writing, its materiality and the sensual experience are significant aspects of script and scripture. In four case studies the paper develops various aspects of writing as symbolic representation, performativity and agency of script. The four examples comprising various genres of texts are Deuteronomy 27, Deuteronomy 6, Exodus 28 and Numbers 6. The case studies evince the transformation from writing processes to the symbolic meaning of a scripturalized Torah as well as scripture as medium in various ways.

Scripture is read, and read, and read. That is what we expect, particularly of Biblical texts. The ritualized handling of scripture, e.g. gestures like lifting up a Torah scroll or lectionary, touching it, bowing before or kissing it, are usually understood to be *post-biblical* practices. They presuppose the attributed value or importance of the text, so that ritual handling is an outcome of its canonization. However, the material importance of writing and "the book" is not only part of its reception history. It is part of scripture itself. In the following paper I will focus on the importance of writing and textualization *within* the Torah (and with some side glances beyond it). Where and how is the materiality of text and writing important and what is its function within the Hebrew Bible, especially in the Torah? I have chosen four different case studies. 1) The "learning-theology" of Deuteronomy

Christian Frevel is Professor of Old Testament Studies in the Department of Catholic Theology of Ruhr University Bochum, Germany.

and its relationship to oral and written Torah – the case of Deuteronomy 27 and the spatial representation of Torah. 2) The self-referentiality of Torah and its interchange with material culture—the case of *tefillin* and *mezuzôt* in Deuteronomy 6. 3) Writing and symbolic representation within a cultic context—the case of second-level performativity in the fabric of the high-priestly garment in Exodus 28. 4) Finally, I will cover a magical experience with words—the case of the *Sotah*-ritual in Num 5:11–31, a practice that has very much to do with later practices of magic with scripture in Judaism, Christianity and Islam.

Scripturality and the spatial representation of Torah in Deuteronomy

The book of Deuteronomy is full of learning (Braulik 1997, Finsterbusch 2005a, Frevel 2012). It is the biblical book which focusses most on memory, generational change, and continuous tradition. It addresses remembrance, repetition, and representation of scripture more often than any other book in the OT. The book situates itself explicitly as a means of memorization. Israel is a community of shared memory, and – because apart from Moses all eye-witnesses to the revelation at Horeb had died out – it is all the more important to pass on the shared memory to the next generation (Lohfink 1991). This commemorative theology is present, for instance, in the so-called "children's sermon" (Deut 6:20–25). Reminders and signs of memory are very important in the thinking of Deuteronomy. It is a truism that scripture and writing take a special role in these processes of keeping the memory for generations, but the emphasis on writing and writing processes in Deuteronomy is most striking (Sonnet 1997).

Moses writes Deuteronomy down and hands it over to the priests (Deut 31:9). When Israel crosses the Jordan—at this crucial liminal point of entering the promised land—Israel is required to erect big plastered stones and to write all the commandments of Moses' Torah carefully and plainly on it. Where these stones should be erected, whether in the middle of the Jordan (Josh 4:9 presuming the identity of these stones with the ones mentioned in Deut 27), in Gilgal (Josh 4:29), at the riverside in the vicinity of Jericho (Deut 27:2–3), on top of Mount Ebal (Deut 27:4 MT), or on the opposite Mount Gerizim (Deut 27:4 Sam), is not quite clear (for the full evidence see Ulrich 2012, 361–364).

From the textual variants it becomes rather obvious that the inscribed stones were a matter of identity politics and were connected with claims of authenticity. Deuteronomy 27 is part of the "negotiations" between Judeans and Samarians (Nihan 2007) and perhaps it refers to or even includes a *hieros logos* of the Gerizim sanctuary. There are various textual traditions and variants in v. 4 (Ulrich 1994, Knoppers 2013), which show that it was not just a later Samaritan sectarian reshaping of tradition to read בהרגרזים "on Mount Gerizim." While the εν αργαρ[ι]ζιμ of the Greek Papyrus Giessen 19 is usually described as a Samaritan reading, the Old Latin also attests *Garzin* in one manuscript (Codex Lugdunensis) and this is most probably giving witness of an original non-Samarian reading of "Gerizim" instead of "Ebal" (Ulrich 2012, 362; Kartveit 2009, 302–303). Recently, a small fragment of a scroll containing Deut 27:4b–6 popped up (Charlesworth 2009), allegedly stemming from Cave 4 in Qumran and dating to the late second/early first century BCE. Although its authenticity is questioned by some scholars with important arguments (see Ulrich 2012, 364–365 for discussion), it also prominently reads הרגרזים "Mount Gerizim" in one word in its center. Perhaps, as befits the importance of the Samari[t]an tradition, the attestation of Gerizim was at least as original or even more original than the בהר עיבל "on Mount Ebal" reading: "There is a growing consensus that the reading 'Mt. Gerizim' is older than the reading 'Mt. Ebal'" (Müller 2016, 199). While the Gerizim is associated with blessing in Deut 11:29; 27:11, it may be even more convincing to put the Torah on stones at this place instead of the place of curse (Knoppers 2013, 202–203; Otto 2017, 19–21). Be that as it may, it is identity politics which is obvious here: the one, who owns the (place with the) original copy of the Torah on plaster, as it is said in Deut 27:4, has the correct original copy!

Hence the textual tradition witnesses claims from various sides. There is an ongoing discussion about dating the change from an original Gerizim to Ebal (Müller 2016, 201–202), and it ranges from middle of the fifth century BCE to the alleged destruction of the Gerizim sanctuary at the end of the second century BCE (Kartveit 2015, 217). The issue is strongly linked to the textual tradition of Josh 8:30–34 where Mount Ebal plays a major role. Thus it may belong to the early phase of argumentation between Judeans and Samarians on the legitimacy of their respective traditions and their claim for the authenticity of Torah. However, the text of Deuteronomy 27 is not a unity, and the variability is not only due to the history of *textual* transmission. Most recently, Eckart Otto (2017, 1930–1936) and Reinhard Müller (2016, 202–207) have argued for a diachronic differentiation. We cannot engage in the detailed discussion of diachrony in this paper, but it becomes clear that Deuteronomy 27 plays a special role in both diachronic and in synchronic respects, which are strongly linked to the self-authorization of the text of Deuteronomy. In my understanding, the location either on Mt. Ebal or Mt. Gerizim in Deut 27:4–8 may be a later addition from the fourth century but there is no consensus on this at the moment (see Otto 2017, 1925–1930).

The crucial point I would like to emphasize here is the link between this identity politics and scripturalization, visual scripturality and the materiality of the text. On the very day that Israel crosses the Jordan (ביום אשר תעברו את הירדן Deut 27:2), the people (העם) must erect the plastered stones and write on them this Torah (התורה הזאת) in the course of their crossing (בעברך). Although it is difficult to decide where the stones exactly stood (in the middle of the river, at the riverside of the Jordan), entering the land is marked with the Torah (as a means of application). If we adopt the assumption that there was a discourse about the understanding of the Torah between Samari[t]ans and Yehudites (and perhaps other groups we do not know of yet), then it becomes comprehensible to place the *copy* of the Torah in v. 4* either originally on Mt. Gerizim or in a later reception phase of the text on Mt. Ebal.

Interestingly enough, Deuteronomy emphasizes the concept that it was a *copy* of the book (ספר, Deut 28:58, 61; 29:19–20, 27; 30:10, and particularly Deut 31:19, 24). The fiction that a certain original remains in the background of the process of assignment enables other groups to claim the tradition (as long as they perform the inscription-ritual of voluntary agreement). Be that as it may, the role of writing in this verse is clear: it is an act of adopting, imposing and laying claim to the *written text*. At the same time, it ties the Torah closely to the land; the ritual is a means of spatialization. Those who enter the land from the east by crossing the Jordan (be it literally or just within the text) are confronted by the text and its authority. In reading it, they get performatively involved with accepting its application. The role of scripturalization and the people's relation to it is a special feature of Deuteronomy.

This can also be shown for the copy of the Torah in the law of the king in Deut 17:18 (see Samuel 2014, 105–108; Otto 2016, 1423–1456). To guide his governance, the king must make himself a copy (וכתב לו את משנה התורה הזאת) from the original which was written by Moses (claim of authenticity) and handed over to the Levitical priests (claim of authority and, in the end, superiority by originality). The subject who does the writing changes in reception history (Fraade 2011, 285–319). In the Temple Scroll (11Q19) the king does not write himself and the term *copy* (משנה) is not mentioned. Only "this torah" shall be written before the priests (התורה הזואת על ספר מלפני הכהנים 11Q19 56:20). Nevertheless, both aspects are crucially important in the understanding of Deuteronomy. The act of writing the scroll by the king himself is an act of performative acceptance of the directives of the Torah. Usually we expect *learning by heart* as the means of internalization

(Carr 2005, 160; Schnepper 2012, 37–40), but here it is rather the *process of writing* which aims at adoption and permanent representation. The writing (v. 18) and reading (v. 19) process demanded of the king in Deut 17:19 may first and foremost aim at internalizing the Torah as guiding principle. It may even be related to a public ritualized reading by or to the king during "audiences," but this is only guesswork.

Learning the Torah is a part of an iterative performance that claims the Torah's impact on his reign. The crucial aspect, though, is the process of writing, which Deuteronomy sees as both an initial, formative and perpetual adoption of the Torah for kingly government. At the same moment that the rule of the king is subordinated to the rule of the Torah, the king is subordinated to the priests by the attribution of the "original" to the Levitical priests (cf. Deut 31:25–26). One cannot escape a hierocratic tendency in this fact, and from this perspective a post-exilic dating makes much sense (Samuel 2014, 103–118; Otto 2016, 1459–1488). Note that the point of time when this ritual must take place is peculiarly unspecified, in fact, not even mentioned. Usually interpreters place it within the process of accession or inauguration ("when he sits down" or "when he is seated"), but the Hebrew text has a circumstantial sentence (והיה כשבתו על כסא ממלכתו "and it shall be in his sitting on the throne of his kingdom") making it a permanent condition, although the process of writing is performed only once.

In this way, the text strengthens the view that the reign of the king must be informed by the Torah during his entire dominion. By this act of implementation, the Torah is applied to the regime in space and time. And, as in the example above, it remains possible for other "kings" or territories to subordinate their dominion under the rule of the Torah also. Thus the strategy of copying the Torah does not only enable the king to be a scribe, but also allows the Torah to perform a unifying function for particular political or religious entities. Material textuality is a means of authorization as well as of dissemination and finally also of concretization.

These two examples of the written Torah evince the importance of the text as a whole. They have shown a particular emphasis on the process of writing and how the text was employed as a controlling, demanding, limiting, or formative authority. The authority of the text itself is based on the authority of Moses, and it is imposed upon particular issues. The next example will show that this strategy of authorizing by scripturalization and safeguarding its impact by performativity is part of Deuteronomy and a feature of scriptural materiality within the Hebrew Bible. First, we will describe Deuteronomy's representation of Torah in everyday life, and then move on to the cultic realm.

Self-reference with material culture:
Transforming the symbolic meaning of a scripturalized Torah

As I already said, textuality plays a key role in the Torah and especially in Deuteronomy, so it is not a coincidence that we focus on Deuteronomy once again. In what follows, I will take a closer look at the Shema and the *tefillin* by focusing on textualization and the materiality of texts, though I am not aiming at a comprehensive study of this issue.

After the Shema's core sentence in Deut 6:4, "Listen Israel, YHWH our God YHWH is one," v. 6 requires setting "these words (הדברים האלה) in your heart." Although it is not clear, most interpretations think this phrase refers to the Shema proper in Deut 6:4, Deut 6:4b or Deut 6:4-5 (Vejola 1992, 175–179, Otto 2012, 793, 803–804). Alternatively, the text of "these words" could be not *exclusively*, or not *only* the Shema. Either it could combine the Shema with other small portions of text or comprise a more or less larger part of Deuteronomy (cf. Deut 1:1; 4:9; 4:30; 5:22; 12:26; 30:1 etc.), for instance the Decalogue or parts of the book (cf. Deut 5:26; 6:26; 12:26). This is suggested by the fact that the demand to write "these words" (דברי אלה) can also be found in the parallel in Deut 11:18. However, it is difficult to decide.

In any case, the addressees must put (שׂים) the words in their hearts, which means that they must learn it by heart or put the text in an amulet. Writing texts on amulets is a common practice which has parallels in Egypt, Greece, Mesopotamia and many places in the Southern Levant (Berlejung 2015). Beyond the storage aspect, textualization is generally related to the impact of the content. In contrast to common amulet practices, the text of Deuteronomy emphasizes the educational aspect of the text (Carr 2005, 121; Finsterbusch 2005a, 239–281). The words should influence the people's whole existence and particularly the education of the next generation: "and you must inculcate them into your children, and speak about them when you sit in your house, and when you walk by the way, and when you lie down, and when you rise" (Deut 6:7). All directions and movements—horizontally and vertically—should be contingent on the one God and be guided by steadfast love of God.

The following sentence is crucial to our topic. The words mentioned shall be attached to the body: "And you shall bind them as a sign upon your hand, and they shall be as frontlets between your eyes" (Deut 6:8). Beyond storage and in addition to an apotropaic function, the text-amulet becomes a means of remembrance, a tool for memorization, a performative appropriation, an outer token of internalization, a medium of transfer, a visible sign, a badge of membership, etc. It is important not to limit its function to one single feature or role.

Because this paper focuses on textualization and its functions, let me first briefly mention four different aspects of representation of the text in Deuteronomy 6:

a. "You must inculcate them into your children" (v. 7a): The rare verb שׁנן which is used here for the diligent teaching is often associated with weapons (Deut 32,41; Isa 5:28; Ps 45:6 *et al.*). The word is made a sword (cf. Hebr 4:12) to impress the message on or into the next generation. Usually it is understood as the demand for repetition of the words. Repetition by heart is a cultural technique of memorization and transmission of tradition. Its purpose is to learn the text by internalization. This is an important part of the maintenance of tradition apart from scripturalization. The phrasing here is inclusive of both oral and written practices.

b. "You must speak about them wherever you are, at home, on the street, going to bed and getting out of it" (v. 7b): Another technique of tradition maintenance is to expound and interpret it regularly, which is required here. The function of commentaries is to keep the text alive.

c. "Bind them as a sign on your hand" (v. 8a): Here the practice seems to be quite clear: the words must be represented on a kind of brace-let and this must be worn around the lower arm or wrist. יד which literally means "hand" can denote the whole arm or just the part of the forearm around the wrist (cf. Isa 44:5; 49:16). It may hint at Egyptian bangles (or rigid bracelets) which are decorated with the cartouche of the pharaoh. However, to the best of my knowledge this practice is not reflected in ancient Jewish ritual practice. In contrast, this commandment was always connected with the *tefillin* (see below).

d. "Write them on ..." (v. 9): While v. 8 does not mention scripturaliza-tion literally so that the sign can be just visual, material or symbolic, v. 9 demands a process of writing on doorposts and gateways. This is very much related to Deuteronomy 27 (see above) and goes even beyond it in several respects. While the instructions for scripturali-zation in Deut 27:3, 9, which address Israel as a whole, are performed once, the practice mentioned here is performed (by individuals) many times. Since it relates to every house and gate, it dissemi-nates the message. In addition, it is a means of public visualization. Like the writing in Deuteronomy 27, the text is being related to a gateway, a passage, or an entrance. Hence entering the land, a city or a house is informed by the Torah or even portions of it. Together with the practice of the *tefillin*, it makes a totality of representation obvious. There is no space for and in "Israel," either outwardly or inwardly, that will not be steeped in the Torah.

The relationships between these various means of symbolic and literal representation, of memorization and performativity to scripturalization makes it reasonable to assume that the *tefillin*-practice of Deut 6:8 was also related to scripturalization since early times. So let us now turn to the *tefillin*.

"And they shall be as frontlets between your eyes" (Deut 6:8). The usual translation of טטפת as "forehead" or "frontlet" is already informed by the *tefillin*-practice (Cohn 2008). However, we have to deal with a chicken-and-egg problem here. Did Deut 6:8 produce a new practice of *tefillin* as an outcome of this prescription or did the words reflect an already existing practice of wearing a particular sign or amulet like a bracelet or armlet (Keel 1981, 212–215)? It is impossible to answer this question definitely. The meaning and etymology of the plural טטפת *ṭoṭāfot* remains disputed if not obscure (see Otto 2012, 809–810) because the word is mentioned only three times, all in the same context (Exod 13:16; Deut 6:8; 11:18). If we assume that the verse represents a synonymous parallelism, we have to take לטטפת as synonymous to לאות "signs." The Greek version did not completely understand the word either and translated the second part of the verse καὶ ἔσται ἀσάλευτον πρὸ ὀφθαλμῶν σου, where ἀσάλευτος means something immoveable. Interestingly enough many recent Hebrew dictionaries translate טטפות with "phylactery," which revives the chicken-and-egg question. "Phylactery" transliterates the Greek word φυλακτήριον, which is etymologically drawn from φυλασσειν "to guard, to ward off" but does not appear in the ancient Greek translation of these verses. Phylactery can denote any textbox in which text is hidden. The Jewish word is *tefillin*, first attested around the turn of the eras. Etymologically the word derives from תפלה "prayer" and thus points to the (now mostly Orthodox and some Conservative) Jewish practice of winding two leather boxes around the forearm (של יד) and the forehead (של ראש). While it is binding on Jewish males after their Bar Mitzvah, a few women wear *tefillin* in modern Reform Judaism. Today, the texts inside *tefillin* most often include Deut 6:4–6, Deut 11:13–21, Exod 13:1–10, and finally Exod 13:11–16.

The oldest *tefillin* come from Qumran, where twenty-three examples were found, all made from leather. Fourteen have four compartments, two have three compartments, and the rest have one compartment (Adler 2011, 2016; Falk 2014). Other specimens were found in a cave in the Judean desert in

Wadi Murabbaʿat from the time of the Bar Kokhba revolt 132–135 CE and two from Cave 34 in *Naḥal Seʾelim*, and one allegedly from *Naḥal Ḥever* (Adler 2016, 264). In 2014, the latest discoveries by Yonatan Adler revealed nine new *tefillin* from Qumran Cave 4 which had until then not been unrolled. Although some of the content of these parchments is already in line with later rabbinic prescriptions, some have additional texts, as Daniel Falk notes: "The selection of texts shows intention to include the four key passages about binding a sign on oneself (Exod 13:9, 16; Deut 6:8; 11:18), but otherwise there is little evidence for a clear norm about the extent of passages to include or their order. The largest list of excerpts found among the Qumran *tefillin* include: Exod 12:43–13:10; Deut 5:1–6:9; Deut 10:12–11:21; Deut 32" (Falk 2014, 77). This range of text is not meant to be read, since most of the letters are smaller than 1 mm in size. Since the *tefillin* from Qumran differ in the number of compartments, they often resemble one of two later types representing the "arm-*tefillin*" and the "head-*tefillin*," but this classification is attested explicitly only later (Adler 2016, 165–166).

Yehuda B. Cohn has argued that the practice of wearing *tefillin* originated on analogy to Greek magical practices in the late Second Temple period. "Tefillin were an 'invented tradition' of the late–Second Temple era, initially shaped by knowledge of parallel Greek practices, and functioning as a popular amulet for achieving length of days" (Cohn 2008, 8). Whether or not magic is the correct category (if it is a satisfactory "category" at all) to employ may be questioned, like their relation to a prolongation of life. As stated above, the apotropaic function is only one aspect of the *tefillin*, which impose the Torah spatially on every area of life. This becomes obvious in the placement of the sign "between the eyes" (לטטפת בין עיניך) which has attracted scholarly discussion and not only because recent practice places the *tefillin* "on the highest part of the head rather than between the eyes" (Cohn 2008, 44).

To begin with, it is important to notice that, for ancient Israelites, the head is not the entity in which thinking, decision making, reasoning, etc. is located. It is rather the heart which is the emotive, volitive, and cognitive center. Thus the placement between the eyes is strikingly not related to the implementation of the Torah in human behavior. The sign on the forehead designates attribution or relationship, as becomes clear in the description of the high-priestly ornaments in Exod 28:36–37 (see below) and particularly in Ezek 9:4. There the prophet must "put a mark on the foreheads of the men who moan and groan because of all the abominations that are committed in it." This sign is called a *tāw* (תו) which is the last letter of the Hebrew alphabet, written in paleo-Hebrew script as a cross (✗). Thus the attachment of the "words" between the eyes can be understood as the symbolic designation of people for YHWH by Deuteronomy or the Torah. This public function may be seen alongside the protective and more private function of the amulets (cf. the early Jewish text amulet practice in Kotansky 1994, XVII, 3).

We should also observe that the place between the eyes on the forehead and the wrist are places where jewelry is worn. Usually there were four bodily regions on which jewelry was worn in the Southern Levant: on both wrists and ankles (often two or three bangles), on the neck or chest as an amulet or pendant, and finally on the forehead as a frontlet containing a precious stone or metal object (Kersken 2011, Stol 2016). Jewelry in these places frequently appears in plaques and figurines depicting female figures and in ivory carvings of the "woman at the window"-motif (Keel 2007, 587–588). The precious plaque on her forehead suggests comparing this jewelry with specific designations known from Akkadian literature. For example, the *nu-gig* was a priestess with high status. She wore a special kind of jewelry, which was called *mùš*. The *mùš* was a sort of crown, a kingly attribute which may be comparable to a diadem on the forehead, also worn by the high-*en*-priest (Renger 1967, 183; Stol 2016). Thus, a precious forehead plaque or jewelry attached to a frontlet are specific designations of affiliation or belonging. Accordingly, the commandment to place the words of Deuteronomy between the eyes distinguishes the person as separated for or as belonging to God. This symbolic meaning already appeared in the ritual practice of the *tefillin* in early Hellenistic times. The forehead as the traditional place for signs of devotion and affiliation is transformed by placing on it with the symbolic representation of the script of the Torah.

This analysis makes the function of the *tefillin* resemble the *mezuzôt*-practice which was mentioned before and which I should briefly address in this context. "You shall write them on the doorposts of your house..." (Deut 6:9): Writing on doorposts is an apotropaic practice, which is a necessary but not sufficient background for understanding the material textual aspect of Deut 6:9. Areas of passage and especially entrances were generally thought to be endangered liminal zones in a house or a city (e.g. Gen 4:7). All hazards must be blocked by magic spells, apotropaic figures or protective inscriptions (Keel 1991, 183–184). Blessings, sayings or verses were written above door lintels to protect the house or the person passing through the door. It is a well-known Muslim practice to put verses of the Qur'an on door and window lintels, and especially on house entrances (Lowy 1977, 70; Keel 1991, 183). In Kuntilet Ajrud, a desert way-station in the Sinai region in the eighth century BCE, several inscriptions on plaster were found, one (mostly unreadable) *in situ* on a jamb, others fallen very close to doorways (Meshel 2012,

105). In Jewish practice, this part of the commandment is implemented by the *mezuzah*-tradition. As with *tefillin*, portions of text—today usually Deut 6:4–9 and Deut 11:13–21—are written on parchment, rolled up and stored in a little decorative case, which often has a ש for *Shaddai* "almighty" on its front. The *mezuzah* is fixed on the door frame of every entrance of a Jewish house as well as sometimes of every room inside the house. The practice was already reflected in the Letter of Aristeas from the second century BCE (*Aristeas* 158–159) and by Philo and Josephus in the first century CE (Philo, *De specialibus legibus* IV, 142, Josephus, *Antiquitates* II 213). As with the *tefillin*, the oldest examples of *mezuzôt* come from Qumran, about eight exemplars (4Q149–155; 8Q4; Milik 1977). In addition, we have to mention the *Nash Papyrus* from the second half of the second century BCE, which includes a mixed text of the two decalogues and the Shema, and is usually interpreted as a *mezuzah*.

The second part of Deut 6:9 requires writing the words "on your gates." Gate inscriptions were quite common in the ancient Near East (Marzahn and Jacob-Rost 1985). Famous examples include the Ishtar Gate in Babylon, the Bronze Gates of Balawat in the entrance to the palace of Shalmanassar III, the Karatepe-Arşlan Taş-Inscription, the XPa-Inscription in Persepolis, the inscription of Darius in Susa, and a fragment of an inscription from Ramses II at Jaffa (Marzahn 1995, 29-30). Usually they are dedicatory inscriptions in which the builder devotes the building to a certain deity. This is probably not the intention of the prescription in Deuteronomy 6. Here inscription indicates an assignment of living space to the constitutive words of Deuteronomy as a symbolic means of influencing, occupying, or distinguishing the living space by the Torah. Less convincing in my view is Othmar Keel's comparison with liturgies of admittance (Pss 15, 24) and the presence of the priest or pharaoh as guardians of the righteousness, appropriateness and purity of the cult attendants (Keel 1991, 184–192).

The practice emphasizes that doorways are liminal zones. The materiality of scripture imposes the power and rule of the Torah on the entrant or, better, on the space he or she enters. Living space is singled out as the space which is assigned to the Torah. As in modern practice, seeing and touching the *mezuzah* keeps it present, effective, and significant. This is a particular mode of memorization in Deuteronomy, which is more than meditation or repetition.

Writing and symbolic representation within a cultic context: Second-level performativity in the fabric of the priestly garment

In the last examples from Deuteronomy, the importance of liminal space was emphasized. It was striking that the materiality of text was important from various angles. The next example from the book of Exodus will give additional evidence for a public-private interface combined with the representational aspect of symbols. Vestments, which cover the private body and designate the person publicly as an official, often have a particular meaning (Grigo 2015, 19–84). They are a means of symbolic communication, just as are the garments of a deity (Zawadski 2006, 2013). The description of the high-priestly vestments in Exodus 28 is very interesting in this regard. On the one hand it undoubtedly has some connection to cultic reality, if not in the first temple then in the second temple in Jerusalem. On the other hand, the text is fictional. It helps constitute an ideal cultic world that never existed exactly in this manner. For instance, the ideal of the twelve tribes of Israel which are represented in *one* single cult simultaneously is wishful thinking, by no means a reality either in the first or in the second temple period. Here is not the place to discuss this issue, but there never was such an entity as the twelve tribes in reality. However, the unity of the tribes is represented symbolically within the description of the high-priestly garments. Thus the text forms a reality of its own. The texts which describe the appearance of the high priest should therefore not only (if at all) be understood as a report giving empirical information about the garments, but rather as a construction comprising communication, symbolic representation and mediation. In what follows, I will focus on the aspect of textuality and writing in the description of the garments in Exodus 28. In the manufacture of the high priest's ornate garments, *writing* plays a prominent role three times: first in making the *ephod* (Exod 28:4–12), secondly in the precious breast shield (Exod 28:15–21), and finally in manufacturing the diadem (Exod 28:36; 39:30). I cannot go into the discussion of the diachrony of these priestly texts here, and will instead limit myself to a few notes on each paragraph:

(a) As with other terms discussed in this paper, the etymology of *ephod* is not quite clear. If there is a connection to the Akkadian *epattu* or the Ugaritic *3pd*, the *ephod* may be have originally been a part of pearlies (Scherer 2004). Judging from other OT texts, the *ephod* is a sort of bag or jacket for lots, but as part of the priestly garment it is instead a square apron or skirt (Seow 2013). Following Martin Noth, Othmar Keel points to Egyptian representations of similar parts of the pharaonic vestment (Keel 2007, 937). The *ephod* is said to be gemmed with two onyx (or malachite) stones (אבני שהם Exod 28:9; 39:6). Like valuable seals, the stones are enclosed in settings of gold filigree and then set on the shoulder-pieces of the *ephod* (על כתפת האפד Exod 28:12). Similar to *name seals*, the onyx stones are engraved with the names of the twelve tribes, derived from the sons of Jacob (פתחת פתוחי חותם על שמות בני ישראל, Exod 39:6). Unlike name seals, six names in a row are placed on each of the stones. The function of the stones is described explicitly as "stones of remembrance" (אבני זכרון לבני ישראל Exod 39:7; cf. 28:12). However, the *direction* of remembrance is not quite clear. It could be Aaron himself who should have the Israelites in mind when he acts representatively before the Lord, or it could be the Lord who should remember the Israelites when Aaron is acting in the cult on their behalf. The noun זכרון "remembrance" is not used very often. Usually the subject of remembrance are the people rather than God (cf. Exod. 12:14; 13:9; 17:14; Lev 23:24; Num 17:5; Josh 4:7; Neh 2:20; Esth 6:1; Job 13:12; Ecc 1:11, 2:16; Isa 57:8).

(b) The breastpiece is a piece of fine linen fabric with gold, purple and crimson woven into it. It is comparable to a pectorale, particularly to the Egyptian pharaonic pectorale (Keel 2004, 385). Twelve gemstones, all of different kinds (and we cannot discuss the issue of identification here, see Zwickel 2012), are applied to the breastpiece in four rows. At first glance this can be associated with more or less commonly practiced magic with stones. In later Greek tradition, "magical gems of semi-precious material (quartzes, jaspers, chalcedonies, hematites, among many others) represent a special category of amulets that owes its flowering to the early centuries of the Common Era" (Kotansky 2006, 66). On the one hand, the apotropaic and magic function of amulets is involved here. On the other hand, the representational function is much more important.

The gemstones are engraved with the names of the twelve tribes in the same way as the *ephod* (Exod 39:14). In contrast to the *ephod*, this time only one name is written on each stone. The pectorale functions as an amulet, granting protection and vitality for the bearer. If this is also the main (or so to say original) function of the breastpiece, the names of the Israelites would represent the commission of Aaron in the cult. The names could then be understood as a means of authorization. Being "sealed" by the twelve tribes, Aaron is installed as assigned by the Israelites to perform as their representative in the cult (scil. a "medium"). Although this makes sense, the function of the breastpiece is said to be a bit different, however. Exod 28:29 states: "So Aaron shall bear the names of the sons of Israel in the breastpiece of judgment upon his heart, when he goes into the holy place, to bring them to continual remembrance before the LORD" (RSV). The remembrance זכרון is meant to represent the twelve tribes *permanently* (תמיד) before the Lord, who will recall the people each time Aaron acts on their behalf. Permanence and consistency is very important to any amulet practice (Berlejung 2014, 117).

The breastpiece is now qualified as חשן המשפט, a "breastpiece of judgment," due to the lots, Urim and Thummim, which will be "on Aaron's heart" when he acts culticly: "thus Aaron shall bear the judgment of the Israelites (את משפט בני ישראל) on his heart before the LORD continually" (Exod 28:30). Verses 29 and 30 are obviously linked by many phrases. Verse 30 shares almost all of its words with v. 29 and could be drawn from it. This strengthens the argument that v. 30 is a secondary addition, which may have been motivated by the "judgement" (משפט) which v. 30 expounds on and links to the oracular function of the Urim and Thummin. But diachrony is not the focus of the present paper. With the Urim and Thummim, we encounter another example of a priestly "invention of tradition" by reshaping or transforming a traditional issue anew and linking it to the Aaronide priestly service. Perhaps "bringing the משפט" is indeed related to the Egyptian practice of offering *Ma'at* as a symbol of the divine order of justice and law (Keel 1994, 383–383). Writing the names on them makes the precious gemstones like amulets, but they also perform an obvious representational function. *All of* Israel, which is made up of the twelve tribes and thus formed as a united ideal entity, is linked by this ritual setting to the constitutive order of law, which itself is presented by Aaron in the presence of the deity. Again we face the establishment of Torah as a medium which exceeds present Israel, Judah or *Yehûd* and which tends to become a universal, transcendent principle. This principle has unifying power in making "Israel" a unity beyond political realms. The sophisticated entanglement of medium, mediator and mediation is puzzling, but it conforms to the late priestly theology of substitution, agency, and communication.

The place where the breastpiece is located, על לבו "upon his heart", is most important. The heart is the volitional, cognitive and emotional center of the person—nothing is more central than the heart. The same wording is used in the description of v. 30 so that the Urim and Thummim parallel the Israelites somewhat. Keel correctly compares the inscribed names to a foundation inscription ("Stifterinschrift", Keel 2004, 385, 2012, 936). The high priest is marked by the names of the Israelites as a gift which is permanently presented each and every time *in* the temple cult. By adding the dedicatory or votive inscription, Aaron in a way becomes himself a votive or representative gift given by the Israelite tribes. This emphasizes the mediating function of the high-priest which is absolutely necessary due to the priestly concept of making the holy of holies a taboo zone. The high priest is closest to the holy of holies. He is the only one who can enter the holy of holies once a year. The priest carries the names of the Israelite tribes into the nearness of God and represents them continuously. Thus he functions similarly to votive offerings placed in the holy of holies of other ancient temples.

(c) Finally, writing plays a crucial role in the description of the diadem of the high priest which is part of his headdress. This headdress consists of two parts: a turban-like headgear (המצנפת), to which a diadem (נזר) is attached by a blue cord (Exod 28:36-38; 29:6; 39:30; Lev 8:9; cf. Lev 21:12; Num 6:7). This is a rosette or stylized blossom (ציץ) made of pure gold, on which the words קדש ליהוה are engraved. קדש ל means "singled out for," an inscription which is more or less frequently attested on objects in the Southern Levant from the Iron Age (at Arad, Hazor, Ekron, Jerusalem, etc.). The inscription consecrates or even sanctifies the marked object performatively.

The blossom on the diadem is on the forehead of the high-priest (Exod 28:38). Again the script is identified as the script of a seal (מכתב פתוחי חותם Exod 39:36), which means—strictly spoken—mirror-inverted script. It is not the diadem which shall be designated as "holy" by the script, but rather the bearer of the diadem, the high-priest. He belongs to the Lord, he is even property of the Lord (cf. Lev 27:30, 32; Deut 26:19; Zech 14:21–22). Usually such applications to crowns or headdress have an apotropaic function. Othmar Keel compares it to the Uraeus of the pharaonic crown. But again, the function within the composition of the priestly garment seems to be a bit different. Exodus 28:38 is not easy to translate, but it clearly mentions the function of the engraved diadem together with the office of Aaron. Aaron's duty, which is framed by his forehead (על מצח), is to carry the guilt of breaching the taboo zone of the holy of holies (Exod 28:43; Num 18:1; 22–23). The verse emphasizes the substitutionary function of the high-priest as representative again. He is the one singled out to encounter the holiness of God in the closest manner. This position makes him responsible for the accurate interpretation of all cultic regulations (Lev 10:10–11), which have to be carried out strictly. By this ritual, he acts vicariously to represent all Israel in the holy of holies.

Here again we encounter the sophisticated system of priestly theology, and it is striking that it employs writing to establish its dense system of hierarchy and substitution with regard to holiness. This merits more scrutiny, but in this paper we have to limit ourselves to drawing a rough summary. The use of script in the manufacture of the clothes is a means of attributing the person or social group, which is designated by the script, to the wearer of the garment or to the context in which the person operates. Writing is used as a performative act and forms a permanent commemorative or representative tag. By representing the names of the twelve tribes on the priestly garment, the people are carried into the holy of holies. Within the Torah, this act of writing evolves within a *textual* world. However, it refers to the performativity of the described ritual contexts although it appears first and foremost on the textual level of performance. Whether it was performed in reality (that is the question when, where and by whom it was implemented in the real world) is insignificant. The magical dimension of gemstones, written texts, etc. forms a background for these texts which are not "magic" themselves. This is, by the way, very common for so-called late priestly traditions: they are related to certain ritual and even magical practices, but at the same time transform them on the textual level into a set of meanings that are oriented primarily to the relationship between God and his people and the mediating function of the cult.

The emphasis on writing processes in the description of the high-priestly garment is striking and underappreciated in academic discussion. Like the deuteronomic and deuteronomistic texts in the first part of the paper, the late priestly texts reveal an exceptional awareness of textuality, and not only with regard to the Torah.

Dissolving scripture for drinking purposes

The final case study addresses a sort of magic experience with words within the book of Numbers and a practice which has very much to do with later esteem of scripture in Judaism, Christianity and Islam. It is a ritual from the book of Numbers, the so-called *Sotah* or the "jealousy ordeal" in Num 5:11–31. This ritual should be performed when a husband becomes suspicious of his spouse. It has a long history of interpretation (Rosen-Zvi 2012) and is, in modern times, often misunderstood as oppressive since it very much reflects the patriarchal supremacy of men (Frymer-Kensky 1984). However, there is a line of interpretation which understands the ritual as protection against a husband's arbitrary jealousy towards his innocent wife (Frevel 2016b). Many details require attention to justify this line of interpretation, and only a few can be discussed in this paper. It should be added that the ritual also underwent literary growth that cannot be dealt with here (see Frevel 2016a with further literature).

Although my focus is on the role of writing in the ritual, let me give you some clues to its complex structure. It comprises a number of sequential actions by various actors: the husband leads his wife to the sanctuary (v. 15) and *he* presents the offering (v. 15). The priest, as ritual expert, takes the women out of the discretionary power of her husband and places her under divine judgement (vv. 16, 18). She is thereby removed from the husband's disposal; he loses all possibility for further legal recourse (v. 31). The priest takes "holy water" as a ritual agent in a clay container and mixes it in dust from the floor of the sanctuary (v. 17). Dust as ingredient-agent is attested already in a second millennium oath-ritual from Mari (ARM 10,9; Levine 1993, 2010). The priest then unbinds the hair on the woman's head (v. 18) and places her with her offering at the entrance of the Tent of Meeting, that is, in the liminal border space between the exclusive realm of the divine (the sanctuary) and the realm of the people (the camp). The priest holds the bitter water in his hands and makes the woman swear an oath (v. 19), thereby submitting herself to the ordeal. If she is guilty, the curse should take effect on the woman, having a negative impact on her ability to produce offspring. The accursed water should cause a prolapse of the uterus and disrupt any pregnancy that might have begun (v. 21). If she is innocent, the cursed water has no negative effects and the woman must be taken back by her husband and be able to bear legitimate children. Under the pre-condition that the woman agrees by saying "Amen, amen" (v. 22), the conditional imprecation is *written down*. Then the writing is scraped off into water and given to the woman to drink (vv. 24, 26). The priest must first declare the conditions of the ordeal (vv. 19–20), i.e. the words of the woman's oath. Then the priest must require the woman take *this* oath (v. 21), but the oath is not quoted verbatim. The verse instead threatens the woman with the possible outcome of the ritual, which is the destruction of her reproductive organs. After the woman has agreed by saying the double "amen", the priest writes down *these curses* (את האלת האלה) on a scroll (בספר) and wipes them into the water of bitterness, literally *blotting them out* from the writing material. By drinking the water, the spell takes effect in the women's belly. It is not clear whether the ritual agent is the dust of the sanctuary, the written imprecation, or both.

The writing is most interesting for our context. The priest must literally write (כתב) the imprecation on a "scroll" (ספר, v. 23; note the striking postponement of the subject of writing). To decide upon the writing material is a difficult issue. Although papyrus was produced in Egypt from the third millennium on, and the earliest evidence of writing on papyrus in Mesopotamia comes from the eighth or seventh century BCE, papyrus was not used in the Southern Levant before the late Achaemenid period or even later in the early Hellenistic period, that is, the fourth or third centuries. Thus the writing in a ספר "book, scroll, letter, document" presumably refers to a piece of parchment rather than to papyrus. However, the word ספר could also be understood more generally and may include other writing material like ostraca or wood. Ink (דיו Jer 36:18), which is not explicitly mentioned here, was produced from organic material, using for instance soot or carbon black mixed with water and gum arabic (Sobott *et al.* 2015, Bearman and Christens-Barry 2009). In Late Antiquity and Medieval times, the production of ink made intensive use of gall-nuts (iron gall ink) or other tannins. This so-called metallic ink uses a compound of gall nuts and vitriol (Würthwein 1995, 9), which might be indicated by the description of the water mixed with ink as bitter (Num 5:18, 19, 23, 24, 27). Although inks were mostly water-soluble, it may be difficult to wipe the script off the parchment without leaving a trace. The verb מחה clearly means "to blot out" things, creatures or even writings (Exod 17:14; 32:32–33; Deut 29:19; Ps 69:29), denoting their non-existence. Most interesting is the use of מחה in Prov 30:20 where it is connected to adultery. There the women refuses to confess (introduced by פה) by saying, "I have done no wrong." Thus she fearlessly "blots out" the curses because she is confident that they will not work. By contrast, the woman in the *sotah*-ritual has to drink the water in which the script has been dissolved.

Interestingly enough the content of the writing has an effect which is bound to its material, in this case the ink. Although striking from a perspective of agency, the emphasis on script and its magical effect is still present in various cultures today. I mention for instance the so called *Taweez* or *Taʿwīz* in Muslim societies. Let me quote a passage from Margaret A. Mills paper on this practice:

> *Taʿwīz* (Arabic and Persian) are protective charms which may contain particular words or verses of the Qurʾān, and/or magical alpha-numeric charts or formulas or other graphic designs, written on paper or inscribed on metal objects and worn on the body. Paper *taʿwīz* may be folded and encased in a bright bit of cloth or a small metal container, usually rectangular or triangular in shape. Other ways of delivering protective or curative power of written *taʿwīz* include burning the paper on which the inscription has been written and inhaling the smoke (*dūdī*, "smoky ones"), or writing the formula in water-soluble ink on a piece of paper or directly on the surface of a china saucer, adding water to dissolve the inscription, and drinking the water. Such written *taʿwīz* invoke and extend the third tenet of faith, the written Sacred Word as powerful in the world. (Mills 2003, 294)[1]

---

1. I thank Sajida Fazal, Käte Hamburger Kolleg Bochum, for pointing me to drinking Taweez practices in Pakistan. See further remarks on this practice in the paper of Katharina Wilkens in this collection, "Infusions and Fumigations: Therapeutic Aspects of the Quran."

The curse also functions as a supernatural power in the adultery ritual of Numbers 5. But it is *text* as such, not biblical verses or *scripture*, that is written down. Even if the curse is mentioned in the text, the priest is commanded to write portions of ritual text rather than, for instance, the biblical prohibition, "You shall not commit adultery" (Exod 20:13; Deut 5:18). However, the practice has parallels not only in other ancient rituals, but also in the reception history of the Bible. Written text (and particularly holy text) has a supernatural effect in many rituals or ritual-like action. This effect can be addressed as magic—so-called "performative operations that are an integral part of religious symbol systems and religious practice" (Schmitt 2014, 1–2). Magic is understood here as related to order and as a means of control. Magic is a situational symbolic act which is performed ritually. This comprises any means of influencing or manipulating reality by a foreign power that is not at hand without magic. If this understanding is accepted, then we can connect the last three, and perhaps even the first case study on that basis. Writing is more than storing and safeguarding information. Writing forms a sort of materiality that may become an agent or represent the agency of a power behind the written word.

Some conclusions

This paper has shown that writing is very important beyond the information storage aspect of script. Its visual representation, its materiality and the sensual experience of script are significant aspects of script *and* scripture. We ended with magical uses of a written text to underline the supposed agency of script. This is not an odd and isolated phenomenon, but rather an aspect of how the book of Deuteronomy itself deals with script and conceptualizes scripture. Writing in the Torah is by no means limited to the textualization of tradition. We have seen that writing was involved in performative actions, processes and rituals. While the first means of writing or the reflection on writing was indeed storage, the passages in Deuteronomy also evince aspects of memorization, representation, and benchmarking. Writing could be used as a means to claim symbolic representation, ascription, permanence, and consistency. Within the book of Exodus, we only examined the stunning importance of writing in the description of the high-priestly garment. While writing always has performative aspects, we could observe in Exodus 28 that this performativity was conceptualized iteratively by linking it to the cultic agent, Aaron. Thus the representation of Israel was ritually performed in the manufacture of the vestments of Aaron, but also made permanent by connecting it to the vicarious agency of Aaron in the holy of holies. Although the examples were taken from different parts of biblical literature, there are obvious links between the conception of writing in Deuteronomy and the late priestly passages. Both reflect writing's constitutive impact on reality and the representational aspect of writing. The transformation from writing processes to the symbolic meaning of a scripturalized Torah was remarkable, particularly in the examples from the book of Deuteronomy. The writtenness of scripture, which becomes much more important in the later reception of the Bible, has roots in examples within the biblical text itself which engage script as medium in various ways.

References

Adler, Yonatan. 2011. "The content and order of the scriptural passages in Tefillin: A reexamination of the early Rabbinic sources in light of the evidence from the Judean desert." In *Halakhah in light of epigraphy*, edited by Albert I. Baumgarten and Hanan Eshel, Journal of Ancient Judaism. Supplements 3, 205–229. Göttingen: Vandenhoeck and Ruprecht.

———. 2017. "The distribution of Tefillin Finds among the Judean Desert Caves." In *The Caves of Qumran*, edited by Marcello Fidanzio, Studies on the Texts of the Desert of Judah 118, 161–173. Leiden: Brill.

Bearman, Gregory and William A. Christens-Barry. 2009. "Spectral Imaging of Ostraca." *Palarch's Journal of Archaeology of Egypt/Egyptology* 6(7): 1–20.

Berlejung, Angelika. 2015. "Kleine Schriften mit großer Wirkung zum Gebrauch von Textamuletten in der Antike." In *Schriftträger—Textträger: Zur materiellen Präsenz des Geschriebenen in frühen Gesellschaften*, edited by Annette Kehnel and Diamantis Panagiotopulos, 103–125. Berlin: de Gruyter. https://doi.org/10.1515/9783110371345.103

Braulik, Georg. 1997. "Das Deuteronomium und die Gedächtniskultur Israels: Redaktionsgeschichtliche Beobachtungen zur Verwendung von *lmd*." In *Studien zum Buch Deuteronomium*, Stuttgarter biblische Aufsatzbände 24, 119–146. Stuttgart: Verlag Katholisches Bibelwerk.

Carr, David M. 2005. *Writing on the Tablet of the Heart: Origins of Scripture and Literature*. Oxford [et al.]: Oxford University Press.

Chang, Dongshin Don. 2016. *Phinehas, the Sons of Zadok, and Melchizedek. Priestly Covenant in Late Second Temple Texts*. Library of Second Temple Studies 90. London: Bloomsbury.

Charlesworth, James Hamilton. 2009. "What is a variant? Announcing a Dead Sea Scrolls fragment of Deuteronomy." *Maarav* 16(2): 201–212.

Claus, Peter and Margaret A. Mills. 2003. *South Asian Folklore. An Encyclopedia: Afghanistan, Bangladesh, India, Nepal, Pakistan, Sri Lanka*. New York & London: Routledge.

Cohn, Yehuda. 2008. *Tangled Up in Text: Tefillin and the Ancient World*. Brown Judaic Studies 351. Providence: Brown University.

Falk, Daniel K. 2014. "Material aspects of prayer manuscripts at Qumran". In *Literature or liturgy? Early Christian hymns and prayers in their literary and litur-*

gical context in Antiquity, edited by Clemens Leonhard and Hermut Löhr, Wissenschaftliche Untersuchungen zum Neuen Testament. Reihe 2 363, 33–87. Tübingen: Mohr Siebeck.

Finsterbusch, Karin. 2005a. *Weisung für Israel: Studien zu religiösem Lehren und Lernen im Deuteronomium und in seinem Umfeld.* Forschungen zum Alten Testament 44. Tübingen: Mohr Siebeck.

———. 2005b. "'Du sollst sie lehren, auf dass sie tun...' Mose als Lehrer der Tora im Buch Deuteronomium." In *Religiöses Lernen in der biblischen, frühjüdischen und frühchristlichen Überlieferung,* edited by Beate Ego and Helmut Merkel, 27–45. Wissenschaftliche Untersuchungen zum Neuen Testament 180. Tübingen: Mohr.

Fraade, Steven D. 2011. *Legal Fictions: Studies of Law and Narrative in the Discursive Worlds of Ancient Jewish Sectarians and Sages.* Supplements to the Journal for the Study of Judaism 147. Leiden: Brill. https://doi.org/10.1163/ej.9789004201095.i-628

Frevel, Christian. 2012. "Lernort Tora: Anstöße aus dem Alten Testament." In *Religionsunterricht als Ort der Theologie,* edited by Norbert Mette and Matthias Sellmann, 109–137. Quaestiones disputatae 247. Freiburg: Herder.

———. 2016a. "Practicing rituals in a textual world: Ritual *and* innovation in the book of Numbers." In *Ritual Innovation in the Hebrew Bible and Early Judaism,* edited by Nathan MacDonald, 129–150. Beihefte zur Zeitschrift für die Alttestamentliche Wissenschaft 468. Berlin: de Gruyter. https://doi.org/10.1515/9783110368710-009

———. 2016b. "Von der Unvollkommenheit des Vollkommenen. Anmerkungen zur Anthropologie der Rituale im Buch Numeri." In *Die Erfindung des Menschen: Person und Persönlichkeit in ihren lebensweltlichen Kontexten,* edited by Stefan Beyerle, 215–244. Theologie – Kultur – Hermeneutik 21. Leipzig: Theologische Verlagsanstalt.

Frymer-Kensky, Tikva. 1984. "The strange case of the suspected Sotah (Numbers V 11–31)." *Vetus Testamentum* 34: 11–26. https://doi.org/10.1163/156853384X00025

Grigo, Jaqueline. 2015. *Religiöse Kleidung. Vestimentäre Praxis zwischen Identität und Differenz.* Berlin. https://doi.org/10.14361/transcript.9783839428399

Kartveit, Magnar. 2009. *The origin of the Samaritans.* Vetus Testamentum. Supplements 128. Leiden: Brill. https://doi.org/10.1163/ej.9789004178199.i-406

———. 2015. "The Place That the Lord Your God Will Choose," *Hebrew Bible and Ancient Israel* 4: 205–218. https://doi.org/10.1628/219222715X14453513581450

Keel, Othmar. 1991. "Zeichen der Verbundenheit. Zur Vorgeschichte und Bedeutung der Forderungen von Deuteronomium 6,8 f. und Par." In *Mélanges Dominique Barthélemy. Études bibliques offertes à l'occasion de son 60e anniversaire,* edited by Pierre Casetti *et al.,* 159–240. Orbis biblicus et orientalis 38. Göttingen: Vandenhoeck & Ruprecht.

———. 2004. "Die Brusttasche des Hohenpriesters als Element priesterschriftlicher Theologie." In *Das Manna fällt auch heute noch. Beiträge zur Geschichte und*

Theologie des Alten, Ersten Testaments, edited by Frank-Lothar Hossfeld *et al.*, 379–391. Herders biblische Studien 44. Freiburg: Herder.

———. 2007. *Die Geschichte Jerusalems und die Entstehung des Monotheismus*, Orte und Landschaften der Bibel IV, 1. Göttingen: Vandenhoek & Ruprecht.

Kersken, Sabine. 2011. "Schmuck." In *Das Wissenschaftliche Bibellexikon im Internet* (www.wibilex.de). Accessed 17 December 2016.

Knoppers, Gary N. 2013. *Jews and Samaritans: The Origins and History of Their Early Relationships*. Oxford: Oxford University Press. https://doi.org/10.1093/acp rof:oso/9780195329544.001.0001

Kotansky, Roy. 1994. *Greek Magical Amulets. Part I, Text and Commentary*. Wiesbaden: Harrassowitz. https://doi.org/10.1007/978-3-663-20312-4

———. 2006. "Amulets." In *Dictionary of Gnosis & Western Esotericism*, edited by Wouter J. Hanegraaf, 60–71. Leiden: Brill.

Levine, Baruch. 1993. *Numbers 1–20*, The Anchor Bible 4. New York: Doubleday.

Lohfink, Norbert. 1991. *Die Väter Israels im Deuteronomium: Zu einem Buch von Thomas Römer*. Orbis biblicus et orientalis 111. Freiburg, Schweiz: University-Verlag.

Lowy, Simeon. 1977. *The Principles of Samaritan Bible Exegesis*. Leiden: Brill.

Marzahn, Joachim and Liane Jakob-Rost. 1985. *Assyrische Königsinschriften auf Ziegeln aus Assur*. Textedition, Vorderasiatische Schriftdenkmäler, Neue Folge 7. Berlin: Akademie-Verlag.

———. 1995. *Das Ištar-Tor von Babylon*. Mainz: Philipp von Zabern.

Meshel, Ze'ev. 2012. *Kuntillet 'Ajrud: An Iron Age II Religious Site on the Judah-Sinai Border*. Jerusalem: Israel Exploration Society.

Mills, Margaret A. *et al*. 2003. *South Asian Folklore. An Encyclopedia*. London: Routledge.

Milik, Józef T. 1977. *Qumrân grotte 4.II: Tefillin, Mezuzot et Tagums (4Q128-157)*. Discoveries of the Judean Desert 3. Oxford: Clarendon.

Müller, Reinhard. 2016. "The altar on Mount Gerizim (Deuteronomy 27:1–8): Center or periphery?" In *Centres and Peripheries in the Early Second Temple Period*, edited by Ehud Ben-Zvi and Christoph Levin, 197–214. Forschungen zum Alten Testament 108. Tübingen: Mohr Siebeck.

Nihan, Christophe. 2007. "The Torah between Samaria and Judah: Shechem and Gerizim in Deuteronomy and Joshua." In *The Pentateuch as Torah*, edited by Gary Knoppers and Bernhard M. Levinson, 187–223. Winona Lake: Eisenbrauns.

Otto, Eckart. 2012. *Deuteronomium 4, 44-11, 32*. Herders Theologischer Kommentar zum Alten Testament. Freiburg: Herder.

———. 2016. *Deuteronomium 12, 1-23, 15*. Herders Theologischer Kommentar zum Alten Testament. Freiburg: Herder.

———. 2017. *Deuteronomium 23, 16-34, 12*. Herders Theologischer Kommentar zum Alten Testament. Freiburg: Herder.

Renger, Johannes. 1967. "Untersuchungen zum Priestertum in Altbabylonischer Zeit." *Zeitschrift für Assyriologie* 24: 110–188.

Rofé, Alexander. 1985. "Deuteronomy 5:28–6:1. Composition and text in the light of deuteronomic style and three tefillin from Qumran (4Q 128, 129, 137)." *Henoch* 7: 1–73.

Rosen-Zvi, Ishay. 2012. *The mishnaic Sotah ritual: Temple, gender and midrash.* Supplements to the Journal for the study of Judaism 160. Leiden: Brill. https://doi.org/10.1163/9789004227989

Samuel, Harald. 2014. *Von Priestern zum Patriarchen Levi und die Leviten im Alten Testament*, Beiträge zur Zeitschrift für die Alttestamentliche Wissenschaft 448. Berlin: de Gruyter.

Scherer, Andreas. 2004. "Das Ephod im Alten Testament." *Ugarit Forschungen* 35: 589–604.

Schmitt, Rüdiger. 2014. *Mantik im Alten Testament.* Alter Orient und Altes Testament 411. Münster: Ugarit Verlag.

Schnepper, Arndt Elmar. 2012. *Goldene Buschstaben ins Herz schreiben. Die Rolle des Memorierens in religiösen Bildungsprozessen.* Göttingen: V&R unipress.

Seow, Choon-Leong. 2013. "Ephod." In *Encyclopedia of the Bible and Its Reception*, Volumes 6–7. Berlin: de Gruyter.

Sobott, Robert, *et al.* 2015. "Non-destructive studies on ostraca texts, inks and their ceramic substrates." *METALLA Sonderheft* 7: 248–250.

Sonnet, Pierre. 1997. *The Book within the Book: Writing in Deuteronomy.* Biblical Interpretation Series 14. Leiden: Brill.

Stol, Marten. 2016. *Women in the Ancient Near East.* Berlin: de Gruyter.

Ulrich, Eugene C. 1994. "4QJosh^a and Joshua's First Altar in the Promised Land." In *New Qumran Texts and Studies*, edited by George J. Brooke and Florentino Garcia Martinez, 89–104. Studies on the Texts of the Desert of Judah 15. Leiden: Brill.

———. 2012. "The Old Latin, Mount Gerizim, and 4QJosh^a." In *Textual criticism and Dead Sea scrolls studies in honour of Julio Trebolle Barrera. Florilegium Complutense*, 361–375. Supplements to the Journal for the study of Judaism 158. Leiden: Brill. https://doi.org/10.1163/9789004221352_023

Veijola, Timo. 1992. "Das Bekenntnis Israels. Beobachtungen zur Geschichte und Theologie von Dtn 6: 4-9." *Theologische Zeitschrift* 48: 369–381.

Würthwein, Ernst. 1995. *The Text of the Old Testament.* Grand Rapids, MI: Eerdmans.

Zawadzki, Stefan. 2013. *Garments of the Gods: Studies on the Textile Industry and the Pantheon of Sippar according to the Texts from the Ebabbar Archive.* 2 vols. Orbis Biblicus et Orientalis 218. Fribourg: Academic Press.

Zwickel, Wolfgang. 2012. *Edelsteine in der Bibel.* Mainz: Philipp von Zabern.

6

Touching Books, Touching Art:
Tactile Dimensions of Sacred Books in the Medieval West

DAVID GANZ

This essay deals with the role of book decoration in a tactile approach to sacred texts in the Western Middle Ages. For a long time, books and artworks have been discussed as visual objects. Taking into account their intrinsic haptic qualities opens new ways to understand the contribution of the arts to the use of sacred texts in medieval Christianity.

Introduction

Around 1500, two otherwise unknown Franciscan scribes in Austria created a pocket-size manuscript that contained a German translation of the Revelation of John and the Rule of the Franciscan Order (Redzich 2010, 174, 595–597; Rainer 2016). Plunging their pens into gold ink they started tracing large letters in the solemn *textura* type on the then still unbound sheets of parchment: 9–10 short lines per page, 466 text pages altogether (Figure 6.1). For the two friars, the intense work of handwriting—"three are the fingers that write but the whole body is laboring," to put it in the words of a thirteenth-century scribe (Paris, BNF, Ms lat. 3827, 167)—would have had its own spiritual value, as many medieval sources tell us (Eberlein 1995, 166–175). All the imperfections and irregularities that characterize the fabric of the letters (*textura* is derived from the Latin *texere*, "to weave") would have testified that this was the product of individual hands. Obviously, sensual experience of the book should have continued once this small object was used by its owner (very probably a high-ranking member of the order). In a pragmatic context of private devotion and meditation, he needed to carefully grasp and turn the small sheets of parchment with his fingers,

David Ganz is Professor of Medieval Art History in the Art History Institute of the University of Zürich, Switzerland.

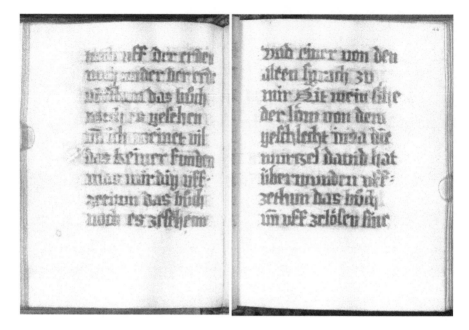

Figure 6.1   The Lamb takes the Book with the Seven Seals (Rev 5:5b-8a), Apocalypse with
Rule of Saint Francis in German, ca. 1500. Munich, Bayerische Staatsbibliothek,
Cgm 111, fol. 43v-44r (© Bayerische Staatsbibliothek München)

while the bright surface of the page and the shimmering letters written on
it would have provoked a sensation of awe.

Yet before the book's proprietor could start deciphering the words and
meditating the meaning of John's visionary account, he would have had a
completely different experience: attached to the front and the back side of
the leather binding were brass plates into which a goldsmith had carved
scenes of the Revelation. Holding the book in his hands (Figure 6.2), the
owner would have seen a sheep approaching a throne on which a digni-
fied elder was sitting, touching with his forelegs a book which the man was
holding on his lap. He would have also recognized that this scene referred
to Revelation 5:6-7, where a Lamb appeared "having seven horns and seven
eyes, that seemed to be slaughtered [...] and took the book out of the right
hand of him who sat on the throne."

The representation on the cover introduced the user to a *mise en abyme*
experience that shaped his approach to the small book in his hands in a particular way. Instead of just signaling its content—the book of Revelation—it
invoked an authoritative biblical model for the activity of taking and opening a sacred text. At the beginning of Revelation 5 when the book with the
seven seals appears in the right hand of God, it is still firmly closed and "no

Figure 6.2   The Lamb takes the Book with the Seven Seals, Apocalypse with Rule of Saint Francis in German, front cover, ca. 1500. Munich, Bayerische Staatsbibliothek, Cgm 111 (© Bayerische Staatsbibliothek München)

man in heaven, nor in earth, neither under the earth, was able to open the book, nor to look thereon" (Rev 5:3). This provokes a strong emotional reaction in the visionary witness, Saint John, who breaks out in tears and has to be comforted by one of the elders. And when the Lamb enters the scene and takes the book, his action is praised by a big celestial chorus of angels, the elders and the four beasts: "And they sung a new song, saying, Thou art worthy to take the book, and to open the seals thereof: for thou wast slain, and hast redeemed us to God by thy blood out of every kindred, and tongue, and people, and nation; and hast made us unto our God kings and priests: and we shall reign on the earth" (Rev 5:9–10).

Of course, the manuscript's owner probably wouldn't have expected that something similar to the materialization of four riders, to an earthquake, to the moon turning dark as blood or to the stars coming down from the sky would happen when he touched the book. Rather, the image on the cover turned touching and opening the book into a trigger for the devotional practice of reading and meditating on John's celestial visions. Looking at the cover and palpating its three-dimensional figures with his fingers, the user would have easily revived the drama around a sealed book which is characterized as the most powerful medium of divine revelation.

The tactility of artworks

In this essay, I will investigate the relationship between the visual arts and tactile approaches to sacred scripture in medieval Western Christianity. As in many other religions of the book, transforming copies of sacred scripture into aesthetic objects was an essential part of Christian book culture, especially in the context of public, communal ritual and private, intimate meditation. Calligraphy, ornament, and figural images were believed to be efficacious tools for converting the mere data of the text into a holy object, capable of mediating between here and there, between the visible terrestrial and the invisible celestial sphere (Brown 2010). While all these elements of book art are traditionally analysed in terms of visual aesthetic experience, I will focus here on the tactile, haptic dimensions of public and private book use.

A short reflection on the reasons for the long disregard of tactility is helpful at this point. When art history evolved as academic discipline around the turn of the eighteenth to nineteenth centuries, it was guided by classicist and idealist aesthetic principles. The reception of the artwork was conceived as a process guided by the eye as the one organ of perception capable of true aesthetic experience. Touch was judged an inferior sense, less cultivated and more prone to be driven by raw desire and sexual attraction—a sensual energy that was reflected in contemporary depictions of Ovid's story about Pygmalion, who fell in love with a nude female figure he had carved in ivory (Blühm 2002):

> Often, he runs his hands over the work, tempted as to whether it is flesh or ivory, not admitting it to be ivory. He kisses it and thinks his kisses are returned; and speaks to it; and holds it, and imagines that his fingers press into the limbs, and is afraid lest bruises appear from the pressure. [...] He dresses the body, also, in clothing; [...] but it appears no less lovely, naked. He arranges the statue on a bed [...] and calls it his bedfellow, and rests its neck against soft down, as if it could feel. (Ovid 2000, X: 243–297)

The institution of the art museum that evolved around 1800 created a disposition that would have prevented visitors from repeating this fetishizing experience: paintings were put into frames and hung on the walls, sculptures were displayed on pedestals, behind barriers or in showcases, and eventually received "do not touch" signs (Chatterjee 2008; Van Eck 2014). Later on, the rise of photography as exclusive medium for the reproduction of artworks—at the expense of three-dimensional techniques such as the plaster cast—has enormously contributed to shifting the focus of art historical analysis mainly to the visual qualities of the artwork. In short, the institutional background of the museum and the technological foundation of photography established a strong framework that coexisted with changing methodological paradigms, from *Stilgeschichte* and Iconology to visual studies and *Bildwissenschaft* (Mitchell 1994; Boehm 1994; Elkins 1999; Belting 2001).

In the last decade, art historians have started to question this long-standing preference, leading to what Jacqueline Jung has coined a "tactile turn" in art history (Wenderholm 2006; Jung 2010; Bacci and Melcher 2011; Rath, *et al.* 2013; Dent 2014; Švankmajer 2014). This reorientation is certainly inspired by new image technologies of the digital age and by a profound change in the cultural role of museums. But it is also part of a broader interdisciplinary tendency to emphasize the principle of embodiment (Bynum 1995; Mascia-Lees 2011) and to explore cultural concepts and practices of multisensory experience (Harvey 2002; Sanger and Walker 2012; Promey 2014; Palazzo 2016). Other important impulses come from theories engaged with the agency and the life of objects (Gell 1998; Law 2002; Latour 2005) and from the recent interest in matter and materiality (Miller 2005; Bennett and Joyce 2010), as well as the concept of material religion (Morgan 2010; Bynum 2011).

Western medieval art can be characterized as a practice that involved a huge variety of object categories. Many of these objects had a practical function and needed to be manipulated when they were used. But nowhere was the nexus between the use of medieval artworks and tactility so strong as in the case of manuscripts which need to be held and opened, flipped through and closed when users want to access them. It is interesting to notice therefore that the process of musealization which yielded the transfer of so many medieval objects into the modern "temples of art" has marginalized the category of manuscripts. With relatively few exceptions, the richest patrimony of medieval art ended up outside the sphere of "art collections": once they were stored in libraries, the tactile aesthetics of these objects could be easily ignored.

It has been rightly argued that Western medieval culture had no clear cut hierarchy of the senses. Vision was often judged superior to other ways of perception because all inner spiritual and cognitive processes were generally believed to be based on images (Jütte 2005, 20–124). But this ranking could change when the issue of getting into contact with the divine was at stake: the ultimate goal of the human soul was often defined in tactile terms, such as embracing or kissing the godhead (Jung 2010). As we will see, physical contact with sacred books could be charged with such models of direct interaction between terrestrial and celestial bodies.

Infer digitum tuum: Touching books and touching the divine

The book with which I started is a product of the late medieval culture of private devotion that conceived of books as vehicles of an intimate experience at close range: books of a small format that typically were private property and needed to be activated with different organs of the body in order to stimulate the imagination. Paintings of this period define devotional activity as contact with prayer books which seldom are actually looked at and read but rather held and touched while the prayer's gaze is directed elsewhere.

In 1457, the Bamberg-based painter, Hans Pleydenwurff, created a small diptych for Georg von Löwenstein, a canon at Bamberg cathedral (Figure 6.3). On the right wing, the aged canon is represented in precious attire, wearing a brocade coat trimmed with fur. In his left hand, he holds a brev-

Figure 6.3 Hans Pleydenwurff, Man of sorrows and count Georg von Löwenstein, diptych, 1456. Basel, Kunstmuseum, and Nuremberg, Germanisches Nationalmuseum (© Kunstmuseum Basel Photo: Martin P. Bühler) and Germanisches Nationalmuseum Nürnberg.

iary that is wrapped in green cloth. From the gesture of his left hand, it becomes clear that until a moment ago, he had been looking in the open book, saying his prayers, and that he has just switched to a second phase of devotional practice, imagining what he has read (Ringbom 1969; Harbison 1985; Lentes 2002; Rothstein 2005; Sand 2014; Scheel 2014). The result of this effort is depicted on the diptych's left wing: Christ himself becomes visible, presenting the bleeding wounds of his passion and death to the canon. A frame of clouds reminds us of the fact that this is only an apparition to the canon's inner eye (Schmidt 2003; Ganz 2010, 51–52; Bawden 2012, 304–310).

This inner vision is related to the outer experience of touching the book. The position of the canon's thumb acts as an index in a double sense: it points to the activity of reading that has triggered the visual revelation of the divine and to the written words that Löwenstein is remembering during his imaginary experience. Touching the book was a means of bodily memorizing the written word. Late medieval *ars memorativa* taught that the process of storing information in the chambers of the brain could be enhanced by using one's hands and fingers as memory aids (Carruthers 1990; Berns 2000). On a woodcut at the beginning of Heinrich Steinhöwel's *Life of Aesop* published in Ulm in 1476, we see the crookbacked author using his hands as means to recall different episodes of his life (Figure 6.4). But we may also think of the common use of paternosters and rosaries as palpable devices of counting and remembering elements of prayer and meditation, as we see in Rogier van der Weyden's diptych for Philippe de Croy, chamberlain of the Burgundian Duke Philip the Good (Hand, *et al.* 2006, 252–253; Campbell and van der Stock 2009, 315–319): while De Croy squeezes the beads between his praying hands, the mother of God unites her son and the book with her hands. The book has moved from the outer to the inner realm of the diptych here, its clasp serving as toy for the little Christ child to whom the prayer is addressed (Figure 6.5).

It seems particularly meaningful therefore that Pleydenwurff's painting evokes the book as an object consisting of layers of different materials with specific surfaces and textures: folios of parchment inside the book, their edges gilded; a small sheet of paper inserted between the pages with notes written on it; a piece of green cloth—probably silk—wrapped around the book with the two ribbons that serve to close this "shirt"; the thread hanging down from one of them, held by the men's right thumb. As a part of this complex pictorial context, the book assumes the status of a metaphor standing for a body vested with garments, a body that may be identified with the sacred body of Christ (for the late medieval practice of covering books with textiles, see Coron and Lefèvre 1995; Gorreri 2001; Smith 2004; Coilly 2008).

Figure 6.4 Esopus, woodcut, from: Heinrich Steinhöwel, Vita Esopi, Ulm: Johann Zainer 1476. Munich, Bayerische Staatsbibliothek, Rar. 762, fol. 1v (© Bayerische Staatsbibliothek München).

In the dual structure of the diptych, the position of this book-body is extremely meaningful: on the right wing, the small opening of the book occupies a similar place as the bleeding side-wound on the left wing. Putting the thumb into the book becomes a metaphor for touching Christ's body and re-enacting the famous gesture of the doubting Thomas: "Reach hither thy finger, and behold my hands; and reach hither thy hand, and thrust it into my side: and be not faithless, but believing." (John 20:27; see Most 2005).

As this example shows, reading, seeing and touching were closely inter-related in late-medieval culture of private devotional book use. The story of doubting Thomas who recognizes Christ by touching him offers an authoritative biblical analogy for the power of sacred books as media that can be activated by physical contact. Pictorial representations such as the Löwenstein diptych developed models of linking the different perceptual

Figure 6.5   Rogier van der Weyden, Virgin with Child and Philippe de Croy, diptych, ca. 1460. San Marino, The Huntington Library Art Collection, inv. 26.105, and Antwerp, Koninklijk Museum voor Schoone Kunsten, inv. 254 (© Huntington Library Art Collection and Bridgeman Images).

dimensions of book use. Obviously, depicting books was also a means to initiate a self-referential discourse on the role of panel paintings in the foldable diptych format which were so often compared to books in contemporary sources (Eichberger 1998).

Sleeping, kissing, swearing: Art-consuming book rituals

In "adding" to the merely textual apparatus of sacred scripture, pictures and other elements of book decoration were a means of defining contact zones with the divine that could be activated not just by looking but also by touching them. That a picture of a naked suffering man hanging on a cross would appeal much more intensely to the senses and to the soul than the words "and Christ was crucified" was a commonplace in medieval image theory (Duggan 1989; Camille 1996; Brown 1999). In the common version of this argument, the different semiotic potentials of words and pictures were derived from the opposition between ear and eye, hearing and seeing. Yet in addition to that dichotomy, the promise of touching the divine by the physical contact with the devotional object seems to have been of enormous importance. Artful embellishment underlined this promise of the sacred book.

No other object category of medieval art offers such a rich sample of traces of physical contact with its users as manuscripts. On the one hand, this has to do with different preservation policies: whereas artworks in museums were systematically subjected to procedures of cleaning that aimed at removing later additions and at restoring the original, this has happened much less so to books in manuscript collections. But on the other hand, it is the intrinsic need of books to be manipulated with hands and other parts of the body that has created dense layers of use. In recent years, the art-historian and manuscript specialist Kathryn Rudy has begun to systematically explore material indexes of use in late medieval devotional books (Rudy 2010). Looking at the wear and dirt on the pages of manuscripts allows us to reconstruct the manual and corporeal practices in which these objects were involved. Very often these phenomena point to images as particular areas of interest. Artistic decoration obviously could enhance the sacred power residing in the books.

One of the most extreme cases is the so-called Miracle Book from Pürten, a small parish church in Upper Bavaria. The Miracle Book is a Carolingian gospel book written and illuminated in the late ninth century in France (Bierbrauer 1990, 131–132). Until the fifteenth century the manuscript was used for reading the pericopes during mass. In the later sixteenth century however, ecclesiastical authorities—the church was administrated by Augustinian Canons from the nearby Au monastery— began using this book as an object with healing power (Fastlinger 1903; Schreiner 2000, 91–92). A specific ritual activated its potential for persons suffering from epilepsy or mental illnesses. During four successive nights, the manuscript was opened and laid under the head of the sick person (Grube-Verhoeven 1966). For this close contact between the sacred book and the human body, the four opening pages of the Gospels with the images of the evangelists were chosen. In terms of signs of use, a deep difference between the pages containing the written text and the openings bearing the images can now be observed: whereas the former are still in quite good shape, the latter are torn into pieces, their painted surface almost completely rubbed away (Figure 6.6). In the logic of the ritual, the authors' portraits were those places where the most direct contact with divine power was possible. Just as Matthew, Mark, Luke and John had been inspired by celestial messengers that the miniatures visualised as the traditional four beings, an angel, a lion, an ox and an eagle, the sick persons that laid their heads on the Gospels hoped to receive a curative energy entering their minds during the night.

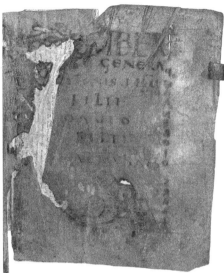

Figure 6.6 Opening with author portrait of Matthew and beginning of Gospel of Matthew, gospel book from Pürten, late 9th century. Munich, Staatsbibliothek, Clm 5250, fol. 18v-19r (© Bayerische Staatsbibliothek München).

Tellingly enough, the one picture that has been completely destroyed is the representation of the fourth Evangelist. Since late antiquity, the gospel of Saint of John was considered to be the most powerful sacred text for magical and medical purposes (Schreiner 2002, 115–122). Especially the opening verses of the prologue were frequently used in textual amulets (Skemer 2006, 87-89). In order to maintain the functionality of the ritual, ecclesiastical authorities decided to replace the lost page with a new one, on which a new author portrait was painted (Figure 6.7). The presence of images was necessary for the effective performance of the ritual.

As can be learned by this—admittedly rather extreme—case, touching is not a neutral contact with artworks: it transforms them by polluting and eroding them. This effect is obviously the reason for the "please do not touch"-signs that so intimately belong to the conservation environment of museums. Yet in the logic of premodern book rituals, there was also a positive outcome from this effect: when touching images meant wearing them, then part of their substance would have been transferred from the book to the body. When touching images meant staining them, then the corporeal excretions of their users would have their memory. Books were capable of conserving traces of use that accumulated over decades and centuries.

Exposing the sacred book of the Gospels to such a transformative practice would not have been conceivable in a period when it was still in use

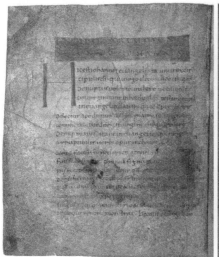

Figure 6.7   Argumentum of Gospel of John and author portrait of John, gospel book from
Pürten, late 9th and 17th/18th centuries. Munich, Staatsbibliothek, Clm 5250, fol.
151v-152r (© Bayerische Staatsbibliothek München).

for the liturgy. In early modern times, a codex with the unabridged text of
the four Gospels written in Carolingian minuscule had no liturgical value
anymore. But Christian liturgy still knew of similar rituals requiring close
bodily contact with sacred scripture. Placing the gospel book on the head,
the neck and the shoulders of a person was part of the medieval ordina-
tion ceremony for bishops and popes (Schreiner 2001). The accompanying prayer invoked the descent of the Holy Spirit. In most cases, the codex
would be opened for the performance of this ritual, but we do not know to
what degree images were involved in it.

The medieval liturgy of the word developed a whole set of actions that
included physical contact with the gospel book or other sacred texts. The
subdeacon and the deacon were responsible for moving the gospel book
from the sacristy to the altar, from the altar to the ambo, from the ambo
back to the altar (Gussone 1995; Lentes 2005; Heinzer 2009). They were also
in charge of carrying the Gospels during processions. Before the reading,
the book needed to be opened, and afterwards it had to be closed. Since
most gospel books were decorated with images on the exterior, these situations would have led to physical contact with these depictions (Steenbock
1965; Lowden 2007; Ganz 2015). Most of the time, this contact would have
been mediated by textiles: cushions on which the books were set and parts
of garments that were used to veil the hands. The exception to this was

the kiss given to the book: when the bishop arrived at the altar, he kissed the book on the altar, and after the reading the deacon kissed it and presented it for kissing to the bishop and other members of the clergy. Most of these kisses would have met the front cover of the book which explains why front covers generally are more worn than back covers (Lowden 2007, 27; Toussaint 2013, 57).

Osculating pages inside the books is well documented in the case of sacramentaries and missals that were used by the priest himself for saying the canonical prayer during which the transformation of the host and the wine took place. Usually they contained an image of the crucifixion at the beginning of the prayer (*Te igitur* ...). Many of these illuminations show traces of discoloration due to frequent contact with the priest's lips (Figure 6.8). Kissing the face of the crucified Christ anticipated the consumption of Christ's body through the Eucharist. The depiction of Christ's face was venerated

Figure 6.8 Crucifixion with prophets and donors, single page from a sacramentary, ca. 1150/1160. Münster, LWL-Landesmuseum für Kunst und Kulturgeschichte/ Dauerleihgabe Bistum Münster, Inv. BM 1745 (© LWL-Landesmuseum für Kunst und Kulturgeschichte Münster).

as if Christ was really there—a kind of real presence that we have to think of as mediated both through the image and through the book which contained the highly efficient words of the prayer. In fact, the priest who would have recited these words was the only person that was allowed to touch the depicted body. The other participants of the liturgy were excluded from this privilege, in the manner of Mary, John, the prophets and donators who look at Christ from a distance in the image. Touching Christ's face corroborated the priest's role of being Christ's first representative. The contact with the pigments on the parchment would have cleansed his lips from every impurity—like the angel putting the glowing coal on Isaiah's mouth (Isa 6:5-7). When late medieval manuscripts introduced a small kiss roundel on the bottom of the page in order to save the precious paintings from erasure, some celebrants obviously continued kissing the miniature instead. For example on the *Te igitur* opening of a missal from the mid-fifteenth century (Figure 6.9), we see a dark shadow of dirt stemming from the fingers that flipped these pages of the book, a smaller dark area around the medallion with the red cross, but also signs of abrasion on the head and feet of Christ (Stollberg-Rilinger *et al.* 2012, 326-327).

By far the most long-lasting and transcultural ritual that required touching a book is swearing an oath on sacred scripture, a topic which is still relatively little studied (Hofmeister 1957, 36-67). In the sixth century, emperor Justinian edited a law that obliged public officials, judges and administrators to take an oath of office, swearing on God the Father, Christ, the Holy Spirit, the Mother of God, and on "the four gospels that I hold in my hands" (*Corpus Iuris Civilis* 1872-1895, vol. 4, 89; Beissel 1906, 4-5; Hofmeister 1957, 38-40; Prodi 1992, 59-60; Humfress 2007). This prescription adapted the Talmudic rule that stipulated touching the Torah for oaths (Greenberg *et al.* 2007, 362). Swearing on books can be seen as replacing older forms of swearing on objects: instead of the book alone, it is always the divine person represented by it that guarantees the truth of the oath.

Somewhat surprisingly, the most famous Western oath book, the Vienna Coronation Gospels which were produced around 800 in the Palace School of Charlemagne, does not show obvious traces of ritual use. Written sources inform us that the gospel book was employed for the king's swearing-in at the end of the coronation ritual (Ramjoué 1968, 13-14, 31-32; for the coronation ritual: Kaemmerer 1961; Erkens 2008). There could have hardly been a more precious and prestigious oath book for the king: The codex is lavishly decorated, its pages dyed with purple, and its text written in gold and silver inks. Moreover, legend linked the Coronation Gospels to the rediscovery of Charlemagne's tomb in the year 1000 when Emperor Otto III gave the order

 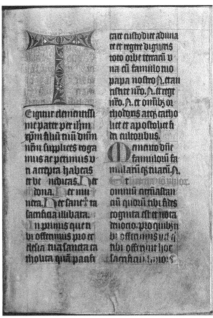

Figure 6.9 Opening with crucifixion and Te igitur, Missale notatum, 1440. Münster, Bistumsarchiv, Depositum Pfarrarchiv Ostenfelde St. Margaretha, Hs 693, fol. 160v-161r (© Bistumsarchiv Münster).

to open it. In later sources, the Gospels were said to have been found in the hands of Charles' intact body, together with other regalia (Cabannensis 1999, 25; Görich 1998). Hence touching the book for the oath would have meant touching a contact relic of the holy founder of the Medieval Roman Empire. The ideal place for performing this gesture would have been the opening of the Gospel of Saint John (Figure 6.10) (Murr 1801, 10 and 14). Yet recent scientific analysis of the manuscript did not prove this assumption: neither the John picture nor the other evangelist miniatures show significant traces of use (for a technical analysis: Grießer, *et al.* 2014). Of course this does not mean that the identification of the Coronation Gospels as an oath book is wrong: probably the coronation was simply too infrequent to leave marks on the pages.

With the significant increase of urban self-administration in late medieval Europe, oath books were widely used for the swearing-in civic officials (Dartmann 2004; Koldeweij 2004). In a sense, the swearing ritual began to emerge out of the sacred sphere of the liturgy. For this purpose, new types of oath books were developed that substituted for liturgical gospel books and missals. Characteristically it was an image— most often the scene of the crucifixion—together with a small portion of the gospel text which

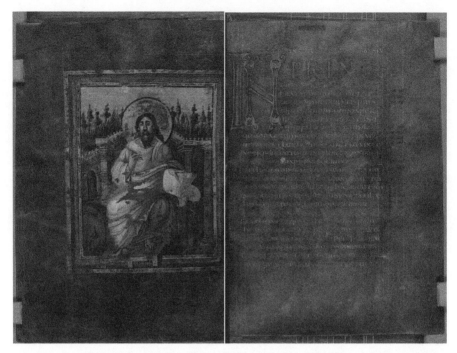

Figure 6.10   Opening with author portrait of John and beginning of Gospel of John, Coronation Gospels, ca. 800. Vienna, Kunsthistorisches Museum, inv. WS XIII 18, fol. 178v-179r (© Kunsthistorisches Museum Wien).

were inserted into these manuscripts, as if they were capable of transmitting the power of the gospel book to the oath book. Since representatives of municipal councils changed regularly and often, these pictures show traces of continual contact with human skin. In the Red Book of Privileges (Roode Priviligienboek) of s'Hertogenbosch, the habit of placing the (left) hand on the space between the body of Christ and the left margin of the page has led to an almost complete erasure of the figure of Mary (Figure 6.11). The small roundel with a cross that should have guided oath takers away from the miniature seems to have been completely ignored (Koldeweij 2004, 159–161).

Another strategy to prevent illuminations from abrasive contact with human hands can be found in the oath book of the city council of Cologne (Siart 2008, 118). Here the crucifixion miniature with the bleeding body of Christ was set against a shimmering golden background and enclosed by a frame that emphasized the evangelical authority of the picture by the representation of the four living beings (Figure 6.12). But before the oath takers would have a chance to look at this picture, a silk curtain had to be removed that covered the page even when it was opened (for the use of cur-

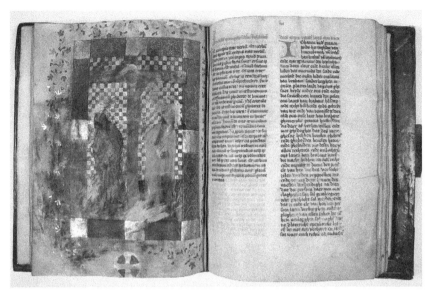

Figure 6.11   Crucifixion and Beginning of Gospel of John, Roode Previlegie-boek, first half of the fifteenth century. 's-Hertogenbosch, Stadsarchief, oudarchief, inv. A 525, fol. 55v-56r (© Erfgoed s'Hertogenbosch, Photo: Anne-Marie Vossen).

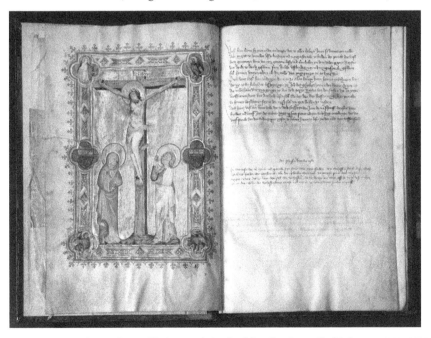

Figure 6.12   Opening with Crucifixion, Oath Book of the City Council of Cologne, 1398–1400. Cologne, Historisches Archiv, V+V V8, fol. 2v-3r (© Rheinisches Bildarchiv Köln, rba_c005529).

tains stitched into manuscripts: Sciacca 2007). Taking the oath would have required a whole sequence of manipulations: opening the book, lifting the curtain, putting the hand on the miniature, withdrawing the hand, lowering the fabric and closing the book.

Networks of hands

As the insertion of the curtain in the Cologne example makes clear, touching art would not have had any significance if it was possible for anyone at anytime. Rituals provided a strong pattern that limited the access to these objects to specific social positions and occasions. Only then, it was generally assumed, would holy books and the actions performed with them fulfill their role as mediators between this and the other world. Even in the case of late-medieval use of privately-owned sacred texts (see the first example in this essay), liturgical rituals were a model to be imitated. In this constellation, art was an important means to build up indexical networks that would have included further participants: connecting the absent hands of a larger group of "creators" and "owners" with "their" book and bringing them in contact with the invisible hands of divine beings (for a similar model of the "Art Nexus": Gell 1998).

The Uta-Codex, an early-eleventh-century manuscript containing the gospel readings for the liturgy, is one of the most intriguing examples for such a network of hands (Pfändtner and Gullath 2012). The fact that this book was created for a female congregation of women, the nunnery of Niedermünster in Regensburg, seems to have been a strong stimulus for the inclusion of other hands in the pictures of this book. When the Uta-Codex was made, the nuns of Niedermünster would have been members of the aristocratic elite but excluded from active participation in the liturgy. Like any other liturgical book, this codex would have passed only through the male hands of the clergy. But on the opening page of the codex (Figure 6.13), the lectionary is held in bare, unveiled hands by a woman, Abbess Uta of Kirchberg, who donated the book (for a detailed analysis of the iconography and the inscriptions: Cohen 2000, 39–51). Employing a typical pictorial formula for the act of dedication, Uta is offering the book to another woman, Mary. In turn, the Virgin is extending her (considerably enlarged) hand in order to receive this precious present. In the topological structure of the miniature, these two female figures occupy separate areas that represent distinct spheres: Uta is standing in the peripheral area of the outer frame, while Mary is sitting in the central roundel of the miniature. Uta's act of donation, so the picture suggests, is able to move the book from the periphery to the center of the Christian universe because a woman has become the

Figure 6.13   Opening with hand of God and donation scene, Uta-Codex, 1020/30 ca. Munich, Bayerische Staatsbibliothek, Clm 13601, fol. 1v-2r (© Bayerische Staatsbibliothek München).

mother of God. As Mary is holding her son on her lap, she is characterized as the vessel of incarnation here. And as Christ is holding another golden codex in his hand, the focus is put on the "Word" that became "flesh" in this process (John 1:13).

In short, as this miniature portrays it, there could hardly have been a donor and a present more appropriate to the two divine recipients. In line with this suggestion, Uta's name is spelled VOTA in the accompanying inscriptions and therefore aligned with the "vota" mentioned in these texts: the votives, the prayers, the vows that Mary and Christ are about to receive. The same word applies to both the donor and the present, both are the embodiment of each other.

While Mary is extending her hand towards this twofold votive, her gaze (as well as that of her son) is directed to the opposite page: Here, a giant golden hand appears which dominates the big roundel in the centre of the picture (Cohen 2000, 27–38). This motif would have been familiar to every contemporary viewer as the most common representation of God (Schmitt 1990, 93–133): a right hand protruding from the sky, detached from any body, a hand capable of creating without touching, according to the first chapter of Genesis: "And God said, Let there be light, and there was light" (Genesis 1:2). The whole world has been created by a hand, the right hand of God who, as the inscription tells us, "encompassing all time by his everlasting will, has from eternity hallowed all things, which he created by his word" ("Perpetuo totu[m] nutu cingens d[eu]s aevu[m], Sanxit ab aeterno: quae condidit omnia v[e]rbo," Cohen 2000, 30).

Obviously, the pictorial representation of this hand is meant as a metaphorical figure for God's power to create and to rule the world "by his word". But the miniature on the right page changes the status of this metaphor: When the word became flesh in the vessel of Mary's body, contact between human and divine hands became conceivable, as the biblical accounts of Mary Magdalene and Thomas testify. Uta and her sisters could think of this moment when the book was closed and Mary's raised hand would have moved towards the hand of God on the opposite page, eventually touching it (for the contact between closed pages in manuscripts, see Schreiner 2000).

Figure 6.14   Christ enthroned with jewelled book cover, Uta-Codex, book-box. Munich, Bayerische Staatsbibliothek, Clm 13601 (© Bayerische Staatsbibliothek München).

As with so many other lavishly decorated books of the liturgy, the main use of the Uta-Codex seems to have consisted of carrying and displaying it without opening the book for reading: its pages are still in astonishingly good condition and do not show signs of wear. The primary "interface" for seeing and handling such a book was its spectacular and sophisticated binding. In the case of the Uta-Codex, this would have been a book box in which the manuscript was locked (Figure 6.14). The monumental sculptural decoration of the lid shows Christ as the ruler of heaven, enclosed in a wide frame decorated with gemstones, enamels and filigree, and equipped with his regalia: the mandorla, the throne and the book. Its high relief underlines in a drastic manner the role of the gospel book as a vessel for the incarnate Word. And here the complex interplay between hands and books continues: Christ is holding an object that seems to be a book whose encrusted cover resembles the jewelled book-box. A closer look reveals that this binding contains no codex and therefore is a cover for Christ's body itself.

Figure 6.15   Rogier van der Weyden, Duran Madonna, ca. 1445. Madrid, Museo del Prado, inv. 2722 (© Bridgeman Images).

In direct line with this, Christ's thumb incises deeply into the cover, thus affirming the close interrelation of the incarnation and the inlibration of the Word in medieval Christianity.

Four centuries later, this concept was still strong, as we learn from paintings such as Rogier van der Weyden's Duran Madonna (Figure 6.15) where the Christ child is actually crumpling the pages of the book his mother was reading (De Vos 1999, 189–191): a seemingly innocent and amusing gesture of illiterate childish behaviour which is much more than that, since it metaphorically hints at Christ being the Word incarnate that transforms the book in an embodiment of himself.

The book as seal

The contrast between the open and the closed book brings me back to the object with which I started. John's vision of the closed book which only the Lamb, as a personification of Christ, is able to open, was a strong model for the handling of sacred books in the liturgy. Looking at earlier representa-

Figure 6.16 Apocalypse Frontispiece, Bible of Charles the Bald, 845. Paris, Bibliothèque nationale, Ms. lat. 1, fol. 415v (© Bibliothèque nationale de France).

tions of the opening scene, we learn that the seals mentioned in the text were initially interpreted as protective marks that prevented the revelation from being released. In the famous Apocalypse frontispiece of the Vivian Bible which originated in the monastery of Tours in the mid-ninth century (Figure 6.16), the seals are represented as clasps that tie the covers of the book together (Dutton and Kessler 1997). But on the late medieval book-cover, the function of the seals has changed considerably (Figure 6.2): Here they are clearly wax seals fixed with cords onto the book. The sealed book is now considered as diploma issued by God.

This significant shift in interpretation is the clue to the elaborate concept of tactility in the Austrian Apocalypse book: looking at this object as a whole (Figure 6.17), one can see seven metal bookmarks fixed with threads that imitate the pointed oval form of the seven seals in the picture. This highly original feature strengthened once more the parallel between the visionary and the real opening of the book. Moreover, it offered additional

Figure 6.17   Apocalypse with Rule of Saint Francis in German, front cover and pendants, ca. 1500. Munich, Bayerische Staatsbibliothek, Cgm 111 (© Bayerische Staatsbibliothek München).

aspects of haptic experience, as the small pendants could be grasped and moved between the fingers, sensing the raised letters that had been written on them: IHS (Jesus Savior of Humankind) on the obverse, and GOTHAIT (divinity) on the reverse.

There is strong evidence that the original, if not unique features of this book were the outcome of a well-established coexistence and partial concurrence between "old" and "new" media of the book—a situation that bears several parallels to the simultaneous use of paper and digital book formats in the early-twentyfirst century. Both the image on the cover and the text inside the book were copied from models created in the new printing technique introduced by Johannes Gutenberg half a century earlier (Eisenstein 1977; Giesecke 1991; Pettegree 2010). The text of Revelation reproduces the

Figure 6.18   Albrecht Dürer, The Lamb and the Twenty-four Elders in Heaven, woodcut, from: heimlich offenbarung iohannis, Nuremberg 1498, Munich, Staatliche Graphische Sammlung, Inv. Nr. 14001 (© Staatliche Graphische Sammlung München).

German translation of the Bible published by the Nuremberg-based book-maker Anton Koberger in 1483. This version of the text was also included in Albrecht Dürer's *heimlich offenbarung iohannis* whose series of monumental woodcuts is cited on the book's exterior (Figure 6.18) (Price 1994; Krüger 1996; Krüger 2002; O'Hear 2011, 142–175; Scherbaum 2013). Obviously, this activity of copying did not aim at mere imitation of an admired model. Instead, the production of the book was conceived as a translation from a machine-made to a handmade-book, highlighting the aesthetic differences such a transfer could imply.

It is in this relationship to print technique that the tactile medium of the seal becomes crucial for the concept of the small manuscript. Sealing and printing share some interesting technical similarities since both of them imply the use of "stampers" carved in a hard material whose surface will be impressed on a different, usually much softer "medium." This relationship as "impression" is highlighted by the material used for the cover and the seven seal plates: brass was a rather exotic choice for metal bindings (in the sixteenth century they were usually made of silver) but the most common one for sealing matrixes. Users who were aware of this practice would have perceived the pendants not just as seals (usually produced in wax) but as sealing matrix made to be impressed into their own hands, and ultimately into their hearts (Bedos-Rezak 2011, 186–202). In the same manner, the concept of a sealing matrix could be applied to the three-dimensional cover.

Eventually, when the book was closed, a second brass plate attached to the back would have become visible (Figure 6.19), decorated with another adaptation of Dürer's *heimlich offenbarung* (Figure 6.20). Here the *mise en abyme* continues with the "mighty angel come down from heaven, clothed with a cloud: and a rainbow was upon his head, and his face was as it were the sun, and his feet as pillars of fire" (Rev 10:1). The angel swears a book oath holding a small open book in his left hand. John who has turned the Island Patmos' shore into an open air writer's studio, his utensils scattered on the ground, takes the book and starts eating it up, obeying the orders given by another angel high in the air. An expression of pain and disgust is distorting his face, alluding to the taste of bitterness with which the book fills his belly (Rev 10:9–10).

Clearly, no one holding the manuscript in his hands would have understood this representation as an exhortation to imitate John literally (for examples of edible sacred texts in early modern Europe see Katharina Wilken's article in this collection). In fact, there was a long tradition of interpreting the act of eating the book as a metaphor for the interiorization of the written text (Wenzel 1995, 228–237). And the roundels in the four

Figure 6.19   John and the Strong Angel, Apocalypse with Rule of Saint Francis in German, back cover and pendants, ca. 1500. Munich, Bayerische Staatsbibliothek, Cgm 111 (© Bayerische Staatsbibliothek München).

corners visualized what the book's owner should have swallowed up into the stomach of his heart: the bitterness of Christ's passion and death, set in contrast to the worldly temptations represented by the bag filled with silver coins which Judas had received for his betrayal. Nonetheless, the book-cover would have also acted as an impressive reminder of the inherent corporality of medieval religious book use: in order to bear spiritual fruit, books had to pass the mouth of the senses and had to be chewed and digested with eyes and fingers. Even in the age of the printed book, sealing the heart with a sacred text had to begin with the body.

Figure 6.20   Albrecht Dürer, John and the Strong Angel, woodcut, from: Heimlich offenbarung iohannis, Nuremberg 1498, Munich, Staatliche Graphische Sammlung, Inv.
Nr. 14008 (© Staatliche Graphische Sammlung München).

References

Bacci, Francesca and David Melcher, eds. 2011. *Art and the Senses*. Oxford: Oxford
University Press.
Bawden, Tina. 2012. "In Bewegung versetzte Betrachter: Überlegungen zur
raumöffnenden Dimension klappbarer Bildträger im Mittelalter." In *Bewegen
im Zwischenraum*, edited by Uwe Wirth, 297–320. Berlin: Kadmos.
Bedos-Rezak, Brigitte Miriam. 2011. *When Ego Was Imago: Signs of Identity in the Middle
Ages*. Leiden: Brill.
Beissel, Stephan. 1906. *Geschichte der Evangelienbücher in der ersten Hälfte des
Mittelalters*. Freiburg i.Br.: Herder.
Belting, Hans. 2001. *Bild-Anthropologie. Entwürfe für eine Bildwissenschaft*. Munich:
Wilhelm Fink.
Bennett, Tony and Patrick Joyce, eds. 2010. *Material Powers. Cultural Studies, History
and the Material Turn*. London: Routledge.
Berns, Jörg Jochen. 2000. *Film vor dem Film. Bewegende und bewegliche Bilder als Mittel
der Imaginationssteuerung in Mittelalter und Früher Neuzeit*. Marburg.

Bierbrauer, Katharina. 1990. *Die vorkarolingischen und karolingischen Handschriften der Bayerischen Staatsbibliothek*. Wiesbaden: Reichert.

Blühm, Andreas. 2002. "Vom Leben zum Bild—vom Bild zum Leben." In *Wettstreit der Künste. Malerei und Skulptur von Dürer bis Daumier*, edited by Ekkehard Mai and Kurt Wettengel, 142–151. Munich: Edition Minerva.

Boehm, Gottfried, ed. 1994. *Was ist ein Bild?* Munich: Wilhelm Fink.

Brown, Michelle P. 2010. "Images to be read and words to be seen: The iconic role of the early Medieval book." *Postscripts* 6: 39–66.

Brown, Peter. 1999. "Images as substitutes for writing." In *East and West. Modes of Communication*, edited by Evangelos Chrysos and Ian Wood, 15–34. Leiden: Brill.

Bynum, Caroline Walker. 1995. "Why all the fuss about the body? A mediaevalist's perspective." *Critical Inquiry* 22(1): 1–33. https://doi.org/10.1086/448780

———. 2011. *Christian Materiality. An Essay on Religion in Late Medieval Europe*. New York: Zone Books.

Cabannensis, Ademarus. 1999. *Chronicon*, edited by Pascale Bourgain, Richard Landes and Georges Pon. *Corpus Christianorum Continuatio medievalis, 129*. Turnhout: Brepols.

Camille, Michael. 1996. "The Gregorian Definition Revisited. Writing and the Medieval Image." In *L'image. Fonctions et usages des Images dans l'Occident médiéval*, edited by Jérôme Baschet and Jean-Claude Schmitt, 89–107. Paris: Le Léopard d'or, D.L.

Campbell, Lorne and Jan Van der Stock, eds. 2009. *Rogier van der Weyden. 1400-1464. Master of Passions*. Exhibition catalogue, Leuven, Museum "M". Zwolle/Leuven: Waanders/Davidsfonds.

Carruthers, Mary. 1990. *The Book of Memory: A Study of Memory in Medieval Culture*. Cambridge: Cambridge University Press.

Chatterjee, Helen J. 2008. *Touch in Museums: Policy and Practice in Object Handling*. New York: Berg.

Cohen, Adam Seth. 2000. *The Uta Codex. Art, Philosophy, and Reform in Eleventh-Century Germany*. University Park: The Pennsylvania State University Press.

Coilly, Nathalie. 2008. "La reliure d'étoffe en France, dans les librairies de Charles V et de ses frères, fin XIVe-début XVe siècle." In *La reliure médiévale. Pour une description normalisée*, edited by Guy Lanoe, 277–286. Turnhout: Brepols.

Coron, Sabine and Martin Lefèvre, eds. 1995. *Livres en broderie. Reliures françaises du Moyen Age à nos jours*, exhibition catalogue, Bibliothèque de l'Arsenal, Bibliothèque Nationale de France. Paris: Bibliothèque Nationale de France.

Corpus Iuris Civilis. 1872–1895. *Corpus Iuris Civilis*. Edited by Paul Krüger *et al*. Berlin: Weidmann.

Dartmann, Christoph. 2004. "Schrift im Ritual. Der Amtseid des Podestà auf den geschlossenen Statutenkodex der italienischen Stadtkommune." *Historische Zeitschrift* 31: 169–204.

De Vos, Dirk. 1999. *Rogier van der Weyden. The Complete Works*. Antwerp: Mercatorfonds.

Dent, Peter, ed. 2014. *Sculpture and Touch*. Farnham: Ashgate.

Duggan, Lawrence G. 1989. "Was Art Really the 'Book of the Illiterate?'" *Word & Image* 5: 227–251. https://doi.org/10.1080/02666286.1989.10435406

Dutton, Paul Edward and Herbert L. Kessler. 1997. *The Poetry and Paintings of the First Bible of Charles the Bald.* Ann Arbor: University of Michigan Press.

Eichberger, Dagmar. 1998. "Devotional objects in book format: Diptychs in the collection of Margaret of Austria and her family." In *The Art of the Book: Its Place in Medieval Worship*, edited by Margaret M. Manion and Bernard J. Muir, 291–323. Exeter: University of Exeter Press.

Eisenstein, Elizabeth. 1977. *The Printing Press as an Agent of Change. Communications and Transformations in Early Modern Europe.* 2 vols. Cambridge: Cambridge University Press.

Elkins, James. 1999. *The Domain of Images.* Ithaca: Cornell University Press.

Erkens, Franz-Reiner. 2008. "Königskrönung und Krönungsordnung im späten Mittelalter." *Zeitschrift des Aachener Geschichtsvereins* 110: 27–64.

Fastlinger, Max. 1903. "Das Mirakelbuch von Pürten." *Beiträger zur Geschichte, Topographie und Statistik des Erzbistums Munich und Freising* 8: 1–13.

Ganz, David. 2010. "Weder eins noch zwei. Jan van Eycks Madonna in der Kirche und die Scharnierlogik spätmittelalterlicher Diptychen." In *Das Bild im Plural. Mehrteilige Bildformen zwischen Mittelalter und Gegenwart*, edited by David Ganz and Felix Thürlemann, 41–65. Berlin: Reimer.

———. 2015. *Buch-Gewänder. Prachteinbände im Mittelalter.* Berlin: Dietrich Reimer.

Gell, Alfred. 1998. *Art and Agency: An Anthropological Theory.* Oxford: Clarendon Press.

Giesecke, Michael. 1991. *Der Buchdruck in der frühen Neuzeit. Eine historische Fallstudie über die Durchsetzung neuer Informations- und Kommunikationstechnologien.* Frankfurt a.M.: Suhrkamp.

Görich, Knut. 1998. "Otto III. öffnet das Karlsgrab in Aachen. Überlegungen zu Heiligenverehrung, Heiligsprechung und Traditionsbildung." In *Herrschaftsrepräsentation im ottonischen Sachsen*, edited by Gerd Althoff and Ernst Schubert, 381–430. Sigmaringen: Jan Thorbecke.

Gorreri, Silvana. 2001. "Vestiti col saio o di seta. Legature monastiche e di lusso per codici di preghiera." In *Cum picturis ystoriatum. Codici devozionali e liturgici della Biblioteca Palatina*, edited by Leonardo Farinelli, 66–74. Mantua: Il Bulino.

Greenberg, Moshe, Haim Hermann Cohn and Menachem Elon. 2007. "Oath." In *Encyclopaedia Judaica*, edited by Michael Berenbaum and Fred Skolnik, vol. 15: 358–364. Detroit: Thomson Gale.

Grießer, Martina, *et al.* 2014. "Technologische Untersuchungen zu Erhaltungszustand, Pergament, Färbung und Miniaturen." In *Das Krönungsevangeliar des Heiligen Römischen Reiches*, edited by Sabine Haag and Franz Kirchweger, 131–149. Wien: Kunsthistorisches Museum.

Grube-Verhoeven, Regine. 1966. "Die Verwendung von Büchern christlich-religiösen Inhalts zu magischen Zwecken." In *Zauberei und Frömmigkeit*, edited by Hermann Brausinger, 11–57. Tübingen: Tübinger Vereinigung für Volkskunde e.V.

Gussone, Nikolaus. 1995. "Der Codex auf dem Thron. Zur Ehrung des Evangelienbuches in Liturgie und Zeremoniell." In *Wort und Buch in der Liturgie. Interdisziplinäre Beiträge zur Wirkmächtigkeit des Wortes und Zeichenhaftigkeit des Buches*, edited by Hanns Petzer Neuheuser, 191–231. St. Ottilien: Eos.

Hand, John Oliver, Catherine A. Metzger and Ron Spronk. 2006. *Prayers and Portraits: Unfolding the Netherlandish Diptych*. Exhibition catalogue, Washington, National Gallery Washington. New Haven, CT: Yale University Press.

Harbison, Craig. 1985. "Visions and meditations in early Flemish painting." *Simiolus* 15: 87–118. https://doi.org/10.2307/3780659

Harvey, Elizabeth D., ed. 2002. *Sensible Flesh: On Touch in Early Modern Culture*. Philadelphia: University of Pennsylvania Press.

Heinzer, Felix. 2009. "Die Inszenierung des Evangelienbuchs in der Liturgie." In *Codex und Raum*, edited by Stephan Müller, Lieselotte E. Saurma and Peter Strohschneider, 43–58. Wiesbaden: Harrassowitz.

Hofmeister, Christian. 1957. *Die christlichen Eidesformen. Eine liturgie- und rechtsgeschichtliche Untersuchung*. Munich: Zink.

Humfress, Caroline. 2007. "Judging by the book. Christian codices and late antique legal culture." In *The Early Christian Book*, edited by William E. Klingshirn and Linda Safran, 141–158. Washington: The Catholic University of America Press.

Jung, Jacqueline E. 2010. "The tactile and the visionary: Notes on the place of sculpture in medieval religious imagination." In *Looking Beyond: Visions, Dreams, and Insights in Medieval Art & History*, edited by Colum Hourihane, 203–240. University Park: Penn State University Press.

Jüte, Robert. 2005. *A History of the Senses: From Antiquity to Cyberspace*. Cambridge: Polity Press.

Kaemmerer, Walter, ed. 1961. *Quellentexte zur Aachener Geschichte, vol. 3: Die Aachener Königs-Krönungen*. Aachen: M. Brimberg.

Koldeweij, Jos. 2004. "Gezworen op het kruis of op relieken." In *Representatie. Kunsthistorische bijdragen over vorst, staatsmacht en beeldende kunst, opgedragen aan Robert W. Scheller*, edited by Johann-Christian Klamt and Kees Veelenturf, 158–179. Nijmegen: Valkhof Pers.

Krüger, Peter. 1996. *Dürers "Apokalypse." Zur poetischen Struktur einer Bilderzählung der Renaissance*. Wiesbaden: Harrassowitz.

———. 2002. "Die Apokalypse." In *Albrecht Dürer. Das druckgraphische Werk, Bd. 2: Holzschnitte und Holzschnittfolgen*, edited by Rainer Schoch, Matthias Mende and Anna Scherbaum, 59–105. Munich: Prestel.

Latour, Bruno. 2005. *Reassembling the Social. An Introduction to Actor-Network-Theory*. Oxford: Oxford University Press.

Law, John. 2002. "Objects and Spaces." *Theory, Culture & Society* 19: 91–105. https://doi.org/10.1177/026327602761899165

Lentes, Thomas. 2002. "Inneres Auge, äußerer Blick und heilige Schau. Ein Diskussionsbeitrag zur visuellen Praxis in Frömmigkeit und Moraldidaxe des späten Mittelalters." In *Frömmigkeit im Mittelalter. Politisch-soziale Kontexte, visuelle Praxis, körperliche Ausdrucksformen*, edited by Klaus Schreiner and Marc Müntz, 179–219. Munich: Wilhelm Fink.

———. 2005. "'Textus Evangelii.' Materialität und Inszenierung des 'textus' in der Liturgie." In *"Textus" im Mittelalter. Komponenten und Situationen des Wortgebrauchs im schriftsemantischen Feld*, edited by Ludolf Kuchenbuch and Uta Kleine, 133–148. Göttingen: Vandenhoeck & Ruprecht.

Lowden, John. 2007. "The word made visible: The exterior of the early Christian book as visual argument." In *The Early Christian Book*, edited by William E. Klingshirn and Linda Safran, 13–47. Washington, DC: The Catholic University of America Press.

Mascia-Lees, Frances Elizabeth, ed. 2011. *A Companion to the Anthropology of the Body and Embodiment*. Malden, MA: Wiley-Blackwell.

Miller, Daniel, ed. 2005. *Materiality*. Durham, NC: Duke University Press.

Mitchell, William J. T. 1994. *Picture Theory. Essays on Verbal and Visual Representation*. Chicago, IL: University of Chicago Press.

Morgan, David, ed. 2010. *Religion and Material Culture: The Matter of Belief*. London: Routledge.

Most, Glenn W. 2005. *Doubting Thomas*. Cambridge, MA: Harvard University Press. https://doi.org/10.4159/9780674041257

Murr, Christoph Gottlieb von. 1801. *Beschreibung der ehemals zu Aachen aufbewahrten drey kaiserlichen Krönungs-Zierden des lateinischen Evangelien-Buches, des arabischen Säbels Karls des Großen, und der Capsul mit der Erde, worauf das Blut des heiligen Stephans soll geflossen seyn*. Nürnberg/Altdorf: Monath und Kussler.

O'Hear, Natasha F. H. 2011. *Contrasting Images of the Book of Revelation in Late Medieval and Early Medieval Art: A Case Study in Visual Exegesis*. Oxford: Oxford University Press. https://doi.org/10.1093/acprof:oso/9780199590100.001.0001

Ovid. 2000. *Metamorphoses*. Translated by Anthony S. Kline. ovid.lib.virginia.edu. Internet Edition. Accessed 20 December 2016.

Palazzo, Éric, ed. 2016. *Les cinq sens au Moyen Âge*. Paris: Les Éditions du Cerf.

Pettegree, Andrew. 2010. *The Book in the Renaissance*. New Haven, CT: Yale University Press.

Pfändtner, Karl-Georg and Brigitte Gullath. 2012. *Der Uta-Codex. Frühe Regensburger Buchmalerei in Vollendung. Die Handschrift Clm 13601 der Bayrischen Staatsbibliothek*. Luzern: Quaternio.

Price, David. 1994. "Albrecht Dürer's representations of faith: The Church, lay devotion and veneration in the apocalypse (1498)." In *Zeitschrift für Kunstgeschichte* 57: 688–696. https://doi.org/10.2307/1482722

Prodi, Paolo. 1992. *Il sacramento del potere. Il giuramento politico nella storia costituzionale dell'Occidente*. Bologna: Il Mulino.

Promey, Sally M., ed. 2014. *Sensational Religion. Sensory Cultures in Material Practice*. New Haven, CT: Yale University Press.

Rainer, Thomas. 2016. "Apokalypse und Franziskanerregel in Deutsch." In *Kunst & Glaube. Ottheinrichs Prachtbibel und die Schlosskapelle Neuburg, exhibition cata-*

logue, Neuburg, Bayerische Schlösserverwaltung, edited by Brigitte Langer and Thomas Rainer, 308–309. Regensburg: Schnell & Steiner.

Ramjoué, Fritz. 1968. *Die Eigentumsverhältnisse an den drei Aachener Reichskleinodien.* Stuttgart: W. Kohlhammer.

Rath, Markus, Jörg Trempler and Iris Wenderholm, eds. 2013. *Das haptische Bild. Körperhafte Bilderfahrung in der Neuzeit.* Berlin: Akademie.

Redzich, Carola. 2010. *Apocalypsis Joannis tot habet sacramenta quot verba. Studien zu Sprache, Überlieferung und Rezeption hochdeutscher Apokalypseübersetzungen des späten Mittelalters.* Berlin: De Gruyter.

Ringbom, Sixten. 1969. "Devotional images and imaginative devotions: Notes on the place of art in late medieval piety." In *Gazette des Beaux-Arts* 111: 159–170.

Rothstein, Bret L. 2005. *Sight and Spirituality in Early Netherlandish Painting.* Cambridge: Cambridge University Press.

Rudy, Kathryn. 2010. "Dirty books: Quantifying patterns of use in medieval manuscripts using a densitometer." In *Journal of Historians of Netherlandish Art* 2: http://www.jhna.org/index.php/past-issues/volume-2-issue-1-2/129-dirty-books. Internet Edition. Accessed 17 December 2016.

Sand, Alexa. 2014. *Vision, Devotion, and Self-Representation in Late Medieval Art.* Cambridge: Cambridge University Press. https://doi.org/10.1017/CBO9781139424769

Sanger, Alice E. and Siv Tove Kulbrandstad Walker, eds. 2012. *Sense and the Senses in Early Modern Art and Cultural Practice.* Farnham: Ashgate.

Scheel, Johanna. 2014. *Das altniederländische Stifterbild. Emotionsstrategien des Sehens und der Selbsterkenntnis.* Berlin: Gebr. Mann.

Scherbaum, Anna. 2013. "Die frühen Zyklen. Apokalypse und Marienleben." In *Der frühe Dürer. Ausstellungskatalog Nürnberg, Germanisches Nationalmuseum,* edited by Daniel Hess and Thomas Eser, 434–457. Nürnberg: Verlag des Germanischen Nationalmuseums.

Schmidt, Peter. 2003. "Inneres Bild und äußeres Bildnis. Porträt und Devotion im späten Mittelalter." In *Das Porträt vor der Erfindung des Porträts,* edited by Martin Büchsel and Peter Schmidt, 219–239. Mainz: Philipp von Zabern.

———. 2009. "Der Finger in der Handschrift. Vom Öffnen, Blättern und Schließen von Codices auf spätmittelalterlichen Bildern." In *Codex und Raum,* edited by Stephan Müller, Stephan, Lieselotte Saurma-Jeltsch and Peter Strohschneider, 85–125. Wiesbaden: Harrassowitz.

Schmitt, Jean-Claude. 1990. *La raison des gestes dans l'Occident médiéval.* Paris: Gallimard.

Schreiner, Klaus. 2000. "Buchstabensymbolik, Bibelorakel, Schriftmagie. Religiöse Bedeutung und lebensweltliche Funktion heiliger Schriften im Mittelalter und in der Frühen Neuzeit." In *Die Verschriftlichung der Welt. Bild, Text und Zahl in der Kultur des Mittelalters und der Frühen Neuzeit,* edited by Horst Wenzel, Wilfried Seipel and Gotthard Wunberg, 59–103. Vienna: Kunsthistorisches Museum.

———. 2001. "Das Buch im Nacken. Bücher und Buchstaben als zeichenhafte Kommunikationsmedien in rituellen Handlungen der mittelalterlichen

Kirche." In *Audiovisualität vor und nach Gutenberg. Zur Kulturgeschichte der medialen Umbrüche*, edited by Horst Wenzel, Wilfried Seipel and Gotthard Wunberg, 73–95. Vienna: Kunsthistorisches Museum.

———. 2002. "Litterae mysticae. Symbolik und Pragmatik heiliger Buchstaben, Texte und Bücher in Kirche und Gesellschaft des Mittelalters." In *Pragmatische Dimensionen mittelalterlicher Schriftkultur*, edited by Christel Meier *et al.*, 277–337. Munich: Wilhelm Fink.

Sciacca, Christine. 2007. "Raising the Curtain. On the Use of Textiles in Manuscripts." In *Weaving, Veiling, and Dressing. Textiles and their Metaphors in the Late Middle Ages*, edited by Kathryn M. Rudy and Barbara Baert, 161–190. Turnhout: Brepols. https://doi.org/10.1484/M.MCS-EB.3.1875

Siart, Olaf, ed. 2008. *Goldene Pracht. Mittelalterliche Schatzkunst in Westfalen*, exhibition catalogue, Münster, LWL-Landesmuseum für Kunst und Kulturgeschichte/ Domkammer der Kathedralkirche St. Paulus. Munich: Hirmer.

Skemer, Don C. 2006. *Binding Words. Textual Amulets in the Middle Ages*. University Park: Pennsylvania State University Press.

Smith, Helen. 2004. "'This one poore blacke gowne lined with white': The clothing of the sixteenth century English book." In *Clothing Culture 1350-1650*, edited by Catherine Richardson 195–208. Ashgate: Aldershot.

Steenbock, Frauke. 1965. *Der kirchliche Prachteinband im frühen Mittelalter. Von den Anfängen bis zum Beginn der Gotik*. Berlin: Deutscher Verlag für Kunstwissenschaft.

Stollberg-Rilinger, Barbara, *et al.*, eds. 2012. *Spektakel der Macht. Rituale im Alten Europa 800-1800*, exhibition catalogue, Magdeburg. Darmstadt: Wissenschaftliche Buchgesellschaft.

Švankmajer, Jan. 2014. *Touching and Imagining. An Introduction to Tactile Art*. Translated by Stanley Dalby. London: Tauris.

Toussaint, Gia. 2013. "Elfenbein an der Schwelle. Einband und Codex im Dialog." In *Marburger Jahrbuch für Kunstwissenschaft* 40: 43–61.

Van Eck, Caroline. 2014. *Art, Agency and Living Presence. From the Animated Image to the Excessive Object*. Berlin: De Gruyter.

Wenderholm, Iris. 2006. *Bild und Berührung. Skulptur und Malerei auf dem Altar der italienischen Frührenaissance*. Berlin: Deutscher Kunstverlag.

Wenzel, Horst. 1995. *Hören und Sehen, Schrift und Bild. Kultur und Gedächtnis im Mittelalter*. Munich: C. H. Beck.

7

Infusions and Fumigations: Literacy Ideologies and Therapeutic Aspects of the Qur'an

KATHARINA WILKENS

Written texts, especially sacred texts, can be handled in different ways. They can be read for semantic content; or they can be materially experienced, touched, or even be inhaled or drunk. I argue that literacy ideologies regulate social acceptability of specific semantic and somatic text practices. Drinking or fumigating the Qur'an as a medical procedure is a highly contested literacy event in which two different ideologies are drawn upon simultaneously. I employ the linguistic model of codeswitching to highlight central aspects of this event: a more somatic ideology of literacy enables the link to medicine, while a more semantic ideology connects the practice to theological discourses on the sacredness of the Qur'an as well as to the tradition of Prophetic medicine. Opposition to and ridicule of the practice, however, comes from representatives of an ideology of semantic purity, including some Islamic theologians and most Western scholars of Islam. Qur'anic potions thus constitute an ideal point of entry for analyzing different types of literacy ideologies being followed in religious traditions.

Introduction

In most Muslim countries, the curative practice of imbibing or fumigating written segments of the Qur'an is very well-known and popular among all sections of society. Verses of the Qur'an are written on a piece of paper which is either dipped into water and drunk or fumigated and inhaled. In another variation, the verses are written onto plates or boards with liquid ink which is then washed off, collected and drunk. What caught my attention from the beginning of my research was the great discrepancy between

Katharina Wilkens is a Research Associate and Lecturer in Religious Studies at Ludwig Maximilians University, Munich, Germany.

the popularity of this practice throughout the Muslim world and how rarely academic literature mentions it.

Art historian Finbarr Barry Flood (2014) has recently observed the opposition between ink potions, edible Catholic images, Byzantine relics and other phenomena, on the one hand, and a Western, Saussurean distinction between signs, signifiers and objects, on the other hand. He argues that in "orthodox, post-Enlightenment modernity, devotional practices centered around animated matter call into question epistemological and ontological models of subject-object relations that have been deeply internalized and naturalized in Euro-America as a legacy of the Reformation and the Enlightenment" (Flood 2014, 460). I will complement his analysis in significant ways by adding medical parameters that take the efficacy of healing through these practices into account.

Drinking the Qur'an is classified in Islamic theology as magic, *siḥr*, usually as permitted magic, sometimes as illicit magic. In ethnography and Islamic studies, the practice has also been subsumed quite naturally under superstitious magic. But I believe this classification places too much emphasis on sympathetic links and impressions of efficacy, while it obscures aspects of the practice that involve semiotic ideologies, religious aesthetics and mediation, and shifts between secular and religious worldviews.

Drinking the Qur'an and ritual healing

Though I refer here mostly to drinking the Qur'an, I am in fact speaking about a range of practices known in a number of religions with broad variations through time and space. Physically ingesting words is a practice also known in many other scriptural traditions such as Catholicism, Sikhism, Buddhism or Daoism as well as in the Old Testament, ancient Egyptian religion and many other ancient Near Eastern traditions. But nowhere has the idea of imbibing ink for therapeutic purposes been as common as in Islamic societies, and nowhere else has it lasted as strongly into the twentieth and twenty-first centuries. In the face of modern medicine and the near-universal spread of literacy for social communication, this Islamic healing ritual is undergoing some changes, but it is not disappearing as many proponents of a disenchanted modernity would have it.

Besides drinking the ink with which Qur'anic verses were written, fumigating inscribed paper with incense sticks or breathing Qur'anic verses over water and then drinking it are popular practices in South East Asia and the Middle East.[1] The principle is always the same: Qur'anic verses are transferred onto a medium and then physically embodied by the patient.

1. In the Sikh tradition, *amrit* is a comparable practice in which hymns from the Guru

116

Qur'anic ink potions have remained popular in many Islamic countries over the centuries despite virulent questions of legitimacy, contestations between clerical authorities, debates on necessary scholarly abilities of the healers, the actual success rates of the practice and its social acceptability. In actuality, this practice is performed and interpreted in many ways. The verses can be specific or non-specific to the cause; a specialized Qur'anic healer may be required, or the patient may be allowed to treat herself/himself; the cure can be restricted to certain afflictions such as witchcraft and *jinn*-possession or it can be applied to all physical and mental diseases. It is highly contested in orthodox theology as well as between local clergymen. Public denial and private consumption is thus a common pattern of behavior.[2]

Qur'anic healing, no matter which form it takes, is a part of medico-theological tradition called Prophetic medicine, *al-ṭibb al-nabawī* (Perho 1995). The major works relating to this tradition—and all bearing the same title *Ṭibb al-nabawī*—were written in the fourteenth to sixteenth centuries, Jalāl al-Dīn al-Suyūṭi, Ibn Qayyim al-Jawziyya and al-Dhahabi being the most cited scholars to today.[3] In its intent it is a medical discipline centered on diet and personal habits, which makes it viable again today both in the context of urban lifestyle recommendations and in conservative, anti-Western circles. Other scholars, with both theological and medical backgrounds, have argued vehemently against this practice, subsuming it under forbidden magic or simple superstition.

In partially literate societies, the degree of learning among Islamic healers can vary enormously. In general, though, this does not seem to reflect upon the efficacy of the remedy. Many healers not proficient in Arabic and who have not memorized the entire Qur'an will always repeat the same few, well established verses. More scholarly healers can work with a greater repertoire of verses. A number of lists with specific recommendations have circulated among healers for many centuries, usually based on texts by Ibn Qayyim al-Jawziyya, al-Suyūṭi and others. A variety of such lists are now available online. Some healers are completely illiterate, or at least illiterate in the Arabic script. Bedouin female healers in Saudi Arabia at the beginning of the twentieth century, for example, were illiterate, but employed

---

Granth Sahib are spoken over water sweetened with honey and stirred with a sword. This is drunk by initiates, but also by people seeking healing (Myrvold 2010, 212–213).

2. I have discussed some of these in Wilkens 2013 and Wilkens (forthcoming), where I also provide more ethnographic detail on drinking the Qur'an from my fieldwork on religious healing in Tanzania 2003/04.

3. Translations are readily available for Ibn Qayyim al-Jawziyya (1998) and al-Suyūṭi (Elgood 1962). The text by al-Jawziyya has been translated and published by others as well as it is very popular today.

Qur'anic potions with great success (Doumato 2000, 141–142). They simply wrote something that looked like script onto a plate, washed the ink off and gave it to the (usually female) patients to drink while reciting some verses (*ruqya*). Another such case has been reported by medical historian Walter Bruchhausen in southeast Tanzania, where female healers in non-Muslim areas imitate Arabic calligraphy without being Muslims themselves and without being able to write in Arabic (2006, 263–266). Nonetheless, the remedy is immensely popular and is actually a forerunner of Islamic conversion in border regions. A more typical situation is that of—usually male—healers with a basic education in the Qur'an, but who are distinguished from scholarly Qur'anic experts at the larger mosques.[4] The tradition of Prophetic medicine is kept alive by these healers who make use of modern editions of the texts by classical authors with additional modern commentaries.

A unique path for distributing Qur'anic remedies is pursued by a company in Malaysia, the Annusyrah Bottling Plant.[5] They specialize in writing verses with saffron ink onto plain china plates, washing them off with rose water, and bottling the mixture. The liquids are produced and bottled under sterile conditions. The product range caters to spiritual and physical illnesses indicated on the labels; no healer is needed to administer the remedies. The local imam, advertised as a championship winner in Qur'an recitation, regularly speaks additional verses over the unbottled water to enhance its efficacy. This commercial enterprise thus acts as an intermediary between the Qur'anic specialist and the patients.

In general, the verses are prescribed and written out by specialized healers. In online environments, though, dependence on such authoritative figures may be minimized, not least because the technology of writing is universal today. In a Shi'ite forum, for example, someone asks: "Do you know if you have to write it yourself or can you get someone to write it for you?" He receives the answer: "Bro, it does not matter who writes it. Sometimes this is written for a sick person to drink and he/she cannot write it."[6] In other forums, technical questions of suitable brushes, preparation of ink and best writing surfaces are discussed in great detail by people who write out such verses privately.

4. For Senegal, see Dilley 2009; for southern Sudan, see el-Tom 1985; for southern India, see Flueckiger 2006; for Nigeria, see Abdalla 1997. This was also what I witnessed in urban Tanzania during my own fieldwork.

5. The official website is www.annusyrahmalaysia.com. An English language overview is provided by the directory of *halal* companies in Malaysia, http://www.perakhalal.com.my/articles/annusyrah.htm (both sites last viewed February 25, 2014).

6. ShiaChat.com, posted 26 March 2012, http://www.shiachat.com/forum/index.php?/topic/235000273-write-the-surah-then-drink-it, last viewed December 12, 2016.

Drinking the Qur'an is firmly embedded in a wide range of practices involving performative and iconic dimensions of scripture (Watts 2013). Qur'anic scholar Jane Dammen McAuliffe (2003) is eloquent on the number of ways the Qur'an as a physical book is looked at, held, touched and treasured, as well as the ways the words of the Qur'anic text are listened to, emotionally absorbed, inhaled, imbibed and worn on the body. Listening to the Qur'an being sung by professional readers (often from cassettes) and wearing amulets for protection are by far the most common and generally well-known of such practices. Divination, warding off evil, protecting fertility, and a host of other rituals also involve scriptural amulets or written permutations of Qur'anic letters, together with numbers and astrological signs.

A short overview of material Qur'anic practices must suffice at this point to demonstrate the deep and multiple groundedness of Qur'anic healing practices in Islamic theology and popular culture.[7] The word of God exists as a textual corpus independent of the book; it is considered to be co-eternal with God and un-created. Intoning or listening to verses is a blessing, *baraka*, in itself. Consequently, speaking verses, *ruqya*, is the most common healing practice (McAuliffe 2003, 342). The material body of the Qur'an is called *muṣḥaf* and it is cherished in specific ways (Suit 2013). Connected with this is the performative art of calligraphy, which renders Quranic verses visible in public spaces. *Baraka*, blessing, generally has a material dimension. It can be passed on through interacting with the *muṣḥaf* of the Qur'an as well as through Sufi mystic sheikhs. *Dhikr*, the remembrance of God, is a mystic prayer practice which can be employed in healing rituals in contexts overlapping with Qur'anic healing. Last but not least, hermetic traditions were part of Islamic theology from the beginning and became part of discourses on magic and mystical theology (Peters 1990, Lory 2012). Some Islamic authors argue that letters of the alphabet have an inner essence or quality, *khawāṣṣ*. But even more than this, letters are said to have a relationship to the upper world, and chapters from the Qur'an are regarded as angels of a higher level. Letters are also characterized according to humoral medical theory: for example, verses consisting mostly of cold letters can be used against fever. Astrological squares are also very often part of Qur'anic healing practices.

Qur'anic preparations are immensely popular due to their medical efficacy. A healer on the island of Zanzibar explained the medical efficacy of the ink potion as the result of a combination of belief and trust in the treatment, which must be present before the physiological circulation of the

---

7. A thorough overview is provided by Abu Zayd (2002) and O'Connor (2004). I have also gone into more detail in Wilkens (forthcoming).

ink through the body after drinking the infusion.[8] Here, the link between drinking the Qur'an as a typical form of medicinal infusion and the theology of the healing power of God is stated explicitly. When looked at from this perspective, the preparation of ink infusions, edible icons and fumigations is clearly comparable to medical preparations—even if the chemical effect is minimal. In typical home cures, substances such as herbal infusions and inhalations quite obviously play a central role.

Drinking the Qur'an is typical for a religious healing ritual. From a bio-medical point of view, these rituals pose a number of problems, not least that of their medical effect. While most biomedical preparations have significant chemical effects on our bodies, some depend on additional processes between mind and body; we need only think of the placebo effect, suggestibility, self-healing, and other phenomena that are currently being explored by medical scientists and psychologists. In this subsystem, the mark of success is the degree of healing or alleviation that can be achieved. As with biomedical procedures, this does not have to apply to every individual procedure or treatment, but a positive effect must be detectable in a high number of cases.

Placebo studies and biomedical studies of ritual healing are a fairly recent development.[9] Most studies focus on aspects of prayer, meditation and mindfulness; none on the specific practice of drinking the Qur'an. Laurence Kirmayer argues that since the biomedical system is premised on a disenchanted, materialist ideology, placebo studies focusing on ritual and symbolic healing have a strong bias against their object of study (Kirmayer 2016, 137). In all non-biomedical systems the world over, however, ritual healing is essential to most procedures due to its effectiveness. The specific rituals and methods adapt continuously to new cultural contexts, scientific discoveries and political requirements.

For example, in the recent past ingesting sacred words or images for the purpose of healing was a common practice in Alpine Catholicism. Images of Mary, the Mother of God, were bought and blessed at pilgrimages sites and then eaten (see further below). This practice was always part of a range of other sacramental rituals centered on sacred images and other objects of saint veneration. But during the twentieth century, ingesting substances not intended primarily for consumption, as in the case of the Marian printed images, became obsolete. In the Islamic context, however, the great importance attached to the physical properties of the Qur'an, the persistence of

8. Interview Hanna Nieber with Talib Ali, 2014, presented at the International Association for the History of Religions meeting in Erfurt 2015.

9. For an overview of the state-of-the art, see Raz and Harris 2016 and Kaptchuk 2011.

astrology, and the growing popularity of Prophetic medicine make it seem unlikely that the practice of drinking the Qur'an for medicinal purposes will die out any time soon.

Drinking the Qur'an is a good case with which to study dynamic attitudes towards various functions of literacy, as well as changing attitudes towards medical usefulness in a religious setting. The use of Qur'anic potions and the debates surrounding them provide us with a unique opportunity to reconstruct the specific intermodality of literacy ideologies, theologies and medical systems, and the dynamic adaptability of this practice in the face of modernization, secularization and globalization.

Literacy ideologies and modern boundaries

The idea of ingesting ink and paper literally revolts people not brought up in this tradition. In a well-known quote by Shakespeare from the comedy "Love's Labour's Lost"—a play on love, language, scholarship and mockery —a man called Dull is described condescendingly by Sir Nathaniel in the following words:

> "Sir, he hath never fed of the dainties that are bred in a book; He hath not eat paper, as it were; he hath not drunk ink; his intellect is not replenished; he is only an animal, only sensible in the duller parts."[10]

The significant words here are "as it were": eating paper and drinking ink are metaphors only. Anything else would be ridiculous in the mocking voice of Shakespeare. This quote is not about actually drinking ink or eating paper in order to train the "intellect" or gain intellectual knowledge. Rather, the metaphor of eating reinforces the opposition between intellect and more physical or sensual kinds of knowledge. But looking to education and how children are taught literary skills, the haptic experience of learning to read and write is part of their intellectual training. Islam, Judaism and Christianity all share traditions of baking cookies shaped like letters, licking honey off letters or licking the letters themselves off hand-held writing boards.

Qur'anic potions are very common in Senegal. Here, as in many other West African countries, the verses are written on wooden boards, washed off, collected and drunk. But this is not done for therapeutic purposes alone. Rudolph Ware, a scholar of Islam who has studied Qur'anic education in Senegal from the twelfth century onwards, sees this as part of the learning process itself. When children drink the ink or lick it directly off the boards at the end of the daily lesson, they are believed to incorporate the lesson

---

10. William Shakespeare, Love's Labour Lost, Act IV, Scene II.

together with the sacredness of the eternal word: "The logic of this whole approach—of equating the body and the text, of teaching the text via the body—must seem quite perverse to many modern Muslims. [...] The idea that one could 'learn' through osmosis makes no sense in this understanding because it violates central conceptions of what knowing is." (Ware 2014, 67) In classical Islamic scholarship, the idea of drinking the Quran is present in all law schools. Sometimes the academic discourse links the practice to the process of learning.[11] In other cases, licking the ink off the writing boards is recommended in order to save the texts physically from enemies. I have already discussed its therapeutic aspects in the context of Prophetic medicine.

Literacy rates are globally on the rise (no matter in which alphabet), and the dominant function of writing lies in transporting semantic content. Knowledge is acquired by reading books and learning what is presented in them. All aspects of book-keeping and bureaucratic administration depend on written records. In social communication, literacy is required for writing letters and posting messages on virtual boards. The academic endeavor is manifestly built around the written word. Historians and philologists read texts and all academics produce written texts. Academic knowledge is by definition knowledge that has been written down.

Socio-economic milieus, professions, education and other factors all influence the number of functions the writing of text can assume within a single society. Whether these different functions clash ideologically is a problem of specific conventions and situations, not a systematic one. For example, in Western Europe today (and in other regions around the world), it is not at all unusual to bake cookies in the shape of letters or to cook letter-shaped noodles in a soup. This has nothing to do with actually writing texts or reading them, that is with the semantic aspect of writing, but instead with the performative side of the writing system, the visibility and tangibility of the letters themselves.

James Watts (2013) has argued that some books, and religious scriptures in particular, have an iconic value which also does not rest on semantic content alone and thus does not conform to the idea of arbitrary signs being distinct from the signified. Holy books are cherished and kept safe; they are used in rituals as physical objects; they are signs of power and wisdom to those who hold them. In schools around the world, children are taught to keep all books in good order and neither to mark them nor lose them. Book cases in living rooms indicate social status. But the dominant

---

11. The title of his book, *The Walking* Qur'an, is taken from an old saying that incorporating the Qur'an in any way makes the person into a "walking Qur'an."

semantic, academic ideology of writing seldom acknowledges its material form in the letters, the paper, the ink, and the bindings. Reflecting this sentiment implicitly, Rudolph Ware speaks of an epistemic chasm (2014, 68) that divides those Western and Islamic scholars who focus on the semantic dimension of texts from other Islamic scholars, both classical and contemporary, who take the performative, and particularly the iconic, dimensions of texts into account.

Webb Keane (2003, 2007) has pointed out some differences in cultural understandings of language. He argues that not all cultures start from the assumption that signs are arbitrary, as expressed for example in the theory of Saussure, but rather assume an essential link between the word, or rather the sound of the word, that is the signifier, and the signified. Keane goes on to observe that the Saussurean distinction acquires an ideological aspect when this type of linguistic understanding is politically favored over others. In the colonial encounter, the distinction between linguistic ideologies was instrumentalized in the discourse of establishing cultural dominance over so-called primitives. People who cannot even distinguish between arbitrary sounds and reality in their magic rituals can never rule themselves independently, so the colonializing ideology runs. This representation is of course oversimplified, but nevertheless it clearly reflects the cultural and political impact of one linguistic ideology aspiring to hegemony over another.

I propose the concept of "literacy ideology" by analogy with semiotic ideologies as a heuristic tool to explain different approaches to written texts and literacy in general, according to a variety of ascribed functions and culturally encoded values. Birgit Meyer sees the need for an increased awareness of the role played by media in all processes of communication. Literary media and the use of writing is a case in point. Ideological boundary work between religions, as well as between religious and secular identities, should be studied through "tensions and clashes over body techniques" (Meyer 2009, 29). In modeling the practice of drinking the Qur'an as a specific sensational form in urban Zanzibar, Hanna Nieber reflects on the differences between various scriptural practices among Christians and Muslims in order to be able to describe their aesthetic particularities comparatively.

Based in a general way on arguments by Webb Keane in respect to semiotic ideologies, Flood (2014) has also remarked on the epistemological and ontological opposition between ink potions, edible Catholic images, Byzantine relics and other phenomena, on the one hand, and a Western, Saussurean distinction between signs, signifiers and objects, on the other hand. By including the materiality of mediation processes in his analysis as proposed by Birgit Meyer, Flood elaborates a theory of mimesis and identity.

The Self identifies with the divine message of the Qur'an not only by mimicking it through speaking, reading and writing, but by participating in that message through logophagy (or iconophagy in the Marian Christian cases). Flood describes a process of "becoming". Though he cogently points out the distinction between the ideological systems, he fails to draw sufficient attention to the boundary work entailing harsh political, and often violent, clashes. Ink potions and Christian icons are not only regarded suspiciously by Protestant, Western philologists and scholars of religion, but more importantly by scholarly colleagues within their own religious traditions.

Catholic sacramental "*Schluckbildchen*", or edible images, from the tradition of Marian veneration may serve as an example of this type of inner-religious discourse in the Alpine region of Europe. Catholic rites of healing include "*Schluckbildchen*" and "*Schabmadonnen*". *Schluckbildchen* are cheap, mass-produced, stamp-sized images on large sheets of paper that have only recently vanished from general use. They used to be sold at pilgrimage sites, mostly in the Alpine region of Europe. These images were bought by pilgrims, blessed at the shrine, and then stuck into bread and eaten for therapeutic purposes (Schneegass 1983). *Schabmadonnen*, or rubbing Madonnas, are small clay figurines also sold at pilgrimage shrines. The blessed figurines are rubbed and the crumbled clay is mixed into water and drunk. As recently as 1904, the Vatican allowed *Schluckbildchen* under the condition that *vana observantia* (empty or superstitious intentions) be excluded (Mirbt 1911, 400). A century later, Swiss Catholic theologian Josef Imbach (2008) describes various Marian rituals and explains their theological foundation. Typically, he draws a distinction between "folk religion" as acceptable ritual practice and "magic" as theologically unlawful. The blessing of herbs for use as home remedies against various ailments on the feast day of Mary's Assumption is classified by him as "folk religion". But he classifies *Schluckbildchen* and *Schabmadonnen*, which serve similar purposes, as "magic" (2008, 185). It seems that the ingestion of non-foodstuffs as medicine—as opposed to blessed herbal remedies with their therapeutic function —disgusts Imbach. No other explanation on theological grounds is actually provided in the book.

Islamic and Christian rules against magic and superstition are almost interchangeable. Theologians in the tradition of Prophetic medicine classify Qur'anic potions as permitted magic, or *al-sihr al-ḥalāl*. As al-Suyūṭī argues, intentionality is important. Using the Qur'an as medicine is permitted as long as *shirk* is excluded, meaning that healing must be attributed to God alone and that the words of the incantation must be in plain Arabic, not any kind of gibberish (Elgood 1962, 154, see also Zadeh 2009). The use of magic, *siḥr*, is one of the most contentious issues in the field of Qurʾanic medicines, talismans and incantations. Al-Suyūṭī himself cites contradictory *ḥadīths* from Aḥmad ibn Ḥanbal, saying at one point that drinking a Qurʾanic potion for medicinal purposes is "well & good" (Elgood 1962, 155), but that wearing amulets is an "abomination" (Elgood 1962, 156f.). But because ibn Ḥanbal is also quoted as saying that ʿAyesha, the young wife of Moḥammed was "complacent in the practice," al-Suyūṭī concludes by simply stating that ibn Ḥanbal "himself was far from strict" (Elgood 1962, 156).

It must be kept in mind that magic, *siḥr*, has a wide spectrum of meanings, and that usage in the Qurʾan differs from that in the *ḥadīth* literature, which differs again from that among later theologians and astrologers.[12] While the Qurʾan is rather negative and classifies many rituals and the tradition of poetry in pre-Islamic religion as forbidden magic in contradistinction to Islam, the *ḥadīth* literature quite often gives reports of the Prophet using talismans, incantations and subtle poetry to attract followers. Negative aspects of magic include all rituals performed with the help of demons and directed against God or the welfare of fellow humans. Later, Ibn Khaldūn included tricking the senses, but also subtle forces of the psyche, hidden qualities of objects, particularly the stars, and the binding of spirits and demons. Thus, the boundaries of licit and illicit magic depend on the choice of sources and their specific interpretation.

Applying the term magic to certain practices is part of discursive and aesthetic boundary formation. Keane (2003, 419) points out that semiotic ideologies and representational economies reflect differences in the agency accorded to certain things. Randall Styers sees this process at work when certain practices are classified by scholars as magic in opposition to an enlightened understanding of materiality: "The dominant scholarly theories of magic have had as a central theme the prescription of idealized norms for modern subjectivity. [...] This subject demonstrates a requisite respect for the abstract regularity of the material world, while repressing any awareness of the mystifications of the commodity form. Subjects who fail to conform to these norms are denigrated as trapped in decidedly non-modern and subversive forms of magical thought." (Styers 2004, 13)

Drinking the Qurʾan has been classified as "magic" twice over: first, by Islamic theologians referring to innate qualities of the Qurʾanic words and their capacity to heal; and second, by modern academics with a purist semantic understanding of scripturality (as exemplified by Saussure[13]) who

---

12. For an overview see Fahd 1997 and O'Connor 2004, 164–167.

13. Christian theological debates on "magic," which touch on various aspects of materiality, instrumentality and the nature of the divine, are one of the roots of the academic

see the materiality and the mundane instrumentalization of the Qur'anic medicines as major incriminating factors (Eneborg 2014; Kruk 2005). The basis of the label "magic" in both cases is quite different, but the same name has clouded issues of interpretation and has prevented Qur'anic medicines, talismans and the like from becoming valid objects of academic study. Ethnographers and collectors of folkloristic practices are happy to list everyday rituals among Muslims at great length (as well as among Christians, of course). A century ago, these descriptions were hardly ever theorized, and implicit categorizations shed light on the naturalized ideologies of scholars vis-à-vis their objects of study. The description by James Robson, dating from 1934, of "magic cures in popular Islam" demonstrates this point. In his introduction, he expresses his intention of not wanting to ridicule so-called magical practices among Muslims (Robson 1934, 33). But at the end of his description, he does allow himself a revealing comment:

> "Whenever Jāḥiẓ[14] refers to magic, he ridicules it, and being a humorist, he can do so to good effect. But in spite of men like him, the common people, and also many who ought to know better, still believe wholeheartedly in the use of magic. Those who have had contact with Moslem communities know this well. And if any further proof is needed, one may point to the large number of books printed on the subject, for publishers are not in the habit of producing books which they do not expect to sell." (Robson 1934, 43)

Robson draws a parallel between inner-Islamic criticisms of "magic" and his own disenchanted misgivings on the subject. But this did not lead to discussions of the differences in these two arguments, or of the arguments on the side of the magical practitioners; instead, the subject of "popular magic" was dropped in philological studies altogether, the boundary having been put firmly in place.

Remke Kruk, a renowned scholar of Islam, has also remarked on the great number of books on magical cures and Prophetic medicine which have been continuously published in the second half of the twentieth century and the beginning of the twenty-first century. She contends that the "existence of sorcery and *jinn*, spirits, is a basic tenet of Islam and still plays an important role in Islamic life" (Kruk 2005, 47). But she also makes the observation that there are no scholarly introductions to Islam that pay significant attention to this fact. She asks whether "there [is] an agenda here?

---

understanding of magic as of the nineteenth century. This fact adds further layers of complexity to the understanding of Qur'anic potions as "magic," but cannot be elaborated here any further.

14. Al-Jāḥiẓ is a widely known ninth century scholar and writer from Bagdad. Robson cites from his book on animals, *Kitāb al-Hayawān*.

Do authors consider it an aspect of Islam that does not contribute to the image of Islam as a viable religion for the modern world?" (Kruk 2005, 47). Her suspicions are echoed by Pierre Lory, who states that magic in Islam is not a simple "superstition," or even un-Islamic, but perfectly normal and thus worthy of philological study (Lory 2012, 184). In the study of African Islam, the implicit ideology that condemns material text practices is exacerbated by a racial bias against so-called primitive religion. One of the major aims of Rudolph Ware's study is to prove that Qur'anic education in Senegal is firmly grounded in Muslim mainstream theology, which is taught at an academic level equal to, or even surpassing, that of the Arab heartlands. He argues that iconic or material aspects of Qur'anic education derive from a specific semiotic ideology (though he does not use this term) well-known in all Arab seats of learning which does not fully endow semantic purity. Contrary to assumptions made by scholars of Islam, mainstream Arab theologians endorsed a semiotic ideology which included iconic-somatic aspects of language and writing throughout the centuries. Drinking the ink off the writing boards in Senegal thus never had anything to do with "Islam noir" or African Islam as imagined by French colonial scholars of Islam. It is also obviously not based on misconceptions of literacy by illiterate people, but rather on central doctrines on the nature of scripture (Ware 2014, 58–60).

Once the fact is established that the iconic dimension of the Qur'an has to be taken into account, the next step is more plausible: the Qur'an as medicine. From a purist biomedical as well as a purist semantic point of view, this would indeed be nonsense, as so many Western scholars have thought. But it is neither simplistic superstition nor the ascription of "wrong" agency to written letters by illiterate people. Based on Islam's outstanding focus on the Qur'an as the Word of God, this practice has reached a degree of popularity not achieved in similar practices of scriptural medicines in other religions. Drinking the Qur'an seems to be a combination of a literacy ideology that favors the iconic aspect of writing, and specific elements of ritual healing that do not depend on the physiological effects of biochemical medicines. I propose a model which permits a description of how various modes of literacy ideologies can coexist while their specific rules and boundaries are kept intact.

Efficacy of therapeutic and literary blends

I have argued that both the biomedical system and the academic literacy ideology dismiss Quranic medicine as ineffective or superstitious. But texts and medicines have several dimensions and corresponding functions which can be put to different uses. People are capable of combining distinct ideologies and dimensions depending on their circumstances, aims and means.

No actor in the scene I am setting here is unaware of the ideological chasms, but the actors are capable of producing specific blends and of disentangling them again. In the following section I will reconstruct some of the rules that govern such specific encounters and the resulting blends or fusions.

Following Shirley Heath, I regard Qur'anic potions as "literacy events" in order to single out specific structures and motivations in this type of situation. A literacy event is "any occasion in which a piece of writing is integral to the nature of participants' interactions and their interpretive processes" (Heath 1982, 93). Heath contends that more often than not, an accompanying speech event will define the use of the written text, sometimes even to the extent of eliminating the need to actually read the text oneself (Heath 1982, 93f.). The semantic content of the text is thus replaced by the oral communication of the participants in the combined literary and speech event. Though Heath studies the way administrative forms are filled in the African American community, her observations apply to Qur'anic potions in equal measure.

With Qur'anic medicine, it is the oral communication between healer and patient (or between interested people in general) which defines the use to which the Qur'anic verses are put. The motivation is medical, not academic. But healing cannot occur without the theological framework defining the sacred presence of the Word of God through writing. Simultaneously, it will not work if specifically medical elements, such as analogy with herbal infusions, are missing. Semantic, performative, and especially iconic dimensions of the Qur'anic text are brought to bear in this literacy event, as well as both ritual and biomedical dimensions of the medical system. Qur'anic potions are thus not about mistakenly mixing up literacy and medical ideologies because of a lack of understanding. It is a conscious combination of specific dimensions in order to add levels of meaning and efficacy.

I base my theoretical model on certain aspects of the linguistic model of code switching. In linguistics, code switching refers basically to the combination of two or more languages or dialects within a single speech situation. These combinations happen on semantic, grammatical, syntactical and pragmatic levels and follow fixed conventions established in multilingual speech communities (Woolard 2004). By employing code switching, precise messages can only be transmitted in communities familiar with the particular type of switch. Social hierarchies expressed in linguistic distinctions, for example, may favor a tendency to use code switching. Code switching is also typical of immigrants, who mix their familiar language at home with the dominant language of their new environment; of school yard conversations among multilingual students; of encounters between rural and urban populations; and not least, of communications via electronic media that often mix global English with the local language.

Code switching is thus always part of a two-way communicational situation, never due to the linguistic inability of an individual. Mistakes made by language learners are not classified as code switching. The term "switching" is misleading inasmuch as current studies strongly emphasize the communicational efficacy of the resulting *blend* rather than the purity and singularity of the primary languages. At the other extreme, fused codes and creole languages can establish themselves in multilingual surroundings; these, too, are not considered as code switching.

The study of code switching has undergone an ideological development that is relevant to my argument here. In the 1940s and 1950s the model of code switching was first described by the renowned and influential linguist Uriel Weinreich who wrote on language contact phenomena (Weinreich 1953). For Weinreich and his contemporaries, code switching was the result of poor discrimination and general linguistic incompetence (Woolard 2004, 74–75). Weinreich described lexical, phonetic and grammatical changes as well as sociolinguistic factors about bilingual speakers in great detail. He analyzed languages in contact as changing or interfering with each other. Nonetheless, purity of speech based on the semantic as well as the pragmatic aspects of language was his ideal linguistic state – never should speakers switch languages within a single sentence (Weinreich 1953, 73).

This depreciative attitude to code switching changed fundamentally in the following decades (Woolard 2004, 75). Studies in social and cognitive linguistics began to emphasize the powerful communicative efficacy of code switching. Cognitive linguists emphasize the surprising flexibility and creativeness of the brain in combining the grammar, vocabulary and syntax of the two or more languages in question. Social linguists point out that switches enable language communities to index messages beyond the semantic scope of the words in a similar manner to inflection, pitch, or volume, as well as facial expressions and gestures.

Relevant research questions from code switching can be transposed to the analysis of drinking and fumigating the Qur'an. These include descriptions of the primary codes, the degree of familiarity with specific situations of switching, the effective gain of the specific blends, the ideological frameworks and social hierarchies that keep the primary codes separate, and the patterns of change over time. Research must investigate both structural and pragmatic aspects within specific socio-cultural settings.

In describing the primary "codes" involved in Qur'anic potions, it is necessary to deconstruct the implicit ideologies of literacy and medicine, and to disentangle their various modes and dimensions, as I have done above. Another interesting debate addresses the question whether legibility is necessary for efficacy. In general, the answer is affirmative (except in the case of people entirely illiterate in Arabic), but in specific cases maybe not. In a Shi'ite chatroom, the question of legibility as paramount to medical efficacy has been addressed specifically: "Using a brush (paint brush) write down the surah on a plate. [...] And obviously what you're writing won't usually fit on the plate. It doesn't matter. You don't have to be able to read it. Just make sure you're writing it correctly."[15] And another author says: "Well, first you need to make sure that when you're writing, you're writing with saffron, and not just pretend-writing!"[16]

Specific qualities of the ink used in Qur'anic potions are another matter of debate. In many Middle Eastern and Asian countries, saffron is an expensive substance highly valued for its color as well as its own inherent healing qualities. In other settings, saffron ink plays no role at all. In West Africa, saffron and porcelain plates are replaced by ash-based black ink and wooden boards. In Zanzibar, healers do use porcelain plates, but replace expensive saffron with red food coloring. In mainland Tanzania, I met many healers who wrote verses on very cheap paper with felt-tip pens or markers. The patients had no qualms about the infusion derived from this mixture. A Sufi sheikh based in London, however, who is accustomed to Western sensitivities, articulates disgust at cheap paper and unsuitable ink on his web page in the following way: "don't use normal ink, use eatable or drinkable water such as saffron water, rose water and do not write on normal paper, as the common sheets of paper contain chemicals, find non-chemical that is not harmful to write on, or maybe a cloth could be used."[17] Here bio-medical and Quranic literacy codes are being invoked simultaneously.

Familiarity with Qur'anic potions and fumigations varies across centuries, countries, social milieus and genders. Conflicts between medical and theological authorities impact this situation. Depending on whose professional field is more dominant in any given society, the practice of drinking the Qur'an will be more or less clandestine or openly permitted. Typically,

---

15. ShiaChat.com, Posted 26 March 2012, http://www.shiachat.com/forum/index.php?/topic/235000273-write-the-surah-then-drink-it/ (as above).

16. ShiaChat.com, Posted 27/10/2009, http://www.shiachat.com/forum/index.php?/topic/234970492-writing-quran-using-saffron/, last viewed December 12, 2016.

17. From Muhammad Sajad Ali ("Sufi Webmaster / Instructor, Herbalist and Healing Therapist" according to his website, http://www.deenislam.co.uk/) posted as a comment on eShaykh, a platform of the Islamic Supreme Council of America (ISCA) on December 1, 2010, http://eshaykh.com/quran-tafsir/ayat-ash-shifa/. The comment section is available through internet archives.

also, it is a practice confined to private or home use when and if medical issues arise. In the public sphere, this practice is irrelevant, ignored, denigrated or denied. A learned Sufi leader I met in Dar es Salaam, Tanzania, who received me in his public consulting room, laughed about ink potions and denied their efficacy. But his wife kept bottles of potions prescribed for their children on the shelf of her kiosk facing the street, which was her familiar space. Among Western scholars, this pattern is similar. Ethnographers with long-term experience of family life know about Qur'anic potions as a matter of course. But philologists or scholars of political Islam whom I have interviewed on this question are very much surprised that such "superstitious" practices should be common in this day and age. Cognizance of a ritual such as Qur'anic potions directly reflects the discourse arenas each scholar has access to, with their specific semiotic and literacy ideologies.

Ingesting and inhaling scriptural medicine exists in numerous sensuous variations. In some forms the practice transcends the boundaries of Islam; in others it is restricted to certain regions within the Islamic world. Historically, drinking ink infusions (often mixed with honey) pre-dates Islam both in ancient Egypt and in ancient Persia. Placing paper on which a sacred text was written or printed into cups of drinking water for medicinal reasons is documented for Mongolian and Tibetan Buddhism (Heissig 1989; Cantwell, this volume), and Daoism (Bumbacher 2012). Burning and fumigating texts is popular in different regions of India. Speaking and thereby breathing holy verses over a bowl of water is most popular in the Arab countries and Turkey. Brass bowls with engraved verses are common to areas with Persian influence, and known to some extent in Turkey (Savage-Smith 2003, Kriss-Heinrich 1962, 129–130). Writing Qur'anic verses on wooden boards—even in the age of cheaply available paper—is typical of West Africa from Senegal to the Sudan, but is not practiced in other parts of Africa or any other region of the Islamic world. Including perfumes, most notably rose water, in the mixture enhances the sensual experience for people in many Arab, Persian and Indian regions. I could extend this list, but suffice to say here that ink medicines are sensational forms that are specific to certain times and places, but not to specific religions.

The Daoist model of medical efficacy rested on the idea that the written supplications that were eaten should reach the gods residing in the body directly (Bumbacher 2012, 65–80). The Islamic idea of healing presupposes that transformative efficacy is inherent to the words spoken by God himself, so that this power may unfold in the body when the words are ingested. Biomedical models of treatment are slowly gaining influence, too. Filling the mixture into disused bottles of cough syrup and following the instructions for the syrup is one example. The above-mentioned Malaysian distributors of ink potions advertise their product as part of the modern wellness and dietary sector.

An interesting question is whether handwriting—as opposed to printing—is thought to enhance the efficacy of the medicine through the link to an individual and trustworthy healer. Though with most local healers this seems to be the case, there are also some counterexamples. In the example of the Malaysian bottling plant, the writing is indeed done by hand only; the process is not automated. But there is no personally known healer. Those who write are simply anonymous employees of the company. The local imam additionally recites some verses over the infusion, but he has no specific renown as a healer. In a case study in southern India another approach was documented. Anthropologist Joyce Flueckiger (2006, 103f.) followed the female Muslim healer Amma over a period of ten years. When mechanical photocopying became cheaper and more easily available, Amma stopped inscribing individual bits of paper for use in fumigations and infusions. Instead she wrote her standard verses only once and copied the page for repeated use. Mechanical printing, as in the case of the Catholic pilgrimage images, seems to be unknown, at least to my knowledge.

Conclusion

Blending textual dimensions and switching between literacy ideologies in a specific healing encounter is something people can do without "misunderstanding" any one of the frameworks (recall magic being defined as misunderstood materiality and drinking the Qur'an as misunderstood scripturality). Blending is thus never about mistakenly mixing codes. Rather, it is a conscious combination in order to add levels of meaning and communicational and medical efficacy; the sacredness of the text is combined with the efficacy of secular medication.

The classification, and often defamation, of this ritual as "magic" or "superstition" is based on notions of how writing and the written word should be handled. Performative aspects of writing can be disavowed or prominently displayed; semantic content can be emphasized or neglected; socio-cultural and political functions can vary. This clash between literacy ideologies has a sociological dimension as well. Depending on which professional opinion (for example, semantic-purist or somatic-iconic as I have described them in the context of Qur'anic healing) is predominant at any given moment, drinking the Qur'an will be more or less clandestine or openly permitted.

Specific blending patterns can die out when circumstances change. In Christianity, ingesting the Sacred has remained possible only for blessed bread and wine in the Eucharist. Ingesting substances not intended primarily for consumption, as in the case of the Marian printed images, has become obsolete. In the Islamic context, the practice of drinking the Qur'an for medicinal purposes seems unlikely to die out in the near future. It will certainly adapt to urban tastes and hygienic standards.

What I have left out is a field of research that is devoted to the many ritual variations of Qur'anic medicines. I have not been able to focus sufficiently on gender differences or on the difference between public and private discourses, though my data indicates that this perspective will shed more light on the complex discursive structure. It seems promising to examine more closely the cultural meanings, habits, metaphors and body techniques attached specifically to drinking and inhaling. I have indicated some developments following from media changes. But these need to be analyzed more precisely. The differences between images and texts, between handwriting and printing, between individual preparations and mass productions dynamically effect changes within the ideological systems. All these aspects will contribute to constructing a more complex and differentiated model of switching and blending.

Starting from the practice of drinking the Qur'an, I have explored the wide range of values attached to the written word, and traced some of the discourses based on different ideologies concerning knowledge, literacy and power. From the perspective of aesthetics of religion, cultural proscriptions are continuously invoked, distinguishing between absurd and effective, disgusting and sweet, barbarous and proper, depending on established ideologies of materiality, devotion, literacy, medical and religious expertise.

References

Abdalla, Ismail H. 1997. *Islam, Medicine, and Practitioners in Northern Nigeria.* Lewiston, NY: Edwin Mellen.

Abu Zayd, Nasr Hamid. 2002. "Everyday Life, Qur'an In." In *Encyclopaedia of the Qur'an*, vol. 2., edited by Jane Dammen McAuliffe, 80–98. Leiden: Brill.

Bruchhausen, Walter. 2006. *Medizin zwischen den Welten. Geschichte und Gegenwart des medizinischen Pluralismus im südöstlichen Tansania.* Göttingen: Bonn University Press/V&R unipress.

Bumbacher, Stephan Peter. 2012. *Empowered Writing. Exorcistic and Apotropaic Rituals in Medieval China.* St. Petersburg, FL: Three Pines Press.

Dilley, Roy. 2004. *Islamic and Caste Knowledge Practices Among Haalpulaaren in Senegal. Between Mosque and Termite Mound.* Edinburgh: Edinburgh University Press for the International African Institute, London.

Doumato, Eleanor Abdella. 2000. *Getting God's Ear. Women, Islam, and Healing in Saudi Arabia and the Gulf.* New York: Columbia University Press.

Elgood, Cyril. 1962. "Tibb-ul-Nabbi or Medicine of the Prophet." *Osiris* 14: 33–192. https://doi.org/10.1086/368625

el-Tom, Abdullahi Osman. 1985. "Drinking the Koran: The meaning of Koranic verses in Berti Erasure." *Africa* 55: 414–431. https://doi.org/10.2307/1160175

Eneborg, Yusuf Muslim. 2014. "The quest for 'disenchantment' and the modernization of magic." *Islam and Christian-Muslim Relations* 25: 419–432. https://doi.org/10.1080/09596410.2014.890847

Fahd, T. 1997. "Siḥr." In *The Encyclopedia of Islam*, new edition, Vol. IX, edited by C. E. Bosworth, E. van Donzel, W. P. Heinrichs and G. Lecomte, 567–571. Leiden: Brill.

Flood, Barry Finbarr. 2014. "Bodies and becoming: Mimesis, mediation, and ingestion of the sacred in Christianity and Islam." In *Sensational Religion. Sensory Cultures in Material Practice*, edited by Sally M. Promey, 459–493. New Haven, CT: Yale University Press.

Flueckiger, Joyce Burkhalter. 2006. *In Amma's Healing Room: Gender and Vernacular Islam in South India*. Bloomington: Indiana University Press.

Heath, Shirley Brice. 1982. "Protean shapes in literacy events: Ever-shifting oral and literate traditions." In *Spoken and Written Language. Exploring Orality and Literacy*, edited by Deborah Tannen, 91–117. Norwood, NJ: Ablex.

Heissig, Werner. 1989. "Heilung durch Zettelschlucken." In *Die Mongolen. Begleitband zur Ausstellung im Haus der Kunst München, 22. März bis 28. Mai 1989*, edited by Werner Heissig and Claudius C. Müller, 232. Innsbruck: Pinguin.

Ibn Qayyim al-Jawziyya. 1998. *Medicine of the Prophet*. Cambridge: The Islamic Text Society. Translation by Penelope Johnstone.

Imbach, Josef. 2008. *Marienverehrung zwischen Glaube und Aberglaube*. Düsseldorf: Patmos.

Kaptchuk, T. J. 2011. "Placebo studies and ritual theory: A comparative analysis of Navajo, acupuncture and biomedical healing." In *Philosophical Transactions of the Royal Society of Biological Sciences* 366: 1849–1858. https://doi.org/10.1098/rstb.2010.0385

Keane, Webb. 2003. "Semiotics and the social analysis of material things." In *Language and Communication* 23: 409–425. https://doi.org/10.1016/S0271-5309(03)00010-7

———. 2007. *Christian Moderns. Freedom and Fetish in the Mission Encounter*. Berkeley: University of California Press.

Kirmayer, Laurence J. 2016. "Unpacking the placebo response: Insights from ethnographic studies of healing." In *Placebo Talks. Modern Perspectives on Placebos in Society*, edited by Amir Raz and Cory S. Harris, 119–143. Oxford: Oxford University Press.

Kriss, Rudolf and Kriss-Heinrich, Hubert. 1962. *Volksglaube im Bereich des Islam. Vol. 2 - Amulette, Zauberformeln und Beschwörungen*. Wiesbaden: Harrassowitz.

Kruk, Remke. 2005. "Harry Potter in the Gulf: Contemporary Islam and the occult." *British Journal of Middle Eastern Studies* 32: 47–73. https://doi.org/10.1080/13530190500081626

Lory, Pierre. 2012. "Verbe coranique et magie en terre d'Islam." *span* 12: 173–186.

McAuliffe, Jane Dammen. 2003. "The persistent power of the Qurʾan." *Proceedings of the American Philosophical Society* 147: 339–346.

Meyer, Birgit. 2009. "From imagined communities to aesthetic formations: Religious mediations, sensational forms, and styles of binding." In *Aesthetic Formations. Media, Religion, and the Senses*, edited by Birgit Meyer, 1–28. New York: Palgrave Macmillan. https://doi.org/10.1057/9780230623248_1

Mirbt, Carl. 1911. *Quellen zur Geschichte des Papsttums und des römischen Katholizismus.* 3rd edition. Tübingen: Mohr.

Nieber, Hanna. 2015. "The body reading the dissolved Qurʾan." Paper presented at the International Association for the History of Religion (IAHR) meeting, Erfurt, Germany.

O'Connor, Kathleen Malone. 2004. "Popular and talismanic uses of the Qurʾan." In *Encyclopaedia of the* Qurʾan. Vol. 4, edited by Jane Dammen McAuliffe, 163–182. Leiden: Brill.

Perho, Irmeli. 1995. *The Prophet's Medicine: A Creation of the Muslim Traditionalist Scholars*. Helsinki: Finnish Oriental Society.

Peters, Francis E. 1990. "Hermes and Harran: The roots of Islamic-Arabic occultism." In *Intellectual Studies on Islam: Essays Written in Honor of Martin B. Dickson*, edited by Vera B. Moreen und Michel M. Mazzaoui, 185–215. Salt Lake City: University of Utah.

Raz, Amir and Cory S. Harris, ed. 2016. *Placebo Talks: Modern Perspectives on Placebos in Society*. Oxford: Oxford University Press.

Robson, James. 1934. "Magic cures in popular Islam." *The Moslem World* 24: 33–43. https://doi.org/10.1111/j.1478-1913.1934.tb00278.x

Savage-Smith, Emilie. 2003. "Safavid magic bowls." In *Hunt for Paradise: Court Arts of Safavid Iran, 1501-1576*, edited by Jon Thompson und Sheila R. Canby, 241–248. London: Thames & Hudson.

Schneegass, Christian. 1983. "Schluckbildchen. Ein Beispiel der 'Populärgraphik' zur aktiven Aneignung'." *Volkskunst. Zeitschrift für volkstümliche Sachkultur* 6: 27–32.

Shakespeare, William. 1595. "Love's Labour Lost." In *Complete Works of Shakespeare*, World Library 1990–1993, Project Gutenberg e-text 1109, available at http://www.gutenberg.org/cache/epub/1109/pg1109-images.html.

Styers, Randall. 2004. *Making Magic: Religion, Magic, and Science in the Modern World.* Oxford: Oxford University Press. https://doi.org/10.1093/0195151070.001.0001

Suit, Natalia. 2013. "Muṣḥaf and the material boundaries of the Qurʾan." In *Iconic Books and Texts*, edited by James W. Watts, 189–206. Sheffield: Equinox.

Ware, Rudolph T. III. 2014. *The Walking* Qurʾan. *Islamic Education, Embodied Knowledge, and History in West Africa*. Chapel Hill: University of North Carolina Press.

Watts, James W. 2013. "The Three Dimensions of Scripture." In *Iconic Books and Texts*, edited by James W. Watts, 9–32. Sheffield: Equinox.

Weinreich, Uriel. 1953. *Languages in Contact. Findings and Problems*. London: Mouton.

Wilkens, Katharina. 2013. "Drinking the Quran, Swallowing the Madonna: Embodied aesthetics of popular healing practices." In *Alternative Voices: A Plurality*

Approach for Religious Studies. Essays in Honor of Ulrich Berner, edited by Afe Adogame, Magnus Echtler and Oliver Freiberger, 243–259. Göttingen: Vandenhoeck und Ruprecht (CSRRW 4).

———. Forthcoming. "Text als Medizin. Ablöschen und Trinken koranischer Verse als therapeutische Praxis." In *Texte vernichten*, edited by Joachim Friedrich Quack. Berlin: De Gruyter (Materiale Textkulturen, open access).

Woolard, Kathryn A. 2004. "Codeswitching." In *A Companion to Linguistic Anthropology*, edited by Alessandro Duranti, 73–94. Malden: Blackwell.

Zadeh, Travis. 2009. "Touching and ingesting: Early debates over the material Qur'an." *Journal of the American Oriental Society* 129: 443–466.

8

Seeing, Touching, Holding, and Swallowing Tibetan Buddhist Texts

CATHY CANTWELL

The iconic dimension of holy books has drawn increasing scholarly attention in recent years (e.g. *Iconic Books and Texts*, James Watts, ed., London, Equinox, 2013). Asian Buddhism provides rich material for considering the ritualization of engagement with sacred texts. In Tibetan Buddhism, this aspect of book culture is perhaps especially pronounced (see, for instance, Schaeffer 2009, especially Chapter 6; Elliott, Diemberger and Clemente 2014). This paper explores the topic in relation to the engagement of the senses in Tibetan context, through seeing, touching, holding and tasting texts. It would seem that it is not the sensory experience in itself, but rather the physical experience of a transmission and incorporation of the sacred qualities from the books into the person which is emphasized in these practices. Parallels and contrasts with examples from elsewhere are mentioned, and there is some consideration of the breadth of the category of sacred books in the Tibetan context in which Dharma teachings may take many forms.

For Tibetans, the iconic dimension of sacred books is a ubiquitous aspect of culture. In pre-modern Tibet, literacy rates probably did not exceed 50% at best,[1] but sacred texts were and are part of everyday life in the community.

1. There are no accurate statistics, and any estimate is likely to be questionable, especially since there are issues over judging the extent of "literacy" when the ability to read and recite various prayers may not necessarily equate to much reading ability, and writing ability lagged behind reading. Helen R. Boyd (2004, 72) gives an estimate of about 50% for pre-modern literacy in Tibet. According to 2000 census data, the Tibetan Autonomous Region's *illiteracy* rate was 48% for men and 60% for women; while the literacy rate

Cathy Cantwell is a Member of the Tibetan and Himalayan Research Cluster at Wolfson College, University of Oxford, UK, and was in 2015–2016 a Visiting Fellow in the Käte Hamburger Kolleg at the Centre for Religious Studies at Ruhr University Bochum, Germany.

Embodying the Buddha Dharma or teaching, and specifically, the Word of the Buddha (Skt/Pali *buddhavacana*; Tib. *sangs rgyas kyi bka'*), texts form a central element of temple and household shrines, (Figure 1) and are to be respected and even worshipped. In a not dissimilar way to the manner in which Sikhs address their sacred scripture as the Guru (Myrvold 2013), Tibetans may talk about holy texts using honorific wording otherwise used for respected persons.[2] In Buddhism, it seems that the worship of books dates back to the earliest period in which the sacred texts were committed to writing. In early Buddhism, texts were memorized and transmitted orally, but once this system was no longer sustainable and texts were written down not long before the turn of the Christian era, there is clear evidence of a cult of the book in the formative period of Mahāyāna Buddhism. Many Mahāyāna sūtras contain such injunctions as that the sūtra should be copied, preserved, respected, praised, circumambulated, with offerings and obeisence made before it.[3] And it is not only in Mahāyāna countries that such traditions have come to surround the holy scriptures: in Theravāda Buddhism, canonical texts are similarly treated, with the creation of expensive and beautiful copies of the texts considered highly meritorious for the sponsor and the copyist.[4] Once produced, such textual collections will be carefully preserved and generally encased in shrines at which they can be worshipped. In the Theravāda case, the ancient Pāli language of the texts

---

of Tibetans in exile is 70% (Central Tibetan Administration 2007, 52, 60). These issues are of course complicated today by the question of which language(s) a native Tibetan speaker may be able to write, given the dominance of Chinese in contemporary Tibet, and the use of Indian languages and English in the subcontinent. Tibetan remains the main language for Tibetan Buddhist texts in both contexts.

2. Examples from a biography of the fifteenth to sixteenth century, Chokyi Dronma, include that when the collection of holy scriptures is to be moved, it is "invited" (*spyan drang*); Chokyi Dronma "meets" (*mjal*) the texts and "offers" (*phul*) them wrappings described as "garments" (*na bza'*) and "sashes" (*sku rags*). (See Elliott, Diemberger and Clemente [eds] 2014, 47).

3. For example, from the Prajñāpāramitā Sūtra in 8,000 lines: "Therefore, then, Ananda, a Bodhisattva who wants to acquire the cognition of the all-knowing should course in this perfection of wisdom, hear it, take it up, study, spread, repeat and write it. When, through the Tathagata's sustaining power it has been well written, in very distinct letters, in a great book, one should honour, revere, adore and worship it, with flowers, incense, scents, wreaths, unguents, aromatic powders, strips of cloth, parasols, banners, bells, flags and with rows of lamps all round, and with manifold kinds of worship. This is our admonition to you, Ananda. For in this perfection of wisdom the cognition of the all-knowing will be brought to perfection." (Conze 1975, 299.)

4. For some images of the Pāli Canon, including a full modern set within a shrine case; a traditional style volume in Thai language with its ornate wooden box; and some folios from a beautifully decorated manuscript copy of a text in Burmese script, see: https://en.wikipedia.org/wiki/Pāli_Canon (accessed 09/04/2016).

has itself taken on a kind of sacredness, enhancing the special nature of the holy scriptures, even though the language is written in different scripts.

Only three senses are discussed in detail in this contribution to the topic, "Seeing, Touching, Holding and Swallowing Sacred Texts," not because hearing is unimportant in engagement with sacred texts. The reverse is if anything the case. The oral dimension of the production, transmission and usage of scriptures has always been central in Buddhism, as is clear from the fact that the texts were not written down in the early centuries. Orality has remained an important feature of engagement with Buddhist teachings, and there are numerous examples in the Tibetan case, some of which will be mentioned in passing here. But for the purposes of this paper, my focus is on sensual contacts with the book as a material artefact. Smelling is also not discussed here. Doubtless, it plays some part in the experience of sensing sacred books, at least in the case of the handling of precious old manuscripts, which may have distinctive smells. Yet smelling is not so obviously ritualized as the other senses, nor does appropriate behaviour in relation to the smelling of texts tend to receive explicit attention.

Seeing

In Tibet, most sacred texts are written in Tibetan language.[5] The canonical texts are generally produced in elaborately decorated large format books, which are not designed for easy reading or portability, but for emphasising their status as representing the holy Dharma, and acting as a support for veneration. The production of manuscript editions of these many volume collections would need to be funded by wealthy patrons or even state sponsorship. Scribes might be trained so that a team working on a particular production would have similar styles of writing, rubrication might be applied to new sections or other decorative features added, and the opening pages of each volume might carry painted miniatures. Every volume of loose leaf pages might be enclosed between hard boards, or even wooden boards, sometimes with an illustrated curtained front folio. Printed books—which in pre-modern Tibet were made by carving wooden blocks for each page, necessitating considerable work and expertise, as well as long-term storage of the blocks—were expensive and did not entirely replace manuscript production. And even in the case of printed editions,[6] illustrations and decorative features might be included on the front pages, to emphasize the sacred

---

5. See, e.g. https://blogs.loc.gov/international-collections/2016/07/a-newly-acquired-tibetan-kanjur-the-dragon-tripitaka/.

6. See, e.g. http://www.orientalstudies.ru/eng/index.php?option=content&task=view&id=2656.

Figure 8.1 Wrapped texts stacked in a display case, between a stūpa (representing Buddha mind) and a sacred image, in the shrine room forming the uppermost storey of the Nyingma temple, Rewalsar, Himachal Pradesh, 1983 (copyright Cathy Cantwell).

nature of the books, and perhaps also to honour the sponsors and monastic establishment which had supported the production.[7] Such attractive books and manuscripts could be seen as appealing directly to the sense of sight, and indeed, to delight the eye. This is sometimes made explicit: Kurtis Schaeffer (2009, 137) cites Bodong Panchen (*bo dong paṇ chen phyogs las rnam rgyal*, 1375–1451) as instructing those producing Dharma volumes under his guidance, "Copy so that one is filled with faith by the mere sight of it." Yet despite this emphasis on the beauty of religious books, they might be opened only very rarely. Tibetan texts are invariably wrapped in large coloured cloths, and kept in shrines or monastic library shelves (see Figure 8.1), sometimes with index leaves attached to the edge of the cloth for ready identification. So in this case, when we think of the "seeing" of Tibetan Buddhist scriptures, this may include a literal sighting of the texts on rare occasions such as when they are unwrapped for a ritual recitation by a large team of monks over a number of days, but generally, the seeing will be of the wrapped items, which one may *know* to be beautifully crafted productions, but the focus is less on the actual

7. Detailed information on the features and production processes of Tibetan manuscripts will soon be available in a comprehensive manual of Tibetan Manuscript Studies, to be published by Cornell University Press, under the title, *Tibetan Manuscripts and Printed Books: An Introduction*, edited by Matthew Kapstein (University of Paris).

Figure 8.2   Tantric text relating to the specific practice to be performed, before its place-
           ment in the three-dimensional maṇḍala construction, Pema Yoedling Dratsang,
           Gelegphu, Bhutan, 2013 (copyright Cathy Cantwell).

perception of the texts themselves, and more on "seeing" them for what
they represent—as supports of the Buddha Dharma.[8] In fact, in some cases,
where a sacred text, as one of the "supports" of the Buddha's presence, may
be incorporated within a sacred maṇḍala for a period of several days while
an intensive practice session is held, the text will not be literally seen at all
for most of the event. (Figures 8.2–8.4) It will be seen briefly on the opening
day of the ritual practice, when the sacred items are ceremonially paraded
around the temple and put into the maṇḍala construction, and it will be seen
on the final day when the items are removed and consecrations bestowed on
the practitioners and the whole congregation, but for most of the time, it is
only the outer decoration of the maṇḍala construction which is actually seen.
So the "seeing" in this case may be more a matter of visualising the text as
being present in the maṇḍala—a visualization which would only have much
relevance for the active monastic participants who are conducting the ritual.
    Another context in which one witnesses a kind of visualized "seeing"
which is not quite ordinary seeing is when an oral transmission of a text

8. It is worth also mentioning here the widespread practice in Asian Buddhism of inserting
    texts within hollow statues of buddhas or bodhisattvas, and also within commemora-
    tive *stūpas*. In this case too, the image or the *stūpa* will become the focus of any worship,
    while the unseen texts are the embodiment of the Dharma or buddha speech, and serve
    to consecrate the image or *stūpa* as a whole.

Figure 8.3   Placement of the text in the three-dimensional maṇḍala construction during the preparatory rituals, Pema Yoedling Dratsang, Gelegphu, Bhutan, 2013 (copyright Nicolas Chong).

Figure 8.4   The three-dimensional maṇḍala construction, with the tantric feast items (*tshogs*) laid out before the afternoon session, Pema Yoedling Dratsang, Gelegphu, Bhutan, 2013 (copyright Cathy Cantwell).

is given. Traditionally, a tantric text should not be studied, practised, or even read without receiving an oral transmission (*lung*), which is bestowed through the teacher reading the text aloud. Such transmissions may be bestowed en masse to a large audience of recipients, and the text or textual collection is generally read at great speed, much too fast to follow the conceptual meaning. Such transmissions primarily fall into the realm of hearing, yet it is sometimes advised that the student should not simply listen but should "see" the words coming from the mouth of the master and visualize them travelling towards and entering their own ears.

Theory and practice in bodily engagement with Buddhist texts

In the Tibetan tradition, texts as supports of the Buddha Dharma take on an added symbolic dimension. One which is shared in most Buddhist contexts is the symbolism of Buddhist texts as embodying the second of the three Jewels or Refuges, that is, the Jewel of the Dharma. Thus, having taken Refuge in the three Jewels—the Buddha, the Dharma and the Sangha —a Buddhist should pay respect to representations of the Buddha, such as Buddha images, to the texts which represent the Dharma, and to monks and the monastic robes which symbolize the Noble or enlightened community.[9] In artistic representations of the "Field of Merit Accumulation" (*tshogs zhing*), which are used in order help the visualization of the Assembly of the objects of Refuge, the Dharma is portrayed by heaped piles of texts,[10] and the practitioner, reciting the Refuge formula, may make numerous prostrations in front of such an image. But in the Vajrayāna or Buddhist tantric teachings, a further dimension is added. Here, the emphasis is on realization of the Buddha nature within all beings and all phenomena, so that all experience should be transformed into Buddha body, speech, mind, qualities and actions. These aspects are symbolized by sacred items which act as the supports for the transformation, and the tantric texts become the support for Buddha speech.[11]

---

9. "Having taken refuge in the Buddha, honour and respect even a tiny piece of broken statue representing him.... Having taken refuge in the Dharma, respect even a fragment of paper bearing a single syllable of the scriptures. Place it above your head and consider it to be the true Jewel of the Dharma. Having taken refuge in the Sangha, consider anything that symbolizes it, be it no more than a patch of red or yellow cloth, as the true Jewel of the Sangha..." (Patrul Rinpoche 1994, 183).

10. See, for instance, http://www.turtlehill.org/ths/tree.html or http://sakyamedia. jugiter.net/foto/Refugetree/index.html#.

11. For example, *The Ritual Practice Framework for the Major Practice Session of the Immortal Life's Creative Seed* ('chi med srog thig sgrub khog, Dudjom Rinpoche Collected Works, Volume Pha: 262) specifies fivefold "supports" (*rten*) for buddha body (consecrated image or painting),

At this stage, I would like to move from Buddhist doctrine to everyday Tibetan life, because a feature which may be peculiarly Tibetan and Himalayan is the extension of attitudes of respect towards books beyond purely Buddhist textual works. Even in principle, respect for religious texts is not restricted to technically canonical literature or "scripture," which in any case is not a simple or closed category since there are many different canonical collections, but extends to all Buddhist teachings, whatever may inspire a person to advance on the spiritual path. Thus, the category is rather fuzzy at the edges. If in doubt, one may treat a book as a holy item in case it may contain some religious teachings or in case a lama's or Buddhist teacher's name may be mentioned. Perhaps in pre-modern times, since the majority of books generally encountered by ordinary folk were Buddhist practice texts, books and writings in general took on much of the symbolic value of religious texts, so that all books came to be treated with respect. There is also some justification for this extension of the category of holy writing, since in the tantric tradition, the letters of the alphabet itself are considered mantra syllables. At the end of many practices, the Tibetanized list of Sanskrit vowels is recited followed by the list of consonants.[12]

In Tibetan context, one should keep texts high up and never put a book on the floor. Should a page drop to the floor by accident, the usual reaction is to pick it up and put it briefly on one's head in recognition of how it should be treated. One must never step over a book and people will often avoid stepping over bags which might contain books. I observed this in a crowded temple where a ceremony was to take place and someone was seeking to pass by people seated crossed-legged on the floor where there was little space. Rather than risk stepping over bags in front of a row of people, a person was more likely to squeeze through behind the row and, if necessary, push peoples' backs down in order to step over them. On one occasion in the UK, I had Tibetan visitors who noticed that I had used some old catalogues to prop up the end of a bed. Fortunately, my visitors were familiar with Europeans, but one commented that this showed that really, despite my immersion in Tibetan culture over many years, I am a European at heart. A Tibetan would never have put written material beneath a bed where one's feet will be placed.

---

speech (longevity tantra or *sādhana* tantric practice text), mind (five-spoked *vajra* implement and a crystal), qualities (*vajra* and bell), and actions (*phur bu* or ritual dagger).

12. The recitation of the Sanskrit vowels (*a ā i ī u ū ṛ r̄ ḷ ḹ e ai o au aṃ aḥ*) and the consonants (*ka kha ga gha nga; tsa tsha dza dzha nya; ṭa ṭha ḍa ḍha ṇa; ta tha da dha na; pa pha ba bha ma; ya ra la wa; śa ṣa sa ha; kṣa*) is considered to compensate for errors in the recitation of syllables during the practice, so this is done at the end, using Tibetan pronunciation rules.

There are various other media apart from books which also provide ways for Tibetans to engage ritually with holy writings. Rolls of paper inscribed with mantras are kept within mantra wheels (*ma ni 'khor lo*) of different sizes, which can be revolved, setting forth the mantras into the world, a common ritual in Tibetan and himalayan contexts. Amulet cases worn against the body may contain mantras, while mantra flags (*dar lcog*) or "wind horse" (*rlung rta*) flags, erected and fluttering in the breeze, proclaim auspiciousness in words and images, including sacred Dharma text. Holy scriptures may be installed, along with other relics and sacred items, in stūpas (Tibetan *mchod rten*), structures which symbolize Buddha mind. Found throughout Tibetan and himalayan environments, stūpas are regularly and repeatedly circumambulated while reciting mantras counted on a rosary. But for the purpose of this short article, the focus is on books.

Touching

The physical touching of sacred texts in an attitude of respect, and especially putting a text to one's head or touching one's forehead against the bottom of a text is more than a gesture of respect.[13] It is through such contact that the blessings or consecrations of the text's sacred power can be transmitted to the individual. This is especially explicit in the case of a tantric empowerment, when for the Buddha speech empowerment the lama puts a text upon students' heads in turn, or in some cases bestows on them the tantric mantra written on a mirror or metallic surface or sometimes drawn on an initiation card. Similar ritual bestowals will take place at the end of a Major Practice Session (*sgrub chen*) or intensive communal tantric practice performed over a number of days by a team of virtuoso meditators and ritualists. During such sessions, the whole practice will be focused on the maṇḍala construction erected within the temple, containing numerous sacred items (as mentioned above) representing various aspects of buddhahood. Throughout, the practitioners will visualize consecrations raining down on the maṇḍala from the buddhas and tantric deities, and in every mantra recitation session a mantra or *dhāraṇī* cord is stretched from the Head Lama's heart to the maṇḍala (Figure 8.5). It entwines around all the items in the maṇḍala, so that the Lama's recitation activates the sacred energies which penetrate through all the maṇḍala articles. On the final day, the "accomplishments" or siddhis are materially bestowed through the Lama taking up each item in turn and placing them on the students' bodies (Figure 8.6), or giving them edible items to eat or drink. The tantric text and/or the written mantra may be placed on

13. See the photograph of Khandro Rinpoche at:
    http://www.tibetanlanguage.org/bookstore/Lang_Lit.html.

Figure 8.5   Mantra recitation session, showing the mantra or *dhāraṇī* cord stretching from the Head Lama's heart to the maṇḍala construction, Pema Yoedling Dratsang, Gelegphu, Bhutan, 2013 (copyright Cathy Cantwell).

Figure 8.6   Bestowing consecration with the flask, Pema Yoedling Dratsang, Gelegphu, Bhutan, 2013 (copyright Nicolas Chong).

the head or, in some cases, against the throat which is considered the speech centre, or the heart, so that the buddha speech consecrations can be imbibed.

Holding

On the holding of texts, I would like to give the example of the community carrying of texts around the village or the agricultural fields, often annually in the spring, as a way of ensuring the blessing of fertility, health and prosperity through the coming year. Often, it is the most extensive twelve to eighteen volume version of the Prajñāpāramitā Sūtra in 100,000 lines (*Śatasāhasrikā Prajñāpāramitā Sūtra*), referred to in Tibetan simply as *'bum* or 100,000, which is carried on a circuit (*'bum skor*) in this manner. Where there is greater sponsorship and more people available, a copy of one of the full canons of Buddha Word (the *bka' 'gyur*) in over 100 volumes may be paraded around the area (a *bka' 'gyur skor ra*).[14]

Following the Chinese invasion of Tibet in the 1950s, when tens of thousands of refugees fled to India, many sought to salvage their community's sacred texts, in some cases carrying them over the Himalayas as they walked to India, Nepal or Bhutan. The Chinese destroyed monastic libraries and printing blocks,[15] and during the Cultural Revolution, there were instances in which Tibetans were forced to go against the attachment to their religion[16] by giving up any privately owned texts and in some cases, desecrating them. There are numerous accounts of the wholesale burning of textual collections, the use of wood blocks as fuel, and even the paving of the floors

14. Lawrence Epstein (1977, Chapter 1) reports the revival of a periodic ritual procession around the community's settlement carrying texts and holy images in the face of drought at a Tibetan refugee camp in Hubli, Mysore, in 1966. More recently, several Himalayan textual circuits have been documented. Martin Mills (2003, 181–185) describes a *'bum skor* in Lingshed, Ladakh. Geoff Childs (2005) reports on the upgrading of a *'bum skor* to a *bka' 'gyur skor ra* in Nubri Valley in highland Nepal, necessitating complex community sponsorship arrangements. For a number of photographs of community members in Thiksey, Ladakh, carrying the Prajñāpāramitā Sūtra in 100,000 lines in 2013, see "Holy Book Walk", https://travelinafarawayland.wordpress.com/2013/06/25/holy-book-walk-june-22-and-23/.

15. "The scriptures in the Tsugla Khang were turned into a bonfire which lasted for four days" (Kunsang Paljor 1977, 55; note that the Tsugla Khang, Tib. *gtsug lag khang*, is the largest cathedral temple in Lhasa); "priceless scriptures were burnt and dumped into manure pits" (Dhondub Choedon 1978, 53); "a group of Red Guards came from Chushar country near Shigatse and ordered us to destroy the Narthang monastery.... The wood blocks were given to the people to burn as fuel" (Statement of Wangyal 1976, 161; note that Narthang monastery had a famous printing press and its holdings included an edition of the entire scriptural canon and commentarial collection).

16. The four "olds" (old thoughts, culture, habits and customs) which were criticized and banned were all features of Tibetan cultural heritage, while the four "news" were all Chinese customs (see Dhondub Choedon 1978, 64–65).

of toilet blocks with stones on which mantras had been carved.[17] Thus, the preservation of the literary heritage became a priority for the exiled community, and indeed, for other Himalayan Buddhists, such as the Bhutanese, who share much the same Buddhist heritage. In more recent times, Buddhist texts which survived the religious persecution in Tibet have come to light, and Buddhist textual production has gained a new lease of life, including digital text production. Paradoxically, the destruction of so much of the Tibetan literary heritage during the second half of the twentieth century, along with the systematic persecution of Tibetans for venerating their texts, has helped to ensure the continuing vitality of the Tibetan cult of the book today.

Swallowing

Finally, I turn to the theme of the consumption of texts. In this case, it is not so much the sense of *taste* which is being used in religious transformation, but the process of swallowing and ingesting the texts. There is a class of texts known as "*Lettering to Eat*" (*za yig*, or rarely, *bza' yig*), which give formulas and accompanying rituals for the ritual specialist to create slips of paper inscribed with mantras or similar magical lettering which can be consumed for protective purposes, especially in the case of ill-health, but also for protection against other negative influences which may afflict the body.[18] Such "*Lettering to Eat*" is generally made on small pieces of paper which are folded into little balls of roasted barley dough mix (*tsam pa*, a Tibetan dietary staple), and swallowed by the patient. These rituals are linked to a broader class of healing rites using mantras. For instance, there are numerous practices for "blowing" mantras into water or ointment which is thought to absorb the mantra letters. Such water can then be administered by mouth, or the ointment can be rubbed onto affected parts of the body. Generally, these rites have the pragmatic purpose of healing, although they are performed

---

17. Phuntsog Wangyal, who travelled to Tibet as part of a Tibetan delegation from the Dalai Lama in 1980, reports: "In places, mani-stones have been used to build pavements or toilets; when the delegates told local officials that not only was this an insult to religion as such but also to Tibetan culture in general, they replied that these stones were being used for the economic development of the country" (Phuntsog Wangyal 1982, 140). Avedon (1984, 359) summarizes many accounts: "Giant bonfires were lit to burn thousands of scriptures, while those not incinerated were desecrated—used as wrapping in Chinese shops, as toilet paper or as padding in shoes. The wooden blocks in which they were bound were made into floorboards, chairs and handles for farm tools."

18. Since writing this section of the paper, I have come across a substantial article on the topic of *za yig* by Frances Garrett (2010). She especially emphasizes that the practice can be seen as an "embodied alchemy of the alphabet" with its efficacy attributed primarily to the letter forms themselves (Garrett 2010, 102–106).

on the basis of a tantric *sādhana* practice focused on developing spiritual wisdom. The more spiritually advanced the practitioner, the more effective their healing products will be. *"Lettering to Eat"* practices are not confined to any one Tibetan school, although they are ubiquitous in the revelatory traditions (*gter ma*) of the Nyingmapa (*rnying ma pa*) and seem to be much less common in the transmitted traditions.[19]

Here, I briefly review three short *"Lettering to Eat"* texts[20] within the revelatory collections of three famous Nyingma masters, whose works are still widely used. The first is from the fifteenth to sixteenth century Pema Lingpa (*padma gling pa*, 1450–1521), the national saint of Bhutan (Figure 8.7). The text is on a single manuscript folio (*padma gling pa'i gter skor*, Volume 3: 333–334), entitled, "The Vajra [indestructible tantric] armour *krod-rdom* Lettering to Eat, effective (when taken on a single) day" (*krod rdom za yig nyin thub rdo rje'i go khrab*). The syllables to be reproduced are given to the left of the page on two lines within an outlined box, which is to be copied exactly, so that the layout of the letters matches exactly. The upper line of letters is written upside down, starting from the upper right margin of the box, while the lower line is written the right way up, starting from the lower left margin of the box. The upper line starts with the syllable, *krod*, while

19. The overwhelming majority of *za yig* texts catalogued by the Buddhist Digital Resource Centre (BDRC: http://www.tbrc.org) are *gter ma* revelations. That said, the tradition may have grown out of early transmitted materials; the eleventh century Bari Lotsawa (*ba ri lo tsā ba*, 1040–1112), who was the second head of the Sakyapa (*sa skya pa*), and is renowned for his translations of tantric texts from Sanskrit, includes a protection text containing a *za yig* within his compendium of rites (*mtshon bsrung za yig sogs mang po*, in Bari Lotsawa 1974: 231–242). Its main focus is protection against weapons, and the need for the Dharma practitioner and the Buddha's dispensation to be protected during difficult times. However, in this case, Bari Lotsawa's text seems to bear a few of the hallmarks of revealed (*gter ma*), as opposed to transmitted (*bka' ma*) texts (such features include the occurence of letters resembling the special revelatory script of "the symbolic script of the space dancers", which is discussed below, the occurence of the revelatory punctuation, *gter tsheg*, in the *"Lettering to Eat"* formula, though not in the main text, and a framing in the final pages reminiscent of Tibetan revelations, with the characteristic aspiration for the text to be found by the appropriate karmic recipient, *las 'phro can dang phrad par shog*), so that any conclusion on its ultimate origin is at this stage premature. The BDRC catalogue includes a few Drigung (*'bri gung*) and Karma Kargyu (*karma bka' brgyud*) *"Lettering to Eat"* texts, although some of these seem to be based on revelatory sources. But even the Gelukpa (*dge lugs pa*) have *"Lettering to Eat"* practices: there is one text available from BDRC which was penned by the third Panchen Lama, Lobzang Palden Yeshe (*blo bzang dpal ldan ye shes*, 1738–1780), again a *"Lettering to Eat"* text for protection against weapons (*mtshon bsrung ba'i bza' yig gi las tshogs nag 'gros su bkod pa*, Lobzang Palden Yeshe *Collected Works* (TBRC W1KG9800), Volume 6: 295–302.

20. I would like to acknowledge the advice of Lopon P. Ogyan Tanzin, with whom I examined these texts and discussed the broader tradition of *"Lettering to Eat"* practices in March 2016. He himself makes and prescribes such lettering to swallow.

the lower line starts with *dhoṃ* [presumably = *rdom*]. The writing resembles mantra syllables, although some of the letter combinations are non-standard for Tibetan script, and both lines lack the usual punctuation mark (*tsheg*) which is generally given between syllables, so that it is as though the letters merge into each other in a continuous stream. While most of the letters are simply mantra type syllables with no apparent conceptual meaning, a few ordinary Tibetan words seem to occur, as is common in Nyingma mantras.[21] The writing on the rest of the page introduces the occasion for the revelation and gives simple instructions for preparing the "*Lettering to Eat*," including how to mix substances for the ink, and the way in which the paper should be rolled up and bound (with red silk thread), so that the syllable, *krod*, is joined with the syllable, *rdom*. The prepared paper is then to be consecrated, and it should be blessed with one's own tantric deity's mantra and the early summary of teachings beginning with the words, *ye dharma*, which is used as a mantra in Tibetan Buddhism.[22] The text advises that the "*Lettering to Eat*" should not be "visible to the sky" (*gnam ma mthong ba byed*) either when writing or eating. According to Lopon P. Ogyan Tanzin, this indicates that one needs to keep any evil spirits away until the lettering has been consumed and is working—so it is best to put a blanket over yourself while you are writing out or swallowing the lettering. An instruction is also given on the consumption: it should not be touched by any tooth, fingernail, or the tip of the tongue.[23] Thus, care needs to be taken in putting the lettering in the mouth and swallowing it, to avoid its coming into contact with the teeth etc.

The second example is a text simply entitled, "Profound Instruction for Lettering to Eat" (*za yig gdams pa zab mo*) by the seventeenth century Terdak Lingpa (*gter bdag gling pa*, 1646–1714; *Collected Works*, Volume 12: 171r-v) (Figure 8.8). Here, the syllables to copy and eat include a small number of standard Tibetan letters, but they are mostly written in the special

---

21. Because of the absence of the *tsheg* punctuation mark, this is not altogether certain, but on the lower line, we seem to have: *gsod mtshon gyi phung po*, "*heaps of weapons for killing*".

22. This is a famous verse from the early Buddhist suttas which summarizes the Buddha's teaching of dependent arising, and thus in Tibetan tradition, it is added like a mantra to the end of practices, and considered to compensate for errors in understanding. In the story in the Pāli Canon (Vinaya, Mahavagga I.23. I.23.1-10), hearing it was enough to give Śariputra a stainless vision of the Dharma and irreversible "stream-entry", when he first met a student of the Buddha and questioned him on the Buddha's teaching: *Of those dharmas [phenomena] which spring from a cause, the Tathāgata has said, "this is their cause, and this is their cessation"; thus the Great Renouncer teaches.*

23. Interestingly, this instruction (*so dang sen mo lce rtse gsum ma thug pa*) is given in exactly the same wording in Bari Lotsawa's "*Lettering to Eat*" text (see above, note 19; Bari Lotsawa 1974: 234, 2v).

Figure 8.7 Pema Lingpa "Lettering to Eat" (*za yig*) text, with the section to swallow highlighted (copyright Buddhist Digital Resource Centre (BDRC), www.tbrc.org/, TBRC work number: W00EGS1017093).

Figure 8.8 Terdak Lingpa "Lettering to Eat" (*za yig*) text, with the section to swallow highlighted (copyright Buddhist Digital Resource Centre (BDRC), www.tbrc.org/, TBRC work number: W22096).

Figure 8.9 Dudjom Lingpa '"Lettering to Eat" (*za yig*) text, with the section to swallow highlighted (copyright Buddhist Digital Resource Centre (BDRC), www.tbrc.org/, TBRC work number: W28732)

revelatory script known as, "the symbolic script of the space dancers" (*mkha' 'gro brda' yig*), a coded language in which many revelations initially appear, before they are de-coded and expanded into full texts in Tibetan by the revealer. The implication, then, is that these words are from the original sacred revelation without any interpretation applied by the revealer, and also that they may in effect encode a much more extensive piece of mystical writing than the number of letters would indicate. A single phrase of "symbolic script" may expand into several pages of text in revelatory works. The letters are not pronouceable in a normal fashion, and lamas giving oral transmission of texts containing "symbolic script" will not attempt to read them, but may count the number of syllables out loud. In this case, the letters are arranged in a maṇḍala-like pattern, with three short lines in the centre, enclosed by two lines on all four sides. The lower set of two lines is written facing outwards, while the inner line on the upper, the left-hand and right-hand sides faces outwards and the outer line in all three cases faces inwards.

The accompanying text begins and ends with symbolic script. The instructions advise that this "*Lettering to Eat*" will help to dispel unconducive conditions and especially, will bring longevity. The syllables should be written on birch bark or Chinese paper. Lopon P. Ogyan Tanzin was puzzled by the mention of birch bark (*gro ga shing shun*);[24] birch bark was used in making some early Tibetan manuscripts and it may still be used for inscribing protective mantras, yet in this case, a more edible material seems preferable. It may be that rather than a practical instruction, birch bark is given as a symbolic marker, linking the text to early generations of Buddhism in Tibet. Apparently, "Chinese paper" (*rgya shog*) indicates very thin sheets, portions of which are easy to swallow. Lopon P. Ogyan Tanzin commented that it is much easier to prepare "*Lettering to Eat*" in contemporary Europe since edible papers, such as rice paper, and edible inks, such as food colouring, are readily obtainable. Having written the syllables, the paper should be anointed with scented water, along with powders of the five precious metals or stones and five medicinal ingredients,[25] and consecrated at the time

---

24. It is possible that there are two categories here, that *gro ga* alone indicates birch bark, while *shing shun* indicates fruit peel. Lopon Ogyan Tanzin read it in this way, although on reflection, it seems more likely that *shing shun* indicates bark, and is linked to *gro ga*. Garrett (2010: 88 note 7) notes the occurrence of birch bark in *za yig* texts.

25. These sets vary somewhat. One list of the five precious metals or stones is gold, silver, coral, lapis lazuli and pearl. Powdered gem stones are considered to have healing properties and are frequently used in Tibetan medicinal pills. One list of the five medicinal ingredients, supplied to me by Lopon Lhundrup Namgyal of Jangsa Monastery, Kalimpong (I have added slightly uncertain or variable identifications; Tibetan classifications of plants do not always neatly correspond to classic botanical species), gives 1. *sle tres*

of the *Victorious* (*rgyal*) constellation.[26] The text concludes by reiterating the benefits of this practice. At the end of the instructions, the final lines give a typical concluding formula, variations of which are often used in revelatory texts, and mark them as such.

My third example is from the works of an influential nineteenth century master from the north-eastern region of the Tibetan plateau, Dudjom Lingpa (*bdud 'joms gling pa*, 1835–1904; *Collected Works*, Volume 1: 471–472) (Figure 8.9). Here, the "*Lettering to Eat*" is given within an outlined box towards the left of the page, and the five syllables, one of which is non-standard Tibetan and probably intended as symbolic script, are positioned vertically on the page. To the left, each syllable is paired with the name of a substance which should be used to anoint it:[27] this list consists of water flavoured with saffron (*gur gum*), sugar or bamboo pith (*ka ra'am gcu gang*), *gu gul* incense, cattle or elephant bile (*ghi waṃ*), and poisonous black aconite (*btsan dug*). Lopon P. Ogyan Tanzin comments that in practice, this may be simplified and the lettering may simply be anointed with saffron water. The writing on the rest of the page gives no instructions about preparing the "*Lettering to Eat*"; it is assumed that the practitioner will be familiar with the traditions for doing this. The text is part of Dudjom Lingpa's cycle on the tantric deity, Dorjé Drollo (*rdo rje gro lod*, or to use the non-standard spelling given here, and frequently in Dudjom Lingpa's work, *rdo rje khro lod*) (Figure 8.10), so that it would be appropriate to use this "*Lettering to Eat*" on the basis of the prior practice of Dorjé Drollo's tantric sādhana. It begins with a few letters in symbolic script, and closes with revelatory seals. It consists almost entirely of a long list of conditions which the "*Lettering to Eat*" will protect against, and the benefits which will be obtained. In brief, all manner of evil and worldly spirits, rites of sorcery, illness, defilements or pollution, bad conditions and any fears will be vanquished, while merits, longevity, wealth, progeny, and wisdom will increase.

Concluding reflections

In the examples of the iconic use of sacred texts considered in this paper, it would seem that the focus is not on an everyday or passive sensual perception of the books. It is clear that the "*Lettering to Eat*" practices, for instance,

---

(*Tinospora cordifolia*); 2. *kaṇḍakāri* (in Ayurveda, this seems to indicate *Solanum xanthocarpum*, but in some Tibetan sources, berry or bramble plants are suggested); 3. *dbang lag*, himalayan marsh orchid (*dactylorhiza hatagirea*); 4. *rgya mtsho lbu ba*, "ocean scum" (a marine resource, probably, *Sepia esculenta*); 5. *shu dag dkar po*, sweet flag (*Acorus gramineus soland*).

26. This corresponds to Pushya Nakshatra in Indian astronomy, or Delta Cancri.

27. The purpose is not specified explicitly; this is according to Lopon P. Ogyan Tanzin.

Figure 8.10   Statue of the tantric deity, Dorjé Drollo, in the shrine for the protective deities, the Nyingma temple, Rewalsar, Himachal Pradesh 1983 (copyright Cathy Cantwell).

are hedged in with special injunctions for the preparation and consumption of the writing. Both Pema Lingpa's and Bari Lotsawa's texts bear witness to a tradition that the person should swallow the paper without it touching the tip of the tongue or the teeth,[28] so there would be little chance to savour the taste. Usually, using traditional papers and inks, "*Lettering to Eat*" will not be a culinary treat, and it will need to be rolled into a dough ball to make it easier to swallow. The primary aim of the involvement of sensual bod-

28. Garrett (2010: 88 note 8) notes that it is common to say that the text should not touch the teeth.

ily engagement with the holy books in this and the other cases discussed in this paper is not the sensory experience in itself, but rather the physical experience of a transmission and incorporation of the sacred qualities from the books into the person. The one slight exception is the communal carrying of the books—in this instance, it is still a matter of receiving the blessings from the texts, but it is the entire community and environment which gains the benefit. The individuals carrying the texts act more as the conduits than as the recipients, although they may also have some sense of a personal benefit in carrying the texts as well as receiving some social recognition for undertaking the task.

As part of everyday life, the ritualized interactions with sacred books express and reinforce Tibetan Buddhist identity and veneration of the Dharma, just as the Chinese State sought (unsuccessfully in the long term) to undermine this by stamping out the practices. In many contexts, incorporation of the sacred qualities of the books is assumed primarily to bring pragmatic benefits, such as protection from evil spirits, improved health and prosperity. Broadly in Buddhist tradition, it is said that Going for Refuge to the three Jewels (Buddha, Dharma and Sangha) helps to protect the person from worldly fears as well as spiritual malaise. Of course, the religious ideal of receiving the blessing of books is to incorporate the wisdom of the Dharma—to *become* the sacred book in one's own bodily and mental experience. This objective is particularly pronounced in contexts such as tantric empowerments and consecrations following tantric practice sessions. With the lama bestowing the consecration through placing the book on the students' heads, their voice should be transformed, becoming Buddha speech. It is clear that the extent to which this may actually be experienced will vary. However, the transmission through the lama's visualization together with the physical bestowal is considered effective even for distracted students who may lack conscious awareness of any transformation at all. Their potential for the development of Buddha speech is still thought to have been ripened by their presence and their receipt of the blessings through bodily contact with the sacred speech embodied in the text.

There are many parallels between the Tibetan book cult and other case studies considered in this volume—lavish productions of the Bible and other holy writings were an important feature of pre-modern Western cultures, and the transmission of blessings through touching and other sensual contacts with holy books is widespread. There are also some contrasts, of which perhaps the most noticeable is that in the Asian examples, including Sikhism, the touching of holy books against the body almost invariably involves the placement of the book on the head or forehead, and never the kissing of the text, which one finds in the Christian tradition. Kissing would be considered expressive of an inappropriate relationship with the text, which should always be treated with deference and respect, and broadly in Indian religions, it would also risk polluting the text. Although Buddhism has less concern with pollution than other Indian religions, Tibetans will avoid breathing or spitting on holy objects. Where close contact is necessary during certain rituals, Tibetans will guard the item(s) by placing a white ceremonial scarf across the mouth and nose, tying it at the back of the head (see Figure 3 above, in which such a scarf is worn when placing sacred items within the maṇḍala). It would also seem that the Tibetan practice of consuming small pieces of sacred writing is rather unusual cross-culturally[29]– parallels are easier to find for more indirect transmission of text by mouth, such as blowing mantras onto water which is then drunk. One also finds the practice of the consumption of inks used for writing holy texts, which were later removed from the page and drunk in liquid (e.g. in Islamic traditions in North Africa; see Katharina Wilkens, this volume). The Tibetan "*Lettering*

29. Although not widespread in other Asian Buddhist contexts, it is possible that the Tibetan tradition developed out of precedents in Indian Buddhism, especially from *dhāraṇī* sources, which were similarly developed in East Asian esoteric Buddhism, while Taoism seems also to have had similar practices. The practice of chewing and swallowing a *dhāraṇī* to overcome a disease is encouraged in a Chinese text of the "Thousand-Handed and Thousand-Eyed Avalokitesvara Bodhisattva's Vast, Perfect, Unimpeded, Great-Compassionate Heart Dharani Sutra" (*Great Compassion Dharani Sutra*: 20). Chinese Taoist and tantric Buddhist sources give witness to the practice of consuming talismans to gain longevity or supernatural powers, or to ward off demons, illness or natural calamities (Mollier 2008, 88 note 122, 105, 116, 127). The swallowing of yantras is described in the context of Chinese esoteric Buddhism, in a section constituting a "Collection of Sacred Yantras" (Trieu Phuoc 2008, 263). Master Dechan Jueren of the Esoteric School of Chinese Buddhism recalled the discipline of having to swallow over 1000 yantras as part of his training, which enabled him to incorporate knowledge within himself (*Swallowing Yantras During the Great Dharani*, talk 2001, Dari Rulai Temple, Los Angeles, translated by Jaliniprabhakumara, http://www.shaolintemple.org.uk/chinese-esoteric-school/lectures-of-dechan-jueren/101-swallowing-yantras-during-the-great-dharani). Frances Garrett (2010, 100–102) gives further Chinese parallels, Taoist and Buddhist, and argues that it is most likely that the Tibetan tradition derived from Chinese rather than Indian sources, since Taoist examples are earlier than Buddhist ones, since there are no extant South Asian examples, and since more of the Tibetan revelations of *za yig* come from Eastern Tibet, and contemporary practice of swallowing letters also seems focused on Eastern Tibet. I am not entirely convinced: so much Indian Buddhist literature was lost that I see no reason why Indian Buddhist *dhāraṇī* texts might not have served as precedents for Chinese and Tibetan esoteric Buddhism in this respect. Also the production and practice of these texts is not confined to the East. Moreover, although Bari Lotsawa came from the East, he travelled to India as a young man and later established his seat at Sakya (*sa skya*) in the southern Tibetan region of Tsang (*gtsang*). However, his text is not a clear case of a transmitted text, let alone a translation from Sanskrit (see note 19 above). I am not sure that there is currently enough evidence to draw firm conclusions on the origins of the practice.

to Eat" practices simply make the principle of physical incorporation of the text direct and immediate, and these practices are considered particularly powerful, perhaps in part as a result.

One issue considered across the papers here has been the question of the extent to which iconic book practices may be confined to the handling of "scriptures" or extended to a broader range of sacred text. As we have seen, in the Tibetan case, at its broadest, any written material will be treated with respect, although there are gradations in which some sacred texts will be treated with more elaborate ritual, or considered capable of transmission of more powerful blessings. There is again perhaps some contrast between Western and Asian traditions in that it is comparatively rare for Asian religions to settle on a single closed canon of scripture, although Sikhism is an exception in this respect. In Hinduism and Buddhism, scriptural collections tend to be large and variable. Although Hinduism has the iconic sacred Vedas as an important symbol, unifying Hindus, many of the most significant and widely used sacred Sanskrit texts in Hindu practice, such as the Bhagavad Gītā, are post-Vedic, and there are large numbers of sacred texts particular to specific Hindu traditions, including much sacred literature in South Indian and other languages. In Buddhism, the category of the Word of the Buddha (Skt/Pali *buddhavacana*) was never solidified into a single group of texts. Various collections were maintained by different Buddhist schools, and those collections often remained relatively open for many centuries. In time, canonical collections developed in different countries, although some Buddhist schools specialized in and revered only a particular text or group of texts. In the Tibetan case, there were a number of canonical collections, each of which frequently had different versions, and was more or less inclusive of certain classes of tantric texts. But in relation to the Tibetan book cult, any canonical collection is treated similarly. The style of very large format books,[30] elaborately decorated and illustrated, and suitable for veneration such as by the circumambulation practices mentioned above, was generally restricted to the production of multi-volume canonical collections, or individual canonical texts, such as the popular Prajñāpāramitā Sūtra in 100,000 lines (see above, p. 147).[31] Beyond the canons, each school

30. For instance, the pages of the Rig 'dzin Tshe dbang Nor bu Edition of the Ancient Tantra Collection (*rnying ma'i rgyud 'bum*), now held at the British Library, are a little variable in size, but measure roughly around 57cm. in length, by 12.5 cm. in height. The Ancient Tantra Collection is a canonical collection specific to the Nyingma (*rnying ma*) school and consisting entirely of their tantras. Some of the larger canons (the *bka' 'gyur* of Buddha Word along with translated commentaries, or *bstan 'gyur*) in which all classes of Buddhist texts are included, have even larger pages.

31. Other popular and important works might be copied as lavishly produced illustrated

and even each monastery might have its own sacred texts, such as the transmitted teachings of their own tradition and the revelations and compilations of their own masters. These texts are kept within the monastic library or on an upper level of the temple, and some will be used in the daily liturgies. Such texts specific to the particular tradition are also used in the ritual bestowal of consecrations during monastic practice sessions and tantric empowerments. Here, the text(s) chosen are those appropriate for the particular practice. While the text is sacred in itself, its power to sanctify is enhanced through receiving consecrations from the buddhas and tantric deities during the course of the ritual, and this is dependent upon the meditation of the lama and his team of tantric masters. High status lamas are considered more efficacious at this,[32] so that an event at which such a lama presides may attract thousands of participants for the final day when the blessings are distributed. A similar consideration applies to a *"Lettering to Eat"* text. In part, the efficacy is to be attributed to the power of the spiritual tradition and the lama who originally revealed the text. But also, much will depend on the lama who prepares the *"Lettering to Eat"* and the tantric practice which he performs to activate it.

We can conclude that all Buddhist texts are considered sacred, but some are more sacred than others, while some may become more sacred in the special context of a tantric ritual or by being linked with a particular tantric master. At its broadest in the Tibetan context, "sacred texts" which should be respected can include any religious writings, manuals used for daily chanting, and wrapped texts kept on altars and high shelves within the home.

Acknowledgements

I would like to acknowledge the support of the Käte Hamburger Kolleg in the Center for Religious Studies at the Ruhr-Universität Bochum during my fellowship year (2015–2016), which enabled me to write this paper. I must also thank Lopon P. Ogyan Tanzin, who brought to my attention the genre of *"Lettering to Eat"* texts (see, p. 148–153), and freely offered the benefit of his time in a lengthy discussion of the examples considered here.

---

manuscripts, although the large format size seems to have been a special feature of canonical texts.

32. It is not altogether this straightforward, since an individual is considered to benefit much more from a lama with whom they have a karmic connection, and a close lineage affiliation, so that it would be more effective to receive transmission from a lama without any established reputation who is close in these respects, than from any lama who is more distant. However, the generalization given here largely holds true for many lay folk who may not have an affiliation to any specific practice lineage.

References

Note: The TBRC reference numbers refer to the electronic texts made available by the Buddhist Digital Resource Centre (BDRC), Cambridge, MA, USA (http://www.tbrc.org).

Bari Lotsawa (*ba ri lo tsā ba*). 1974. *Be'u bum of Ba-ri Lo-tsa-ba Rin-chen-grags: A collection of magico-medical spells, incantations and esoteric formulae transmitted in Tibet through the Lo-tsā-ba of Ba-ri, Rin-chen-grags*, reproduced from a rare manuscript from Darjeeling by Lama Jurme Drakpa, Delhi (TBRC W15562).

Boyd, Helen R. 2004. *The Future of Tibet: The Government-in-exile Meets the Challenge of Democratization.* New York: Peter Lang.

Central Tibetan Administration. 2007. *Tibet: A Human Development and Enviroment Report.* Dharamsala.

Childs, Geoff. 2005. "How to Fund a Ritual: Notes on the Social Usage of the Kanjur (*bKa' 'gyur*) in a Tibetan Village." *Tibet Journal* 30(2): 41–48.

Choedon, Dhondub. 1978. *Life in the Red Flag People's Commune.* Dharamsala: Information Office of H.H. the Dalai Lama.

Conze, Edward, trans. 1975. *The Perfection of Wisdom in Eight Thousand Lines and its Verse Summary.* Bolinas, CA: Four Seasons Foundation.

Dudjom Lingpa. 2004. *Collected Works: gter chos/ bdud 'joms gling pa; sprul pa'i gter chen bdud 'joms gling pa'i zab gter gsang ba'i chos sde.* 21 volumes, Lama Kuenzang Wangdue, Thimphu, Bhutan (TBRC W28732).

Dudjom Rinpoche. 1979–1985. *Collected Works: The collected writings and revelations of H. H. bDud-'joms Rin-po-che 'Jigs bral ye shes rdo rje, bDud 'joms 'jigs bral ye shes rdo rje'i gsung 'bum.* 25 volumes, Dupjung Lama, Kalimpong. (TBRC W20869 0334-0358).

Elliott, M., H. Diemberger and M. Clemente, eds. 2014. *Buddha's Word: The Life of Books in Tibet and Beyond.* Cambridge: Museum of Archaeology and Anthropology.

Epstein, Lawrence. 1977. "Causation in Tibetan religion: Duality and its transformations." Unpublished Ph.D thesis, University of Washington.

Garrett, Frances 2010. "Eating letters in the Tibetan treasure tradition." *Journal of the International Association of Buddhist Studies* 32(1-2): 85–183.

Great Compassion Dharani Sutra ("Thousand-Handed and Thousand-Eyed Avalokitesvara Bodhisattva's Vast, Perfect, Unimpeded, Great-Compassionate Heart Dharani Sutra"). English translation available in pdf form from *The Huntington Archive* (*The John C. and Susan L. Huntington Photographic Archive of Buddhist and Asian Art*, accessed 01/06/2016), http://huntingtonarchive.org/resources/downloads/sutras/05bodhisattvaYana/Great%20Compassion%20Dharani%20Sutra.doc.pdf

Mills, Martin A. 2003. *Identity, Ritual and State in Tibetan Buddhism: The Foundations of Authority in Gelukpa Monasticism.* London: RoutledgeCurzon.

Mollier, Christine, 2008. *Buddhism and Taoism Face to Face: Scripture, Ritual, and Iconographic Exchange in Medieval China.* Honolulu: University of Hawaii Press. https://doi.org/10.21313/hawaii/9780824831691.001.0001

Myrvold, Kristina. 2013. "Engaging with the Guru: Sikh beliefs and practices of Guru Granth Sahib." In *Iconic Books and Texts*, edited by James W. Watts, 261–281. London: Equinox.

Paljor, Kunsang. 1977. *Tibet: The Undying Flame.* Dharamsala: Information Office of H.H. the Dalai Lama.

Patrul Rinpoche. 1994. *The Words of My Perfect Teacher.* Padmakara Translation Group. San Francisco: Harper Collins.

Pema Lingpa (*padma gling pa*). 1975. *padma gling pa'i gter skor. Collected gter-ma rediscoveries of Padma-gliṅ pa: A reproduction of a rare munuscript collection from Manang*, 7 volumes, New Delhi, Ngawang Topgay (TBRC W00EGS1017093).

Phuoc, Trieu. 2008. *The Quintessence of Secret (Esoteric) Buddhism*, (Revised Edition). Matgiao Friendship Association, California (pdf download available: https://selfdefinition.org/tantra/Quintessence-Of-Secret-Esoteric-Buddhism.pdf)

Schaeffer, Kurtis R. 2009. *The Culture of the Book in Tibet.* New York: Columbia University Press. https://doi.org/10.7312/scha14716

Terdak Lingpa (*gter bdag gling pa*). 1998. *Collected Works: smin gling gter chen rig 'dzin 'gyur med rdo rje'i gsung 'bum.* 16 volumes, Dehra Dun, D.G. Khochhen Tulku (TBRC W22096).

Wangyal, Phuntsog. 1982. *The Report from Tibet.* in *From Liberation to Liberalisation: Views on 'Liberalised' Tibet*, 127–163. Dharamsala: Information Office of H.H. the Dalai Lama.

Wilkens, Katharina. "Infusions and fumigations: Therapeutic aspects of the Quran." Paper given to the workshop, *Seeing, Touching and Holding, and Tasting Sacred Texts*, Ruhr-Univeristät Bochum, April 2016.

9

Neo-Confucian Sensory Readings of Scriptures: The Reading Methods of Chu Hsi and Yi Hwang

YOHAN YOO

Chu Hsi (1130-1200) of China and Yi Hwang (1501–1570) of Korea, leading scholars of the Neo-Confucian school of the two countries, emphasized readings of Confucian scriptures. They believed that Confucian scriptures have transformative power when read repeatedly and deliberately. Chu introduced the concept—further developed by Yi—of encouraging a scholar to activate at least three senses when reading a text, over and above the experience of merely reading the characters of the text. They advised Neo-Confucian scholars to try to make contact with the sages and fully internalize their teaching through their senses of sight, hearing, and taste by reading scriptures, though they did not directly appeal to the physical senses. First, the text should be recited aloud so the reciters will hear their own voices, sometimes along with those of their colleagues when several scholars read together. They imagined, furthermore, that the voices they were hearing while reading were those of the ancient sages themselves. Secondly, while hearing the voices of the sages, the reciting scholars should visualize their images, seeking personal communion with them. Finally, the meditative reading of scholars was frequently likened to savoring a text's flavor. The act of reading books was described as eating, biting, chewing, and tasting. When the readers recited the text aloud, pronouncing each syllable using tongues, lips and mouths, they were engaged in a gustatory experience: "chewing" and "tasting" scriptures.

A new perspective on Neo-Confucian readings of scriptures

Studies on Confucian "scriptures" have been exclusively focused on their content, especially on their philosophical and ideological aspects, just like

Yohan Yoo is Professor in the Department of Religious Studies and Associate Dean of the College of Humanities at Seoul National University, Korea.

most other studies of religious scriptures. However, some scholars in relatively recent years have tried to overcome the imbalanced tendency of Western scholarship to be occupied with the content of scripture (Smith 1971; Graham 1987; Watts 2006; Yoo 2010). Wilfred Cantwell Smith, who first pointed out this imbalance, argued that scholars of academic studies of religion should treat scripture as "a living force in the life" of religious people and should pay attention to what people do with scripture (Smith 1971). Agreeing with Smith, in this article I will demonstrate how Confucian scholars try to make the most of scriptures by making sensory images in reading them, while putting to one side traditional Confucian subjects involving abstract concepts or philosophical discourses.

I would like to emphasize that the term "scripture" is very adequate to designate Confucian classical texts, although some may doubt if the term "scripture" is appropriate in the Confucian context. First of all, as Rodney Taylor correctly points out, Confucian books that are linked to the tradition of the sage, who "hears the Way of Heaven and manifests it to the world" (Taylor 1990, 32), can be described as the scriptures of Confucianism.[1] According to Taylor, the Five Classics are "the repository of such manifestations" (32), and the Four Books were thought to represent "the quintessential expression of *li* (理)" (35), which designates principle or truth. Secondly, it should be noted that the Chinese word *ching* (經), which corresponds to the Classics of Confucianism, has also been used for the Buddhist sutras and relatively recently for the Christian Bible, which are generally accepted as religious scriptures.

Here I will pay particular attention to the reading method suggested by Chu Hsi (1130–1200) of China and Yi Hwang (pen name T'oegye, 1501–1570) of Korea, leading scholars of the Neo-Confucian school of the two countries. Both of them were confident that sensory reading of scriptures enabled scholars to have a kind of religious experience in which they could see the sages and hear their voices. As S. Brent Plate reminds us, "there is no thinking without first sensing" and "the primary contact points between the self and the world" are the five sense organs (Plate 2014, 5, 7). It is through the senses that human beings become and remain conscious of objects, and even

---

1. This is the reason Taylor even regards those Confucian books as "holy books" (Taylor 1990, 23). It should be noted that the Chinese word 聖人, which is usually translated "the sage" in English, can be literally translated as "sacred person." As mentioned above, the sage was the person who could hear and manifest the will of Heaven. Among sages, Confucian scholars have counted Confucius and some ancient rulers in the classical texts, including the Three Sovereigns and the Five Emperors whom many contemporary scholars think to have been ancient deities (Küng and Ching 1989, 10), and the three founders of the Chou dynasty.

embody consciousness. Experience associated with religion is also only possible through the senses. Mircea Eliade points out that "broadly speaking, there can be no religious experience without the intervention of the senses. ... Throughout religious history, sensory activity has been used as a means of participating in the sacred and attaining to the divine" (Eliade 1960, 74). Confucian scholars tried to appropriate their senses to contact the sage, or the sacred person, through scriptures, just like shamans who try to connect to the sacred through their "strangely sharpened sense" (Eliade 1960, 81).

In reading scriptures, Neo-Confucian scholars of China and Korea made a practice of mobilizing all available senses by using several parts of their bodies at the same time. They were encouraged to see texts with their eyes, recite them by mouth, hear the voice of their recitation by ear, and often copy the texts with their hands. Furthermore, they tried to commune with the sages and fully internalize their teachings through their senses of sight, hearing, and taste, though in their imagination rather than appealing directly to the physical senses. They visualized the image of the sage, the author of the text, and the wise men who are disciples and discussants of the sage. That is, Neo-Confucian scholars imagined they were seeing sages and wise men teach them right on the spot as they were reading. In addition, scholars tried to auralize the voices of sages and wise men, imagining they were hearing their voices when they were hearing their own voices reading, often along those of their colleagues when several scholars read together. Scholars also loved to compare reading to eating and understanding texts to tasting them, often saying that they were feeling the "taste" of scriptures. Such comparisons were made very often, vividly, and in detail. However, it was not just comparison or metaphor. The scholars created the sensory images of tasting when they were reading, and they imagined they were eating the text. Their "religious experience," in which they thought that they saw and heard the sage and tasted scriptures, depended on their "sensory experience" and "sensory activity" (Eliade 1960, 81). The starting point was their own voices reading, which soon came to be heard as the voice of the sage. Neo-Confucian scholars had "a sensitivity that can perceive and integrate these new experiences" (Eliade 1960, 81).

Confucian practices of visualization and auralization in reading have not drawn the attention of scholars.[2] Though some studies allude to these

---

2. For instance, the entry "Visualization" in the *Encyclopedia of Religion* says only "See Buddhism, Schools of; Daoism; Meditation" (Jones 2005, 9627). In contrast, scholars of Buddhism have discussed visualization practices in reciting sutras, which include envisioning "a buddha or bodhisattvas as a kind of visualized icon to worship or receive teachings" (McMahan 2010; see also Gregory 1986; Yamabe 1999; Hennessey 2011). The influence of Buddhism and Daoism on Chu Hsi is manifest, though he often criticized

practices, it is difficult to find works that focus on sensory readings in Neo-Confucianism. Daniel Gardner points out that Chu advised Confucian readers to make scripture their own in Chu's "Methods of Reading," which corresponds to the tenth and eleventh chapters of his *Classified Conversations*. He briefly introduces Chu's comparison of meditative reading to savoring the flavor and Chu's suggestion that readers of the sages' texts should try to "speak with them face to face" (Gardner 2004, 112). However, Gardner does not articulate the role of the senses in Neo-Confucian reading, though he knows that Chu asked readers to make visual, auditory, and gustatory imagery.

Neo-Confucian readings of scripture, as emphasized by Chu and Yi, began with readers' senses in that they first saw the text and heard their own voices reading. Furthermore, they thought they saw the sages, authors and characters of scripture, heard their voices, and tasted the flavor of scripture. Though they did not see and hear the sages directly or physically, and though they did not literally chew and eat the books, their readings really involved the senses of seeing, hearing, and tasting. As David Morgan persuasively argues, seeing is not limited to direct and physical seeing but "is an operation that relies on an apparatus of assumptions and inclinations, habits and routines, historical associations and cultural practices" (Morgan 2005, 3). It is "the contemplation of images," rather than images themselves, that "exerts the power to arrest the mind" (Morgan 2005, 1). The sense of hearing and tasting can also be understood in this way: these senses too are matters of assumptions, inclinations, and contemplations.

Visualization and auralization in reading

Chu Hsi and Yi Hwang emphasized readings of Confucian classics as the most important form of spiritual practice to attain *li*, principle, and in doing so ultimately to become a sage. They believed the Confucian classics—especially the Four Books and the Five Classics, in which the ancient Confucian sages revealed *li* most clearly—to have transformative power when read repeatedly and deliberately. Readers were supposed to get this

---

them and tried to show that Confucianism is superior (Ching 2000, 152–188). Considering that his doctrine and methods of self-cultivation were undoubtedly affected by Buddhism and Daoism, his suggestions on reading also seem to have something to do with them. However, we should not rush to a conclusion that the neo-Confucian visualization was formed under the influence of Buddhism and Daoism. Visualizing the deities or ancestors in ritual contexts also appears in some early Confucian texts including the *Book of Rites* and the *Analects*. According to "Significance of Sacrifice" in the *Book of Rites*, "In sacrificing, King Wen served the dead in the same way he served the living. ... When he mentioned his father' name, he did as if he saw him" (24.008). And the *Analects* attests that "[Confucius] offered sacrifice to his ancestors as if his ancestors were actually there and offered sacrifice to gods as if the gods were actually there" (3.12).

power through sensory readings of scriptures, specifically by visualizing and auralizing scriptures.

Chu, who is rated as a great master of Confucianism in the Sung Dynasty of China (960–1269) and is thought to have made a synthesis of Neo-Confucianism, first emphasized this reading method. Chu pointed out that Confucian sages had people read scriptures in order to edify them (Chu 1977, 121). People reading scriptures were supposed to experience what the sages had experienced. In addition, according to Chu, "if a scholar reads books of sages properly, he can understand what sages meant as if he converses with them face to face" (Chu 1977, 121). Though it was obvious that Confucian readers did not meet the sages directly, they were encouraged to think as if the sages were present at the place they were reading. They had to imagine the sages were talking to them while they were reading. Chu said, "You should always let the words of the sages be in front of your eyes, roll around in your mouth, and circle round in your heart" (Chu 1977, 121). In the process of visualizing sages as if seeing them and of auralizing the sages as if listening to what they said, the senses of vision and hearing should be mobilized.

Yi developed further this brief suggestion of Chu and made it more concrete and sophisticated. Yi was one of the most prominent figures among Korean Confucian scholars. He developed new prospects for Neo-Confucianism philosophy on the basis of his theories of *li* and self-cultivation (Keum 2013, 11). He was also believed to embody the ideal of the virtuous gentleman, the model for Korean Confucian scholars of the scholar who realized the spirit of Neo-Confucianism in his daily life (Keum 2013, 3, 4). However, while Yi is one of the most respected Confucian scholars in Korean history, it was Chu whom Yi admired and regarded as a model Confucian scholar in terms of both scholarship and life. Yi was not the only Korean scholar who tried to retrace the course of Chu's example. Since Neo-Confucianism had been imported from China to Korea, many other Korean Neo-Confucian scholars placed Chu right after the sages in importance and respected him as the authentic successor of Confucius. For instance, An Hyang (1243–1306), a renowned Confucian scholar of the Goryeo Dynasty (918–1392) who first introduced Neo-Confucianism to Korea, regarded the works of Chu as representing the true tradition of Confucius and Mencius. He even said, "Chu Hsi's merits equal those of Confucius. If one wants to study Confucius, one ought to study Chu Hsi first" (Deuchler 1992, 17). Just like An, Yi also accepted Chu as the standard of Confucian scholarship, thinking of him as a kind of semi-sage. While Chu had argued that the *Four Books* should be learned first before reading the *Five Classics* of original Confucianism, Yi asserted that Confucian scholars should understand Confucian scriptures through studying the *Collected Works of Master Chu*, which he regarded as the most important book for Confucian scholars (Keum 2013, 124).

Following Chu's teaching, Yi emphasized that scholars must maintain their minds in the state of *ching* (敬), alertness or mindfulness, all day long. Most importantly, according to Yi, if scholars remain alert and mindful when they read scriptures, they can see images of the sages appear in front of the readers and hear their voices. In "Diagram of the Admonition on Rising Early and Retiring Late," the tenth diagram of Yi's *The Ten Diagrams on Sage Learning*,[3] Yi quoted Chen Po's suggestion that scholars should see the sages and the wise men face to face when reading.

> At this time open your books and see the sage and the wise men face to face. Confucius is seated, Yen Hui and Tseng Tzu are at the front and the rear. Personally, sincerely, and attentively listen to the words of the sacred teacher. Repeatedly referring to the questions and discussions of the disciples, follow them. (Yi 2009, 139)

Scholars would see Confucius, the main character and speaker of scripture, sit before them and his disciples, supporting characters and speakers of scripture, sit around them. According to this diagram, reading in the state of mindfulness was quite the same thing as listening earnestly to the words of the sacred teacher (聖師).

For this experience, scripture should be read aloud and, of course, in a state of mindfulness. Scripture study in Confucianism has been based on reading texts aloud. Chu often said that reading aloud or reciting is the proper way to read scriptures (Gardner 2004, 118), and Yi emphasized that the texts' meaning would become clear by itself if scholars would read them aloud repeatedly sitting in an appropriate position (Keum 2001, 268). Gardner implies this when he observes that this reading is "capable of drawing the reader into a communication with the sages and worthies of antiquity" (Gardner 2004, 112). When Confucian scholars made a voice in reading aloud, they thought they heard the voice of the sage rather than their own voice because the sage was the speaker in the text. They also could visualize the image of the sage who was speaking to them right at the place of reading. In this sense, Neo-Confucian book reading, which was usually reading aloud in the state of mindfulness, was a kind of spiritual practice in which readers used their senses.

---

3. *The Ten Diagram on Sage Learning* is said to be Yi's masterpiece in which Yi summarized his scholarship of lifetime into ten diagrams and his comments (Keum 2001, iii). In the tenth diagram, "Diagram of the Admonition on Rising Early and Retiring Late," Yi quoted the admonition that had been composed by Chen Po, a Chinese scholar of Sung dynasty, and explained and reinterpreted the admonition in a diagram with his comments. (Kalton 1988, 250; Cheong 2007, 163–164).

Because Yi and other Korean Neo-Confucian scholars thought of Chu almost like a sage, it was natural that Yi tried to see Chu and hear his words in reading *Collected Works of Master Chu*, just as he tried to see and hear Confucius and other sages when he read scriptures of original Confucianism. In *Yeonboboyu* Yi described his attitude when reading *Collected Works*:

> I tried to get genuine knowledge and to achieve complete understanding [of the text] by kneeling down all day long and fully concentrating my mind. My reading was not different from seeing Chu face to face and learning from him directly because I was highly delighted and had devout faith. Therefore, my view became clearer and more precise day by day and my cultivation grew purer and more solid every day. (Requoted from Keum 2012, 47)

By trying to see Chu face to face and learn from him directly, Yi inherited Chu's suggestion that readers should read scriptures as if they converse with them face to face.

Yi emphasized the importance of the letters of Chu among his many other writings, because they made it easier to visualize and auralize Chu as the author and speaker of the text. Yi compiled fourteen volumes of Chu's letters by selecting letters that he regarded as essential for scholars' study and lives from the forty-eight volumes of Chu's letters. In the foreword, he asserted, "[Chu's letters] teach not only his contemporary disciples but also those who hear his teachings a hundred years later, talking face to face and pulling them by the ears [having them listen carefully]" (Keum 2012, 158). Though Yi knew that some of Chu's letters that he selected were quite private and not directly related to academic discussions, he thought that those letters were particularly helpful. When several disciples of Yi asked why he included those private letters in the compilation, he replied, "I inserted leisurely chats on purpose because I expected readers to experience, by savoring the texts, as if they heard Chu's voices while freely visiting him in person and talking with him" (Keum 2012, 159). According to Yi, Chu's letters that included not only academic discussion but also private conversations were very efficient at setting the scene for visualizing and hearing the semi-sage. Though Chu's private letters did not directly concern deep scholarship, they still helped readers see the great teacher and hear his words. Therefore, to Yi and many other Korean Neo-Confucians, the letters amounted to scriptures.

Reading as tasting: Appreciating the true flavor of books

In addition to visual and aural senses, Chu and Yi developed and recommended a reading method that involved another sense. Both of them employed vivid gustatory imagery for tasting the true flavor of the scriptures. If a sense is a matter of assumptions and inclinations, and concentrating on a sensory image can fill the mind, as suggested above, it can be said that Chu and Yi were encouraging scholars to have gustatory sensations flood their mind. Just as readers could communicate with the sages by reading aloud in mindful state, they also could enjoy the taste of the text by employing the same reading method. According to Gardner, "Savoring the flavor fully, the reader will come to appreciate the true taste. Such imagery is especially apt in a culture of reading where the text normally is recited aloud, by the lips and the mouth" (Gardner 2004, 112). In reciting the text aloud "by the lips and the mouth," they thought that they were chewing "nourishment and spiritual sustenance" (Gardner 2004, 112) provided by the sages and finally tasting it.

Chu argued that Confucian readers should make the text their own and that they had to "experience the text personally" (Gardner 2004, 111). And that personal experience of scripture, according to Chu, was likely to lead to savoring its flavor fully and appreciating its true taste. In *Classified Conversations of Master Chu*, many passages compared reading to tasting. The Chinese word 味, which corresponds to the English word "taste," can also be translated by "appreciating" and "understanding," just as the English word carries the same range of meanings. Chu used this word frequently in connection with the practice of reading. Chu asserted that if scholars concentrated on reading they could taste the text and that if they penetrated deeply into it they could savor its authentic rich flavor (Chu 1977, 122). Chu also likened meticulous and thorough reading to savoring food. Reading the text with appreciation was compared to chewing well and savoring the flavor (Chu 1977, 131). Scholars should completely understand each passage one at a time and then repeat the whole chapter pondering its meaning, as if they chewed and then felt its taste (Chu 1977, 138, 139). If they read the text thoroughly again and again, they will naturally recognize what they could not previously understand and they will experience a flavor richer than what they had previously known. Scholars cannot experience this subtle flavor unless they are very experienced in reading (Chu 1977, 126). Once the flavor of the text is experienced, they will "recognize its meaning that naturally comes out of the text" (Chu 1977, 128). This thorough and meticulous reading would lead to recognizing *li*, truth or principle, as well as understanding the text fully.

> Generally speaking, one should read thoroughly and minutely, thinking meanings of the text. Reading like this, one's understanding of the text by itself becomes more exact and profound. After one's reading becomes exact and profound, one can naturally recognize principle (*li*). It is just like eating [嚌] a fruit. If one bites [咬] the fruit roughly at first, one swallows without

knowing its rich taste. But if one chews [嚼] and breaks it into small pieces, its taste naturally comes forth and one gets to know if the fruit is mellow [甛], bitter [苦], sweet [甘], or hot [辛]. At last one can be said to know the taste [味]. (Chu 1977, 124)

In this passage, Chu uses four verbs and four adjectives in order to explain his reading method by employing the metaphor of eating and tasting. While reading itself is compared to eating, reading without understanding the text fully is just biting.[4] Careful and meticulous reading includes two processes of chewing and tasting. He described the experience of tasting vividly, suggesting that there are four distinct flavors: mellow, bitter, sweet, and hot. The readers who follow his reading method can understand exactly and profoundly the text and finally recognize principle, as if they not only eat food but also appreciate its various tastes.

Yi also likened reading to eating and tasting, describing them as if scriptures themselves were food and the object of the gustatory sense. He argued that scholars should enjoy the happiness of knowing "the taste of reading" (Keum 2001, 42). As mentioned above, Yi asserted that scholars should begin studying by reading *Collected Works of Master Chu* and acquaint themselves with them. If they then read the Four Books after having read *Collected Works*, Yi says, then "every word of the sages will be tasty" (Keum 2013, 124).

He described his own reading as eating scriptures. In a poem he wrote when he was fifty-nine years old, he contrasts his own eating of the book with that of a bookworm that was eating the book without knowing its taste.

Being a gray-haired old man who is gravely ill and incapable
I have been eating into the book, making a pair with a bookworm
How can it know the taste though it eats the letters?
Heaven grants me many books in which I find my pleasure.

(Requoted from Keum 2013, 50)

In this poem, Yi's reading is described as eating the book while knowing its taste. Though a bookworm also eats the book physically, this eating cannot rival his own because the bookworm does not know the full flavor. In another poem that he composed when he was sixty-one years old, he wrote, "true taste is in the text / my satisfaction from it is much bigger than that from all kinds of delicacies" (Keum 2013, 51). Yi equates Confucian scholars' reading of scriptures to eating the text and savoring its taste.

---

4. Chu often compared reading to eating food in *Classified Conversations of Master Chu*. For example, he likened reading to drinking wine and to taking medicine. According to Chu, scholars who like reading would keep reading, as a person who likes drinking would not stop after drinking just one glass of wine but would like to drink another. Likewise, one should keep reading as medicine should be taken many times to exert a remedial effect. (Chu 1977, 128)

These two Neo-Confucian masters did not describe the gustatory experience of reading simply for poetic effect. For them, tasting the scriptures was a real experience. As I explained above, Chu emphasized that the personal experience of the text that will result in appreciating its true taste. Similarly, Yi argues that the flavor of the text "cannot be expressed in language." He continues:

> Scholars themselves should try to get at the explanation by tasting its deep flavor and having real experience of it. ... [Asking about the taste of the text] is just like asking other persons how the food they are eating tastes. One can know the taste of the food only after eating what other persons are eating and after tasting what they are tasting. Is it right if one asks other persons how it tastes without eating it oneself at all? Scholars must never fail to experience fully the taste [of the text] first-hand. (Yi 2010, 152)

Experiencing the taste of reading was not just a metaphoric expression. Though Yi mentioned it for the purpose of introducing it to scholars and encouraging them to experience it, Yi thought that it was beyond description. Chu and Yi advised Neo-Confucian scholars to gain direct sensory experience of tasting scriptures.

Chu and Yi likened reading scriptures to eating them and understanding them fully to savoring their true flavor. They not only appropriated metaphors of eating and tasting but also created the gustatory imagery for the taste of books while reading them. To them, reading was a complicated process that involved biting, chewing, eating, and tasting the words of the sages.

Conclusion

Chu and Yi encouraged the Confucian scholar to activate at least three senses when reading a text, over and above the experience of merely reading the characters of the text. First, the text should be recited aloud so the reciters would hear their own voices, sometimes along with those of their colleagues. They imagined, furthermore, that the voices they were hearing while reading were those of the ancient sages themselves and of their disciples, namely "the wise men." Secondly, while hearing the voices of the sages, the reciting scholars would visualize their images, seeking personal communion with them. Finally, the meditative reading of scholars was frequently likened to savoring a text's flavor, with the act of reading being described as eating, biting, chewing, and tasting. When the readers recited the text aloud, pronouncing each syllable using their tongues, lips and mouths, they engaged in a gustatory experience: "chewing" and "tasting" the ancient classics.

While I limited myself to the sensory aspects of Chu and Yi's reading methods, research on the sensory readings of Neo-Confucian scholars should be expanded further. As the influence of Chu and Yi on Confucian scholars was significant, there will be many examples of other Chinese and Korean scholars' sensory reading. Because a sense is "an operation that relies on an apparatus of assumptions and inclinations" and because "the contemplation of images" has "the power to arrest the mind" (Morgan 2005, 1, 3), it is clear that the senses were deeply involved in these scholars' communion with the sages through reading though they did not physically see the sages, hear their words, or actually consume their books. Their religious experience began from reading scriptures by using their senses and aimed at a sensory experience.

References

Cheong, Sunu. 2007. *Gongbuui Balgyeon* [*Discovery of Study*]. Seoul: Hyeonamsa (published in Korean).

Ching, Julia. 2000. *The Religious Thought of Chu Hsi*. Oxford: Oxford University Press.

Chu, Hsi. 1977. *Chu-tzu yü-lei* [朱子語類, *Classified Conversations of Master Chu*]. Edited by Li Jingde in 1473. Seoul: a Facsimile edition (Seoul National University Library, 181. 1346 J868ef).

Confucius. 2003. *Lúnyǔ* (論 語, *Analects*). Translated into Korean and Annotated by Gangsu Lee *et al.* Seoul: Jisiksaneopsa (published in Classical Chinese and Korean).

Deuchler, Martina. 1992. *The Confucian Transformation of Korea: A Study of Society and Ideology*. Cambridge, MA: Council on East Asian Studies, Harvard University.

Eliade, Mircea. 1960 [1957]. *Myths, Dreams and Mysteries*. Translated by Philip Mairet. New York: Harper & Row.

Gardner, Daniel K. 2004. "Attentiveness and meditative reading in Cheng-Zhu Neo-Confucianism." In *Confucian Spirituality* vol. 2, edited by Tu Weiming and Mary Evelyn Tucker, 99–119. New York: The Crossroad Publishing.

Graham, William A. 1987. *Beyond the Written Word: Oral Aspects of Scripture in the History of Religion*. Cambridge: Cambridge University Press.

Gregory, Peter N., ed. 1986. *Traditions of Meditation in Chinese Buddhism*. Honolulu: University of Hawaii Press.

Hennessey, Anna Madelyn. 2011. "Chinese images of body and landscape: Visualization and representation in the religious experience of medieval China." Unpublished Ph.D. theis, University of California Santa Barbara.

Jones, Lindsay, ed. 2005. *Encyclopedia of Religion*. 2nd edition, vol. 14. Farmington Hills, MI: Thompson Gale.

Kalton, Michael C. 1988. *To Become a Sage: The Ten Diagrams on Sage Learning by Yi T'oegye*. New York: Columbia University Press.

Keum, Jangtae. 2001. Seonghaksipttowa *T'oegye Cheolhagui Gujo* [Seonghaksiptto *and the Structure in the Philosophy of T'oegye*]. Seoul: Seoul National University Press (published in Korean).

———. 2013. *T'oegye Pyeongjeon* [*Critical Biography of T'oegye*]. Seoul: Jisikgwagyoyang (published in Korean).

Küng, Hans and Julia Ching. 1989. *Christianity and Chinese Religions*. New York: Doubleday.

Li Ji (禮 記, *Book of Rites*). 1985. Translated into Korean and annotated by Sangok Lee. Seoul: Myeongmundang (published in Classical Chinese and Korean).

McMahan, David L. 2010. "Vision and visualization." http://www.oxfordbibliographies.com/view/document/obo-9780195393521/obo-9780195393521-0175.xml?rskey=afI5rD&result=3&q=visualization#firstMatch. http//doi.10.1093/obo/9780195393521-0175.

Morgan, David. 2005. *The Sacred Gaze: Religious Visual Culture in Theory and Practice*. Berkeley: University of California Press.

Plate, S. Brent. 2014. *A History of Religion in 5 1/2 Objects: Bringing the Spiritual to its Senses*. Boston, MA: Beacon Press.

Smith, Wilfred Cantwell. 1971. "The study of religion and the study of the Bible." *Journal of the American Academy of Religion* 39: 131–140. https://doi.org/10.1093/jaarel/XXXIX.2.131

Song, Jubok. 1999. *Chuja Seodangeun Eotteoke Geureul Baewonna* [*How Master Chu School Studied: Translation and Annotation of "On Reading," Chapter 10 and 11 of* Classified Conversations *of Master Chu* (*Chu-tzu yü-lei*)]. Seongnam: Cheonggye. (published in Korean).

Taylor, Rodney L. 1990. *The Religious Dimensions of Confucianism*. Albany: State University of New York Press.

Watts, James W. 2006. "The Three Dimensions of Scriptures." *Postscripts* 2(2–3): 135–159.

Yamabe, Nobuyoshi. 1999. "The Sutra on the ocean-like Samadhi of the visualization of the Buddha." Unpublished Ph.D thesis, Yale University.

Yi, Hwang. 2009 [1568]. *Seonghaksiptto* [*The Ten Diagrams on Sage Learning*]. Translated from Classical Chinese and annotated by RIKS (Research Institute of Korean Studies, Korea University). Seoul: Sangjisa. (published in Korean).

———. 2010. *Yijasueo* [*Essential Words of Master Yi*]. Edited by Yi Ik and An Jeongbok in 1753. Translated from Classical Chinse by Lee Gwangho. Seoul: Sangjisa. (published in Korean).

Yoo, Yohan. 2010. "Possession and Repetition: Ways in which Korean Lay Buddhist Appropriate Scriptures." *Postscripts* 6(1–3): 243–259.

— 10 —

Scriptures' Indexical Touch

JAMES W. WATTS

Touching and holding books does not usually evoke the language of sensation. Touching a book indexes the reader in relationship to the book. Holding a book of scripture indexes a person as faithful to the beliefs and practices that are commonly associated with that scripture. In portraiture, the direction of a book's indexical function is usually clear. Scribes, professors, lawyers and politicians pose in their libraries, often with book in hand, to depict themselves as scholars. The fact that scriptures are books makes a vocabulary of textual agency available for describing their symbolic function. The indexical link between book and person gains force from the fact that books and people share the quality of interiority. We think of both books and people as material containers of immaterial ideas. Therefore, images of people with books invite viewers to consider the relationship between their invisible ideas. However, art that portrays a god or goddess holding a scripture conveys a tighter indexical relationship, often to the point of collapsing any distinction between them.

Books must be manipulated in order to be used *as books*. Whether in the form of scrolls or codices, books must be picked up and unrolled or opened. They must be held in one's hands or set on a desk, where they often have to be held open. Books are designed to be touched.

Touching books, unlike touching most other objects, does not indicate the reader's control of the book. Instead, it usually represents the book's control of the reader. Touching books *reverses* the usual implications of holding and manipulating an object: it is not so much that you touch the book as that it touches you. The significance of touching a book is really

James W. Watts is Professor of Religion at Syracuse University in Syracuse, New York, and was in 2015–2016 a Visiting Fellow in the Käte Hamburger Kolleg at the Center for Religious Studies at Ruhr University Bochum, Germany.

about indexing the person who reads or holds or, at least, touches the book. Touching a book indexes the reader in relationship to the book.

Indexing readers by ritualizing scriptures

By "indexing," I am using language developed by C. S. Pierce (1867) to categorize signs.[1] An index is connected to its referent by some factual or causal relationship between them. For modern books, the most obvious indexical relationship lies between the book and its author: the existence of a book turns its writer into its author. Books, however, also index their readers as people who know what is in this book, who value this book, and, perhaps, as people who have been affected by this book in one way or another.

Books of scripture index their readers and handlers in especially potent ways. Touching scriptures serves to establish and maintain a person's religious identity. It marks them by their relationship to the book and their relationship through the book to the religion and to its customary beliefs and practices.

The indexical use of scriptures is one example of the broader indexical function of rituals. Roy Rappaport (1999) maintained that rituals customarily serve to index their participants' relationship to the ritual's purpose and to each other. Thus a wedding obviously indexes the couple's new status as married, not only to themselves but also to everyone who witnesses or hears about the wedding. Rappaport observed that the indexical function of rituals does not depend on people's mental agreement with the tradition: you do not have to believe in all the doctrines of the religious tradition or even agree that this couple should get married in order to attend a wedding. Willing participation in the wedding ceremony does, however, index your acceptance of the "canonical order" represented by the ritual. You cannot deny that the couple is married without lying. The ritual indexes its participants' place in the social relationships that it expresses.

---

1. My use of the term "icon" to describe iconic books, however, goes beyond Pierce's definition of an icon as resembling its referent. The terminology of "iconic books" depends instead on Byzantine icon theory and later elaborations of it (Parmenter 2006), in which icons have indexical and symbolic as well as iconic functions in Pierce's terminology. He allowed that signs can function as symbols, icons and indices simultaneously. An iconic book, then, does represent things it resembles, such as other books or books in general. But symbolic uses of books make the book stand for something else, such as knowledge, learning, wisdom, or religion. Indexical use of books points out their factual or causal relationships to people or other things. The Iconic Books Project defines an iconic book as a visible and material object that, like an Orthodox Christian icon and many other kinds of religious art, is believed to put viewers and readers in touch with an immaterial, transcendent reality. In the case of books, that immaterial reality is, in the first place, the conceptual contents of the book's text. In the case of scriptures, that immaterial reality is believed to be spiritual, transcendent, and divine. Such iconic books function as icons, symbols, and indices according to Pierce's description of signs.

According to Rappaport, some ritual objects index the performer and others represent the canon. A few items, such as the crowns of kings, "seem to be intermediate.... Such objects are themselves parts of the canonical order, but their manipulation is in part self-referential" (Rappaport 1999, 145). Books of scriptures are intermediate like crowns. The iconic ritualization of scriptures references the "canonical order" of orthodox beliefs as well as indexing those who hold, touch, and read them in a self-referential manner.

Holding a book of scripture thus indexes a person as faithful to the beliefs and practices that are commonly associated with that scripture. By holding or touching the scripture, a person presents themselves as pious and orthodox by the standards of that scripture's religious tradition. Showing oneself holding the scripture is therefore an important form of self-presentation in many religious traditions.[2] The act of touching or holding the scripture also claims for that person the benefits promised by the scripture's tradition. Many people believe these benefits to be quite real, though they may not define them more specifically than by saying that "it is a blessing" to hold or touch the scripture.

Of course, other religious symbols serve the same purpose. Religious devotion frequently ascribes agency to symbols, images, and amulets. Because we do not normally grant agency to such objects, stories about icons and relics, for example, get classified as miraculous. However, the fact that scriptures are books makes a vocabulary of textual agency available for describing their symbolic function. Conventional discourse readily accepts the agency of books, so their religious effects can be described as due to having extraordinarily effective texts rather than or in addition to miraculous intervention. Investing textual media with religious symbolism changes the discourse of agency around those symbols. To modern rationalists, it makes the power of books appear more "natural" and rational than the power of other religious symbols and objects.

Textual effects depend, of course, on people actually reading the books. Intellectuals in all scriptural religions frequently complain about the low level of scriptural knowledge among their fellow believers. A book of scripture, however, serves simultaneously as a text to be interpreted, a script to be performed orally, and an icon to be venerated (Watts 2006). Most people do not distinguish these different dimensions of scriptural agency, so the conventional semantic agency of books supports claims to the divinely-enhanced agency of scriptures in the performative and iconic dimensions as well.

---

2. Just as in secular culture: portraits of scholars and lawyers in their libraries are clichés of ancient, medieval and modern visual culture.

Taking oaths and vows frequently involves manipulating a book of scripture. Here touch or proximity indexes people in especially obvious ways: touching the book visually proclaims their new office or obligations at the same time that speaking the oath does in the hearing of others. The ritual indexes their new status through the sight of touching the book and the sound of the oath.

Touch conveys greater intimacy than hearing. In human cultures, touching skin to skin conveys both vulnerability and intimacy. When books were written on parchment, that is, on processed animal hides, touching them involved touching skin to skin. The analogy between intimate reading and human intimacy was naturalized by the touch of parchment. Perhaps that is why leather remains a popular binding material for bibles. The sensation of leather in one's hands promotes a feeling of intimacy with the scripture.

The kiss is a more intimate form of touch. The use of lips brings the devotee one step closer to the vulnerability of eating and drinking that exposes the person and book to each other's effects. The kiss is the most intimate public expression, so it is not surprising that people often exhibit their devotion to a book of scripture by kissing it (except in cultures that regard spit as polluting, which therefore frown on kissing scriptures). In liturgical churches, the reader kisses the Gospel before and after reading it aloud. In synagogues, people often kiss prayer books and shawls after using them to touch the Torah scroll. Kissing the wrong scripture can elicit outrage because kissing indexes the person in relationship to the book even more powerfully than touch does. For example, when Pope John Paul II was presented a Qur'an in 1999 and kissed it as if it were a Gospel book (Fides 1999), he outraged many conservative Catholics.

Touching books

Touch and handling are therefore essential to the book's function, essential to reading it. That is not true of all texts: reading billboards or blackboards or Powerpoint presentations requires only looking. Nor do all uses of books require touching: books can be used as icons simply by displaying them. But when a book is displayed in this way, little or any of it can be read. Reading books requires manipulation. So do letters and e-readers. Reading most texts involves the hands as much as the eyes.

However, to speak of "manipulating books" makes people feel uncomfortable. It is an accurate description of how books are used. But while manipulating hammers and forks sounds routine, to speak of manipulating books sounds like doing something wrong. The language of manipulation indicates the reader's control over the book. And while readers do control physical books just as much as carpenters control their hammers, it feels transgressive to admit it.

The problem is that the phrase "manipulating books" suggests that readers control the contents of books. That is not the way that reading is supposed to work. By "supposed to," I am referring to the ways our languages direct how we think about and speak about books. It sounds jarring to assert that readers determine the meaning of the books they read, even though that is self-evidently the case: readers decide that the object they hold is a book, they decide that its markings are letters, they decide which language the letters encode, and they translate the visual signs into mental or spoken language. At every stage, readers can decide differently and sometimes do.

Nevertheless, that description of the reading process does not accord with the cultural presentation of how books work. We think of reading as a process in which the book is active and the reader passive. We think of books as having their own agency. Books "speak" to us. We frequently comment on how a particular book has "changed" our minds or "moved" us. Its stories "touch" us. The book acts upon the reader, often changing the reader's mind or beliefs or commitments.

Many stories of reading sacred texts end in religious conversions. A famous example is that of Saint Augustine in his *Confessions*. It is instructive that the child's chant that inspired him to open randomly and read a verse from Paul's letter to the Romans commanded him first to hold the book: *tolle, lege* "take, read."[3] Though these active imperatives emphasize Augustine's actions, he describes an experience of being acted upon: "a light of serenity infused my heart." Reading is experienced as a passive activity.

When we shift our focus to the reader's activity in reading, we do not usually use the language of touch and manipulation, but rather of eating. We eagerly "consume" or "devour" a good book. Eating is, of course, the

---

3. "So was I speaking and weeping in the most bitter contrition of my heart, when, lo! I heard from a neighbouring house a voice, as of boy or girl, I know not, chanting, and oft repeating. 'Take up and read; Take up and read.' ['Tolle, lege! Tolle, lege!'] Instantly, my countenance altered, I began to think most intently whether children were wont in any kind of play to sing such words: nor could I remember ever to have heard the like. So checking the torrent of my tears, I arose; interpreting it to be no other than a command from God to open the book, and read the first chapter I should find... Eagerly then I returned to the place where Alypius was sitting; for there had I laid the volume of the Apostle when I arose thence. I seized, opened, and in silence read that section on which my eyes first fell: 'Not in rioting and drunkenness, not in chambering and wantonness, not in strife and envying; but put ye on the Lord Jesus Christ, and make not provision for the flesh, in concupiscence.' [Romans 13:14–15] No further would I read; nor needed I: for instantly at the end of this sentence, by a light as it were of serenity infused into my heart, all the darkness of doubt vanished away." Augustine (2001, Book Eight, Chapter 12, Paragraphs 27–28).

most intimate of physical relationships. We do not simply manipulate food: we internalize it and it nourishes us, in fact, becomes part of us. So when I "consume" a book, I am nourished, preserved, or changed. The implication of the metaphor is that I am affected by the book (see the essay by Yohan Yoo in this volume). Unlike food, however, the book remains unchanged. By thinking of reading as eating, we again affirm the book's agency.

So, in contrast to hammers, to speak of touching books does not usually describe the reader's control of the book. Instead, it indicates the book's control of the reader. Many people believe that contact with scriptures or portions of their text can be effective in transforming their bodies and circumstances (see the essays in this volume by Katharina Wilkens, David Ganz and Dorina Parmenter). Touch also establishes an indexical relationship between book and human, in which the book legitimizes a person's identity (see Christian Frevel in this volume). Depending on the book, that identity may be as reader, author, or scholar. Books of scripture index people's religious identities.

Avoiding scripture's touch

Scripture veneration, however, frequently manifests itself in a refusal to touch scripture or in restrictions on how it may be touched. My research on the Torah in antiquity and in traditional Jewish ritual practices provides some interesting examples of scripture's indexical touch and its restrictions. (See also Marianne Schleicher's essay in this volume.)

Jewish scribes who copy Torah scrolls must purify themselves first, according the Talmudic rules. Many other Jews try to avoid touching the scrolls directly. In the course of a synagogue service, cloth covers and pointers mediate between human bodies and scrolls so that the Torah need never be subjected to unmediated touch. The effort to avoid touching Torah scrolls directly while ritualizing various forms of mediated touch suggests that the divine text is powerful enough to affect people through other media, but human touch is not. Touch mediated by covers, prayer book or shawl is believed to convey a blessing, and the manipulation of *mezuzahs* and *tefillin*, boxes that contain hand-written portions of the Torah, is characteristic of Jewish devotion. *Mezuzahs* serve as very public marker of Jewish identity and *tefillin* index Orthodox practice (see Frevel's essay in this volume). Thus various forms of mediated touch index and differentiate Jewish identity through ritual manipulation of the Torah.

Concerns about polluting touch took a paradoxical form in ancient rabbinic literature. The Mishnah defines scriptures as books "that defile the hands" (*m. Yad.* 3:5). This strange way of categorizing the most holy objects in Judaism has stimulated a great deal of debate from rabbinic to modern times. It is clear that the power to defile the hands sets scriptures apart from other books, and so performs a typical function of pollution language in separating holy objects from common ones. John Barton (1997, 107-121) suggested that the rabbis' concern focused specifically on texts that contain the name of God, YHWH, written in Hebrew letters. The custom of never pronouncing the name of God became widespread in ancient Judaism because of awe and fear of its power. So Barton argued that the rabbis also feared touching a text containing the divine name. Defining scriptures as "defiling the hands" establishes a prohibition for the sense of touch to parallel the prohibition on hearing the sound of the divine name. Seeing the divine name in writing was not prohibited: it appears on almost every page of Jewish scriptures, the Tanak. The rules against unmediated touch of the scripture scroll, like the rule against speaking the name, drew attention to the sanctity and power of the name especially at the moment when one sees it written on the page. Thus in rabbinic ritual rules, perception of divinity by the sight of the divine name was controlled by prohibiting its perception by the sense of hearing and by unmediated touch of the sacred scrolls in which it is written.

Fear of damaging or defiling scriptures by touch is not limited to Jewish practices. Many Muslims avoid touching Qur'ans until they can assure themselves of being clean (Suit 2010). Many Sikhs do not own a complete copy of their scripture, the Guru Granth Sahib, because of the many requirements for its proper maintenance (Myrvold 2010b). Nor are such fears peculiar to religious communities. Libraries limit access to their rare books. When they grant access, they often require only mediated touch (gloves) under the supervision of library personnel. Public display of rare books is usually accompanied by the injunction, "Do not touch!" Here fear of manipulation is fear of destruction, and leads to preventing touch entirely. As a result, ancient and rare books in modern libraries and museums can become only aesthetic objects, available only to sight, the most remote and least intimate of the human senses. Viewing such books does not index the viewer, though displaying them does index their owner's wealth and prestige as well as enhance the status of books themselves. (For an aesthetic evaluation of all aspects of iconic books, see Brent Plate's essay in this volume.)

Fear of harm and destruction is, of course, warranted both for rare books and for scriptures. Devoted touches and kisses often wear away the texts and pages of books (see Ganz's essay in this volume). More worrisome to devotees is the possibility of scriptures becoming subject to hostile touch in the form of deliberate desecration and destruction. An act of desecration refuses a scripture's indexical touch and instead violently exerts manipulative control over the book. Desecrators destroy the book to manipulate the scripture's indexical relationship to the community that venerates it. The responses of outrage from the scripture's devotees testify to the power of that indexical relationship (Watts 2009).

It would be natural to regard the indexical function of books, and of scriptures in particular, as a secondary consequence of a book's social and religious prestige. That would be a mistake, for two reasons. First, books in general index those who read and handle them as literate and so, in many cultures, as educated and intellectual. The appearance of a book performs this function even when the contents of the book are not identified. Second, many books and other texts are created for indexical uses. Some books have been written, copied, published, and sold to be touched as much as to be read. I will describe just one famous example from my research on biblical texts to illustrate this point.

Touching written texts in the Torah

The Bible describes the tablets of the Ten Commandments as written primarily for indexical use. Exodus tells the story, and Deuteronomy repeats it. Moses climbs Mount Sinai to hear God's revelation of the law. At the end of forty days, he is given tablets "written by the finger of God" (Exod. 31:18; Deut. 9:10). He descends the mountain with the tablets in his hand to the Israelite camp, where he finds the people worshipping the golden calf. Moses breaks the tablets, which expresses Moses' anger and also illustrates the fact that the Israelites have broken the covenant with God inscribed on the tablets. After setting things straight, Moses returns to the mountain and receives a second set of tablets (Exod. 34) which he deposits in the Ark of the Covenant, a box built especially to hold the tablets (Exod. 25:10-16; Deut 10:1-5).

Nobody in this story or anywhere else in the Bible actually reads the tablets of the commandments. There is no need to, because Moses already wrote down the law on a scroll which he read aloud to the people (Exod. 24:3-4, 7). Before he dies, he writes it down again and gives the scroll to the Levitical priests with instructions to read it aloud every seven years to all the Israelites (Deut. 31:9-13). This Torah scroll is supposed to be kept next to the ark that contains the tablets of the covenant (Deut. 31:24-26).

The Torah thus describes itself as taking two different textual forms, one public and the other hidden. Contrary to what one might expect, the esoteric and exoteric texts do not differ in contents: we are assured that the scroll that is read aloud in its entirety contains all the laws given by God at

Sinai (Exod. 24:4; Deut. 31:24), which must include whatever was written on the tablets.

The tablets and scroll differ instead in their purpose and use. While the scroll is meant for publication, the tablets are a deposit text. It is their existence in Israel's possession that guarantees Israel's covenant with God. The tablets of the commandments are not public monuments in the Bible, despite how they are usually portrayed in Jewish and Christian art and sculpture (though the Torah must also be inscribed monumentally: Deut 6:9; 27:4; see Frevel in this volume). The tablets are created to serve as relic texts (Watts 2006, 155–156). They are hidden away in their ark reliquary where they cannot be seen or touched. As relics, what is most important is that Israel possesses them.

As is typically the case with reliquaries, possessing and touching the ark carries the same indexical power as the tablets of the commandments. Only the priests are allowed to approach the ark (Lev. 16:2, 12–14) and special precautions must be taken when carrying it (Num. 4:5–20). Having the ark reliquary in one's possession has the power to bless (2 Sam. 6:11) or to curse (1 Sam. 5–6), depending on one's intentions. Accidentally touching it has the power to kill (2 Sam. 6:6–7). The ark containing the tablets thus indexes Israel as the people of God's covenant.

The books of Exodus and Deuteronomy equate the contents of the tablets and the scroll to prepare the way for the Torah scroll to assume the tablets' indexical function, as it did in later Judaism (Watts 2015, 2016; for other Pentateuchal texts that emphasize material uses of texts, see the essay by Frevel in this volume). This was already the case in the early Second Temple period when the priest and scribe, Ezra, is described as returning from Babylon with the Torah "in his hand" (Ezra 7:14). Biblical literature thus establishes the ritual pattern in which the powerful form of scripture is the hand-held form, which mythically is the tablets hidden in the ark but in ritual experience is the Torah scroll.

The puzzle of indexical circles between book and deity

The indexical function of scriptures gains strength from the nature of written texts as visual and material representations of their contents. This power is illustrated by visual art depicting books. In portraiture, the direction of a book's indexical function is usually clear. Scribes, professors, lawyers and politicians pose in their libraries, often with book in hand, to depict themselves as scholars. The implication is that they know what is written in the books around them. Rabbis, ministers and saints pose with a book of scripture or commentary to show their piety and orthodoxy. The implication is that they conform to the ideals advocated by their scripture. In the case of author's portraits, books and humans index each other: the human as author and the books as being that author's work. The implication is that all the books' contents are the author's ideas.

The indexical link between book and person gains force from the fact that books and people share the quality of interiority. Books have contents and people have thoughts. We think of both books and people as material containers of immaterial ideas. This belief generates a tendency in many cultures to treat material books like you treat human bodies (see the essays in Myrvold 2010a). Therefore, images of people with books invite viewers to consider the relationship between their invisible ideas.

Art that portrays a god or goddess holding a scripture conveys a tighter indexical relationship. The images adopt the conventional pose of human portraiture. But in the case of a deity holding a book, it is difficult to decide which indexes the other. Such images presuppose that the human form of the deity is a visual analogy for a transcendent reality. The book may or may not have a material existence, but its representation in this context overwhelms its physical form with its transcendent contents. Thus images of Jesus holding the Gospels or Brahma holding the Vedas do not just index the deity by the book or vice-versa. They identify them. Here the indexical circle tightens to the point of collapsing any distinction between them.

Some religious traditions and mystical groups within traditions are more likely to accept the equation of deity and book than others. The New Testament's description of Christ as the "Word of God" (John 1:1) inaugurated a tendency in ritual and art to identify him with the written Gospels. Dorina Parmenter (2006, 170) has pointed out that one ancient Christian text, the Gospel of Truth from Nag Hammadi, describes Christ's death as the crucifixion of a book. Michelle Brown (2010, 59) found a medieval sculpture of the Virgin Mary holding a codex in the usual place occupied by the Christ child.

Other religious traditions go further. Jewish mysticism in the Zohar speculates about the metaphysical relationship between God and Torah (Wolfson 2004). South Asian traditions have been very open to the metaphysical identity of book and deity. The Buddhist texts called Prajnaparamita appear in medieval art in the form of a goddess by that name (Kinnard 2002). Some Hindus have recently begun depicting the Bhagavad Gita as the goddess Maata Geeta (Joanne Waghorne, personal communication).

The appearance of books in divine images draws our attention to the fact that the contents of books seem to transcend their material manifestation. Books' contents survive the material destruction of books because they appear in multiple copies. By copying, the contents of books can be preserved over much longer periods of time than can a scroll or codex. This characteristic of texts has led to the common observation that writing provides people the only demonstrable form of life after death. Because ideas live on in books, books materialize transcendence. Touching and holding books allows people to come into contact with immaterial values. By touching and holding scriptures, they feel like they can touch divinity.

References

Augustine, Aurelius. 2001. *The Confessions of St. Augustine*, translated by Edward Pusey. Vol. VII, Part 1. The Harvard Classics. New York: P.F. Collier & Son, 1909–14; Bartleby.com, 2001. www.bartleby.com/7/1/.

Barton, John. 1997. *Holy Writings, Sacred Texts*. Louisville: Westminster John Knox.

Brown, Michelle P. 2010. "Images to be read and words to be seen: The iconic role of the early medieval book." *Postscripts* 6: 39–66 (Reprinted in *Iconic Books and Texts*, edited by James W. Watts, 93–118. London: Equinox, 2013).

Fides. 1999. "Iraqi Catholic leader decries allied bombing." June 01, 1999. Online at http://www.traditioninaction.org/RevolutionPhotos/Snap/A055rcKoran_1.html.

Kinnard, Jacob N. 2002. "On Buddhist 'Bibliolaters': Representing and worshiping the book in medieval Indian Buddhism." *The Eastern Buddhist* 34(2): 94–116, and plates 1 and 2.

Myrvold, Kristina, ed. 2010a. *The Death of Sacred Texts: Ritual Disposal and Renovation of Texts in World Religions*. London: Ashgate.

———. 2010b. "Engaging with the Guru: Sikh beliefs and practices of Guru Granth Sahib." *Postscripts* 6: 201–224 (Reprinted in *Iconic Books and Texts*, edited by James W. Watts, 261–282. London: Equinox, 2013).

Parmenter, Dorina Miller. 2006. "The Iconic Book: The Image of the Bible in Early Christian Rituals." *Postscripts* 2: 160–189 (Reprinted in *Iconic Books and Texts*, edited by James W. Watts, 63–92. London: Equinox, 2013).

Pierce, C. S. 1867. "On A New List of Categories." In *The Writings of Charles S. Peirce: A Chronological Edition* (6 vols.; Peirce Edition Project; Bloomington, IN: Indiana University Press, 1982), 49-58.

Rappaport, Roy A. 1999. *Ritual and Religion in the Making of Humanity*. Cambridge: Cambridge University Press. https://doi.org/10.1017/CBO9780511814686

Suit, Natalia K. 2010. "*Muṣḥaf* and the material boundaries of the Qurʾan." *Postscripts* 6 (2010), 143-163 (Reprinted in *Iconic Books and Texts*, edited by James W. Watts, 189–206. London: Equinox, 2013).

Watts, James W. 2006. "The three dimensions of scriptures." *Postscripts* 2(2): 135–159 (Reprinted in *Iconic Books and Texts*, 8–30. London: Equinox, 2013).

———. 2009. "Desecrating Scriptures." A case study for the Luce Project in Religion, Media and International Relations at Syracuse University, online at http://surface.syr.edu/rel/3/.

———. 2015. "Iconic scriptures from decalogue to Bible." *Mémoires du livre / Studies in Book Culture* 6/2.

———. 2016. "From ark of the covenant to Torah scroll: Ritualizing Israel's iconic texts." In *Ritual Innovation in the Hebrew Bible and Early Judaism*, edited by Nathan MacDonald, 21–34. Beihefte zur Zeitschrift für die alttestamentliche Wissenschaft 468. Berlin: De Gruyter. https://doi.org/10.1515/9783110368710-004

Wolfson, Elliot R. 2004. "Iconicity of the text: Reification of Torah and the idolatrous impulse of Zoharic Kabbalah." *Jewish Studies Quarterly* 11: 315–342. https://doi.org/10.1628/0944570043028437

Indices

Author Index

Subject Index

A

Aaron (high priest): 68–72, 75
aesthetic: 2, 3, 5, 7, 10, 11, 14, 22, 54, 84, 105, 125, 133
affect theory: 2, 3, 27–28, 33–35
affiliation: 66
agency: 57, 70, 74, 75, 85, 125, 127, 175–178
al-Dhahabi: 117
al-Jāḥiẓ: 126
al-Suyūṭi, Jalāl al-Dīn: 117, 124–125
Aly, Islam: 16–17
amulets: 29, 62, 64–67, 69, 90, 119, 125, 126, 145, 175
An Hyang: 165
Arabic: 117, 118, 124, 130
architecture: 18
Ark of the Covenant: 30, 50, 180–181
art: 2, 5–25, 81–113, 181–182
art history: 84–85
artefacts, artefactual: 40–55
astrology: 119
Augustine: 177, 183
authenticity: 58, 59
authority: 6, 8, 9, 60, 61
authorization: 69
authors: 174
'Ayesha: 125

B

Baggini, Julian: 6, 10, 22
Bari Lotsawa: 149, 150, 153, 156, 159
bark: 152

Barthes, Roland: 20
beliefs: 3, 33, 119, 174, 175
Bhagavad Gītā: 157, 182
Bible, bibles: 2, 9, 13, 15–16, 21–22, 27–37, 155, 180–81
Bible societies: 30
bibliocide: 6, 10
binding: 82, 101
blessing: 11, 119, 147, 155, 157, 175, 178, 181
bodies, embodiment: 12, 13, 15, 22–24, 28, 31, 33, 62, 102, 106, 123, 154, 163, 178, 182
Bodong Panchen: 140
books: 5, 6, 10, 16, 21, 22, 30, 57, 94, 104, 139, 144, 155, 173, 174, 177, 180–183
book arts: 2, 3, 7, 9
book box: 30, 101
book culture: 84, 137
Book of Mormon: 9
books: 19
bowing: 52, 57, 143
Brahma: 182
Buddhism: 116, 137–160, 163–164, 182
burning: 6, 7, 24, 147

C

calligraphy: 17, 19, 84, 119
Calvino, Italo: 20
canon, canonical: 41, 147, 150, 157
cantor: 52
Cathach reliquary: 30

Printed in Australia
AUHW010847201118
305455AU00003B/5